MAPS

GUANGDONG PROVINCE
PEARL RIVER DELTA
Zhaoqing
Guangzhou
Foshan
Dongguan
Huizhou
Shenzhen
Jianmen
Zhongshan
Zhuhai
Macau
HONG KONG

CHINA

N

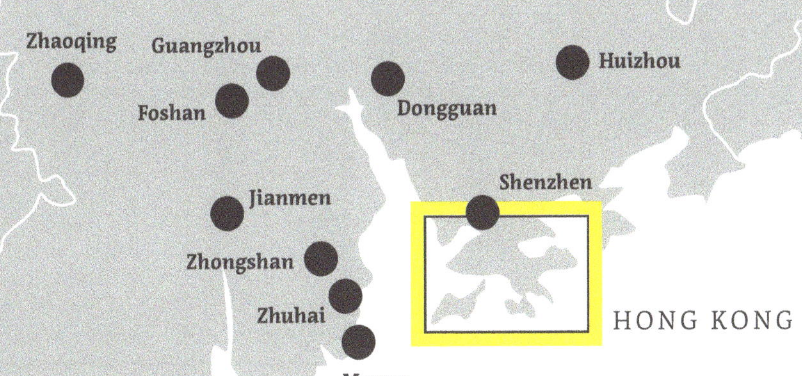

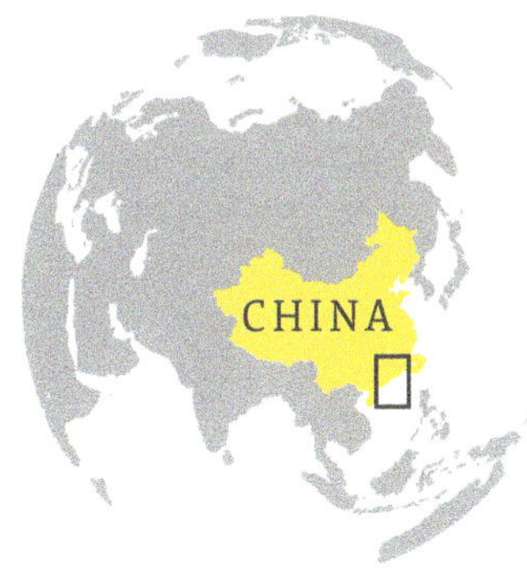

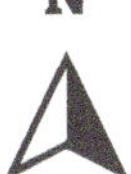

50km

Spark Publishing Inc. is a not-for-profit left-wing publisher based in Melbourne, Australia. Follow us on Instagram @sparkpublishinginc

Design and layout by Viktoria Ivanova
Cover image by Ben Hillier

Title: The Art of Rebellion: Dispatches from Hong Kong
ISBN: 978-0-646-82119-1: Paperback
Author: Ben Hillier

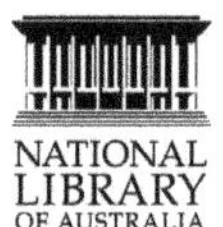

A catalogue record for this work is available from the National Library of Australia

THE ART OF REBELLION

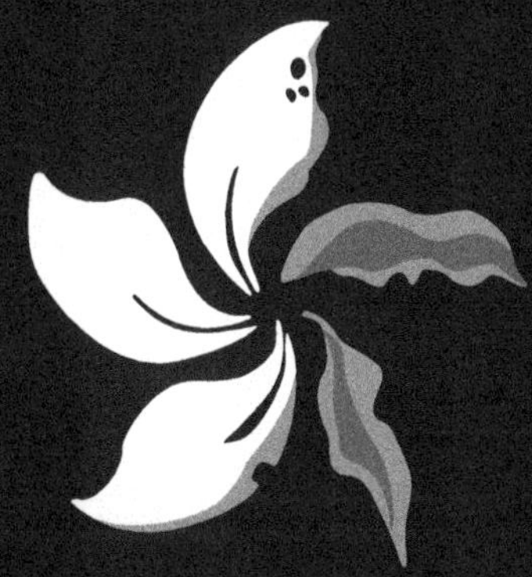

DISPATCHES FROM HONG KONG

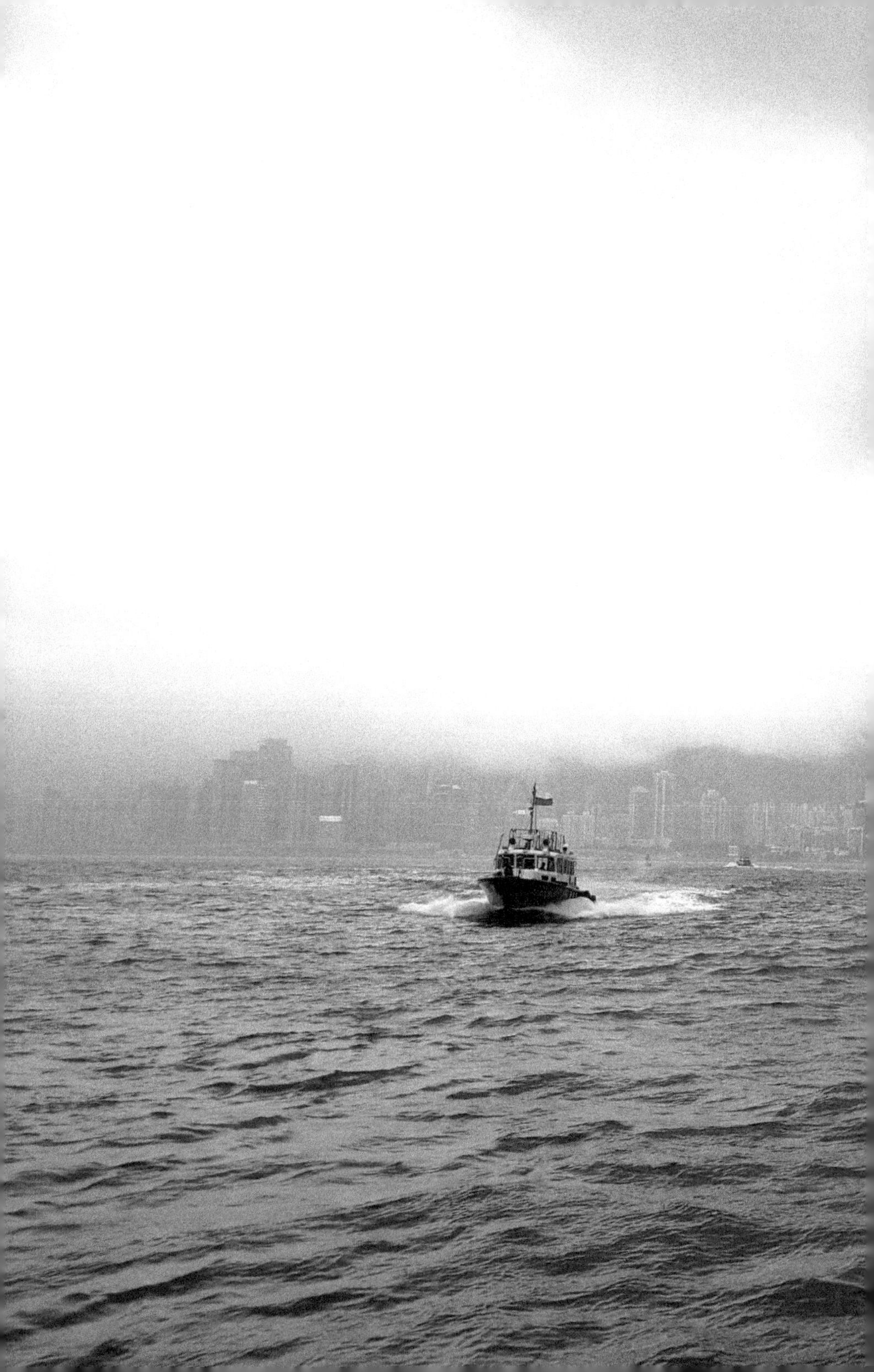

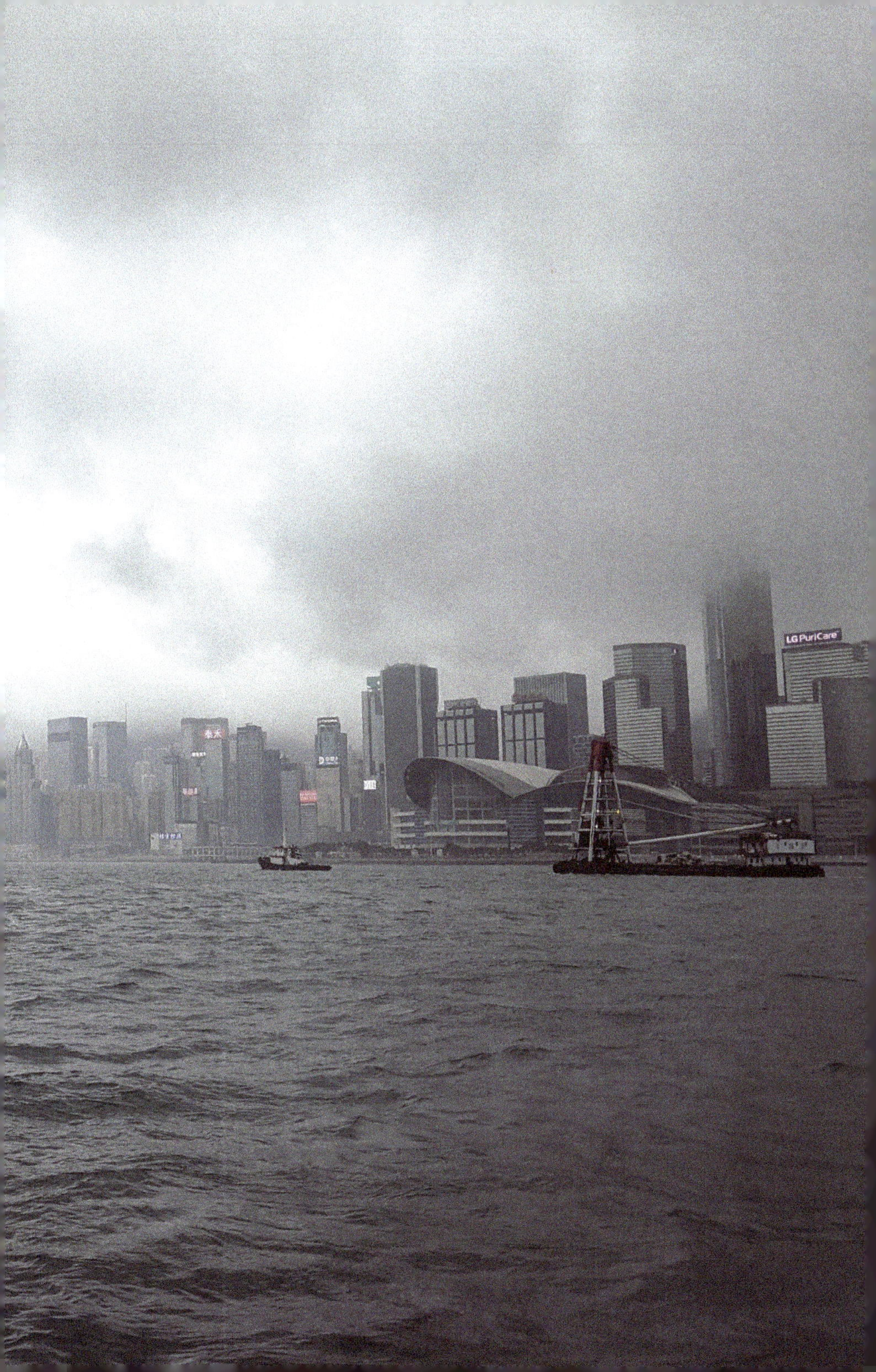
LG PuriCare

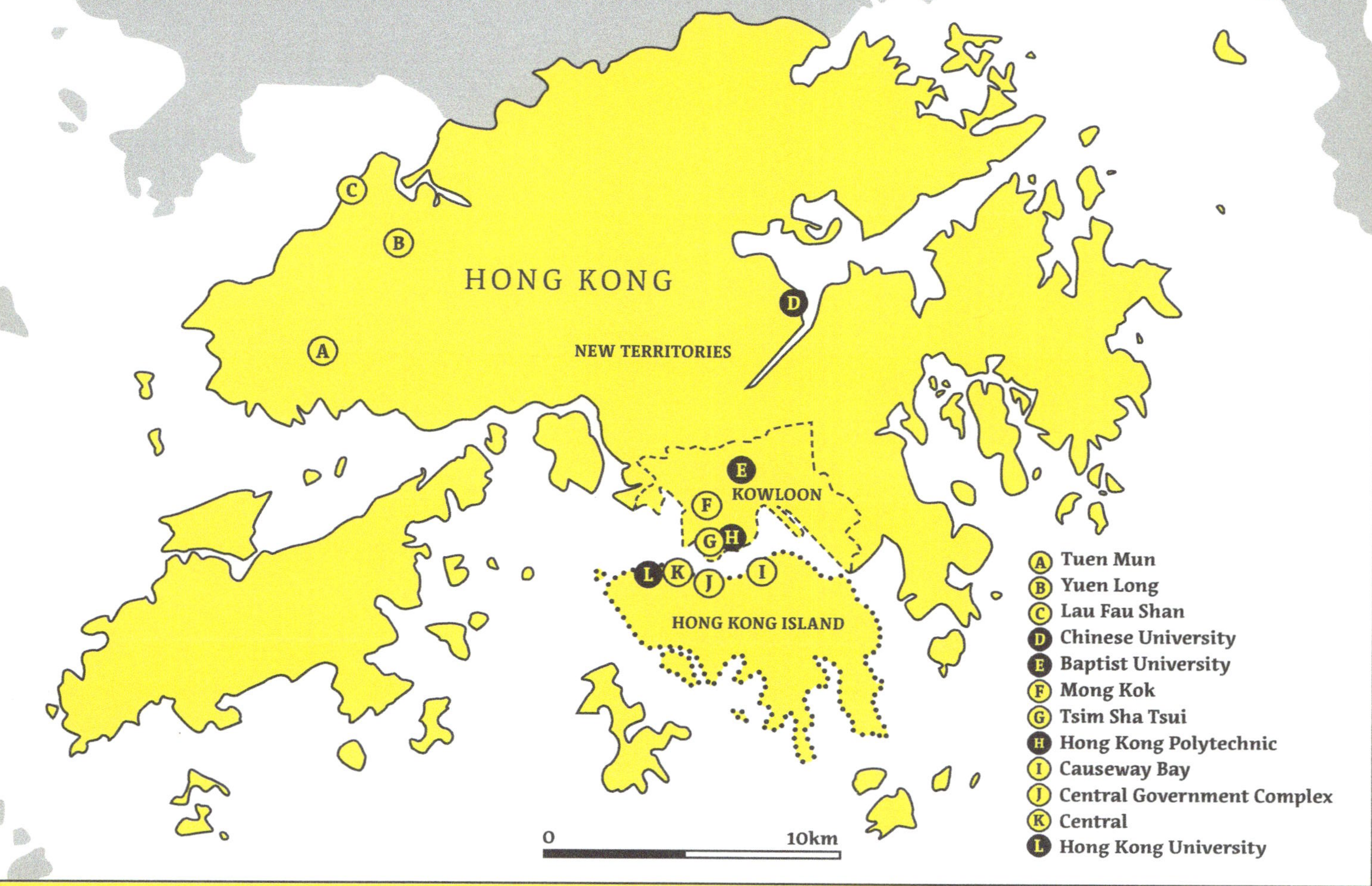
HONG KONG
NEW TERRITORIES
KOWLOON
HONG KONG ISLAND
0
10km
A Tuen Mun
B Yuen Long
C Lau Fau Shan
D Chinese University
E Baptist University
F Mong Kok
G Tsim Sha Tsui
H Hong Kong Polytechnic
I Causeway Bay
J Central Government Complex
K Central
L Hong Kong University

THE ART OF REBELLION

DISPATCHES FROM HONG KONG

BEN HILLIER

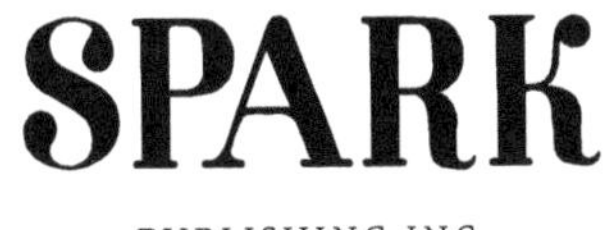

PUBLISHING INC.

ACKNOWLEDGMENTS

I owe a debt of gratitude to comrade Au Loong Yu, activist, analyst, historian and general raconteur. Thanks also to Winnie Yu, president of the Hospital Authority Employees Alliance; to Leo at the Hong Kong Confederation of Trade Unions; to everyone at *Red Flag* and Socialist Alternative in Australia; to Michael Kandelaars; and to Viktoria Ivanova for bringing everything to life with the design, imagery and artwork from the protest movement. If many young Hong Kongers are now renowned for their heroism, it was notable how many seemed more fearful of their mothers finding out that they were on the frontlines than they were fearful of the police. It reminded me that they don't get thanked enough. Thanks, mum. And thanks, nana.

ARTWORK AND IMAGERY

All uncredited images and video stills throughout the book are attributed to Ben Hillier. All other images are credited as USP (United Social Press), an online press and photo agency based in Hong Kong. Their immense catalogue and willingness to allow and encourage their work to be reproduced and shared widely is commendable. Where artwork is uncredited, the artist is unknown, anonymous or has been difficult to trace online. The collection is displayed in no particular order and is far from definitive. What is printed here is just a fraction of the prolific creativity that continues to accompany the resistance.

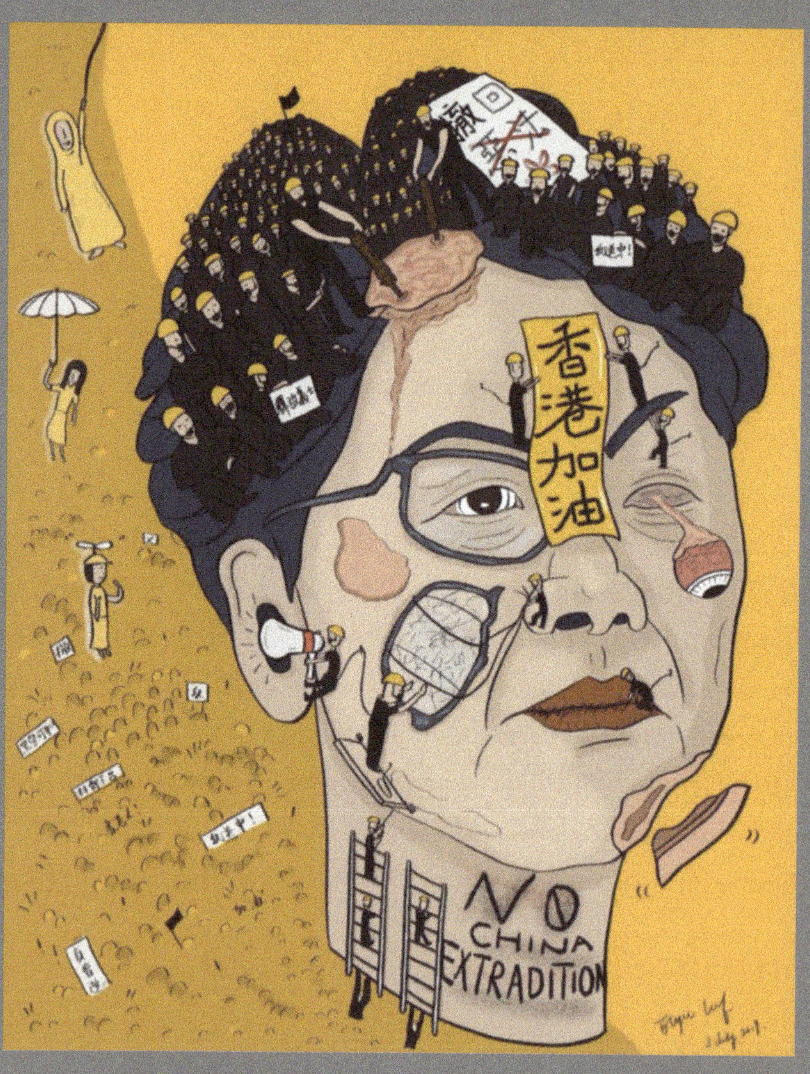

PORTRAIT OF CARRIE LAM
ELYSE LEAF (2019)
@PITAYAPEN

'WHAT HAVE I DONE WRONG'
(RIGHT)

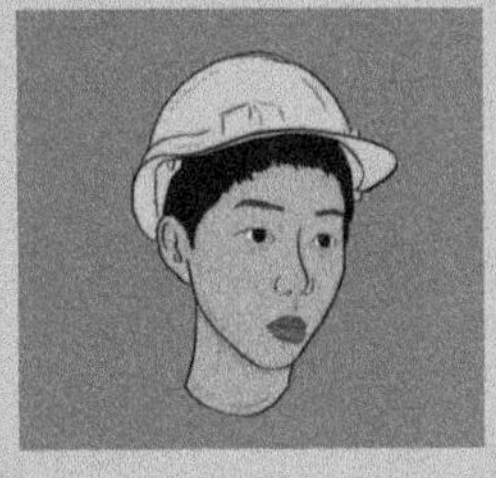

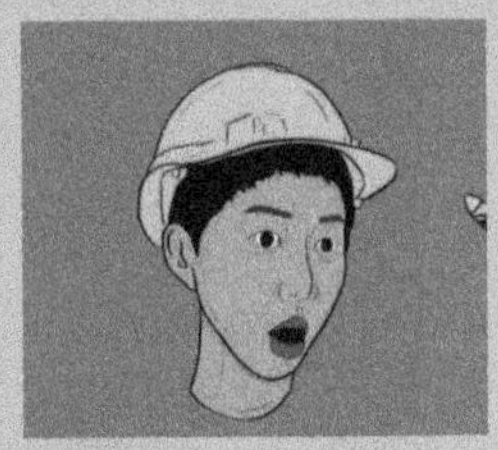

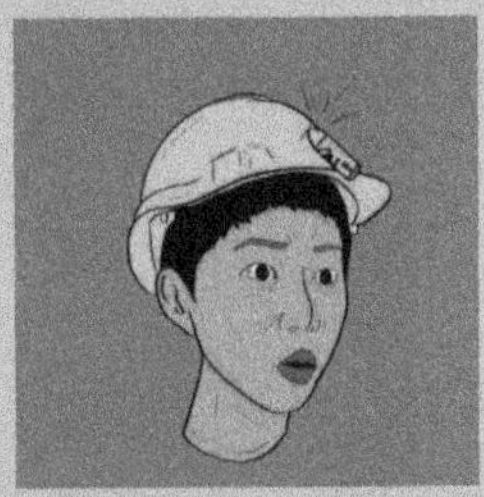

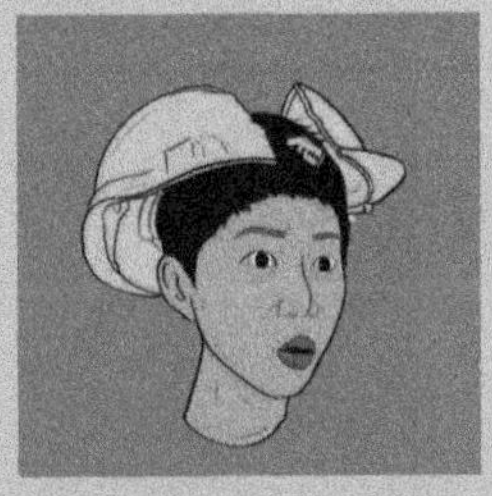

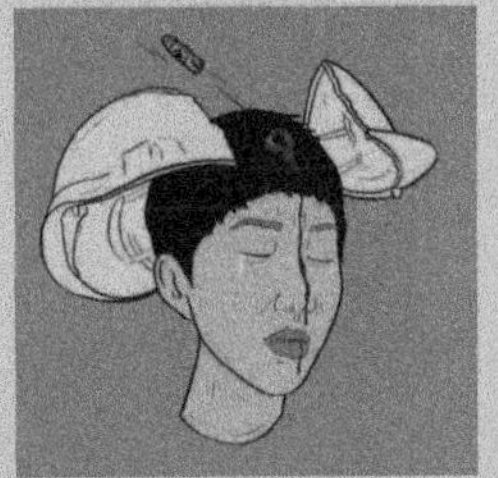

I can't tell you what art does and how it does it, but I know that art has often judged the judges, pleaded revenge to the innocent and shown to the future what the past has suffered, so that it has never been forgotten.

I know too that the powerful fear art, whatever its form, when it does this, and that amongst the people such art sometimes runs like a rumour and a legend because it makes sense of what life's brutalities cannot, a sense that unites us, for it is inseparable from a justice at last. Art, when it functions like this, becomes a meeting place of the invisible, the irreducible, the enduring, guts and honour.

— **John Berger**

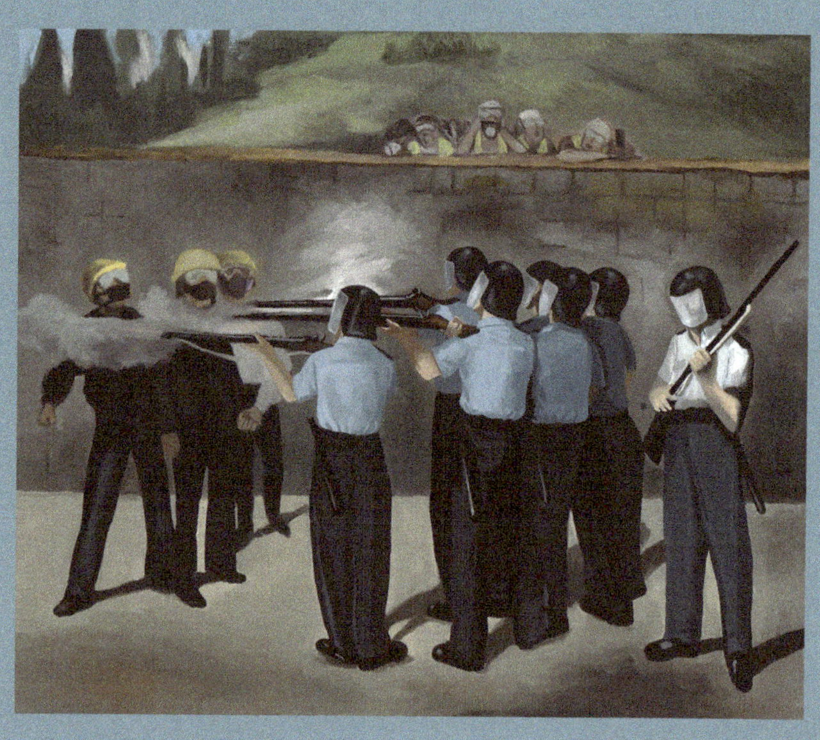

REFERENCING ÉDOUARD MANET'S
'EXECUTION OF EMPEROR MAXIMILIAN'
JUSTIN WONG (2019)

CONTENTS

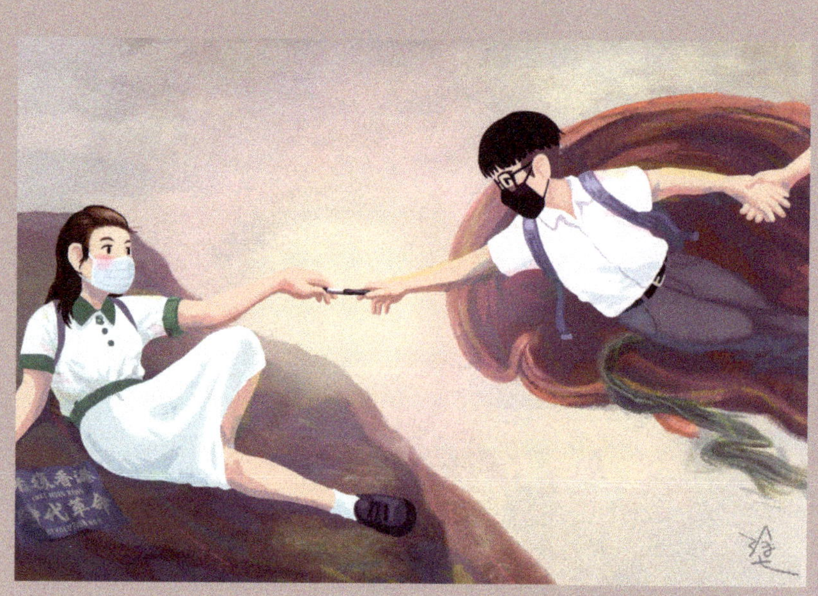

ARTO (2019)

FOREWORD

The articles collected here, the fruit of two short visits to Hong Kong in November 2019 and February 2020, were first published in *Red Flag*. By and large, they were written on the fly and mostly have been left as first published to keep the original mood. Some errors have been corrected where they were too obvious to ignore and threatened to distract or mislead readers. A separate account of the attack on the Chinese University, written by Lokman Tsui and published at GlobalVoices.org, has been included to complement the first piece relating the 12 November events in Mong Kok.

The political and economic situation has been irrevocably altered since the pieces were written. The two February articles, penned when the global pandemic was still only a Chinese epidemic, began to grapple with how the coronavirus was changing the political landscape. It's clear now that many of us were too optimistic about things soon getting back to 'normal'. More significantly, it was difficult to foresee that the police crackdown against protesters, notable at the time, would escalate so rapidly and culminate in Beijing's imposition of an outrageous national security law in July. The final section serves as a postscript in covering this dramatic shift in the situation.

Finally, it's a cliché, and potentially self-defeating to admit at the beginning of a written document, that words cannot adequately convey events. But the true magnitude of the struggle in Hong Kong is beyond the reach of my vocabulary at least. For that reason, the book features artwork and imagery to better convey the life and colour of a city in rebellion. During the quieter moments in Hong Kong, there was always a political spectacle—graffiti, posters, a Lennon Wall, a smashed traffic light or boarded-up bank—bursting forth as a reminder that hearts were in turn breaking and burning all over the territory. Hopefully, something of that is conveyed here.

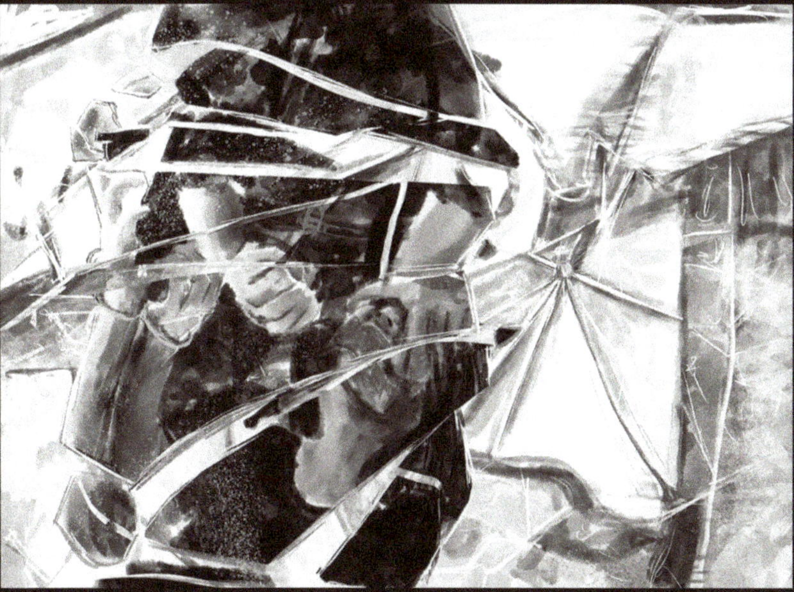

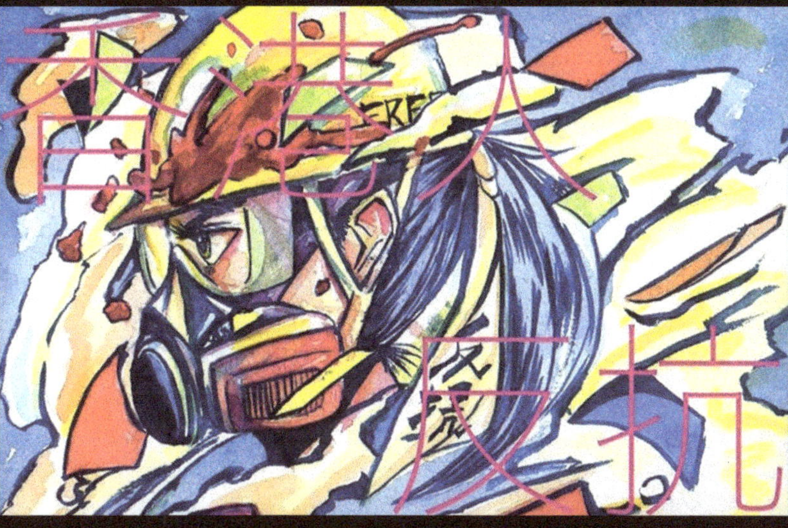
香港人
反抗

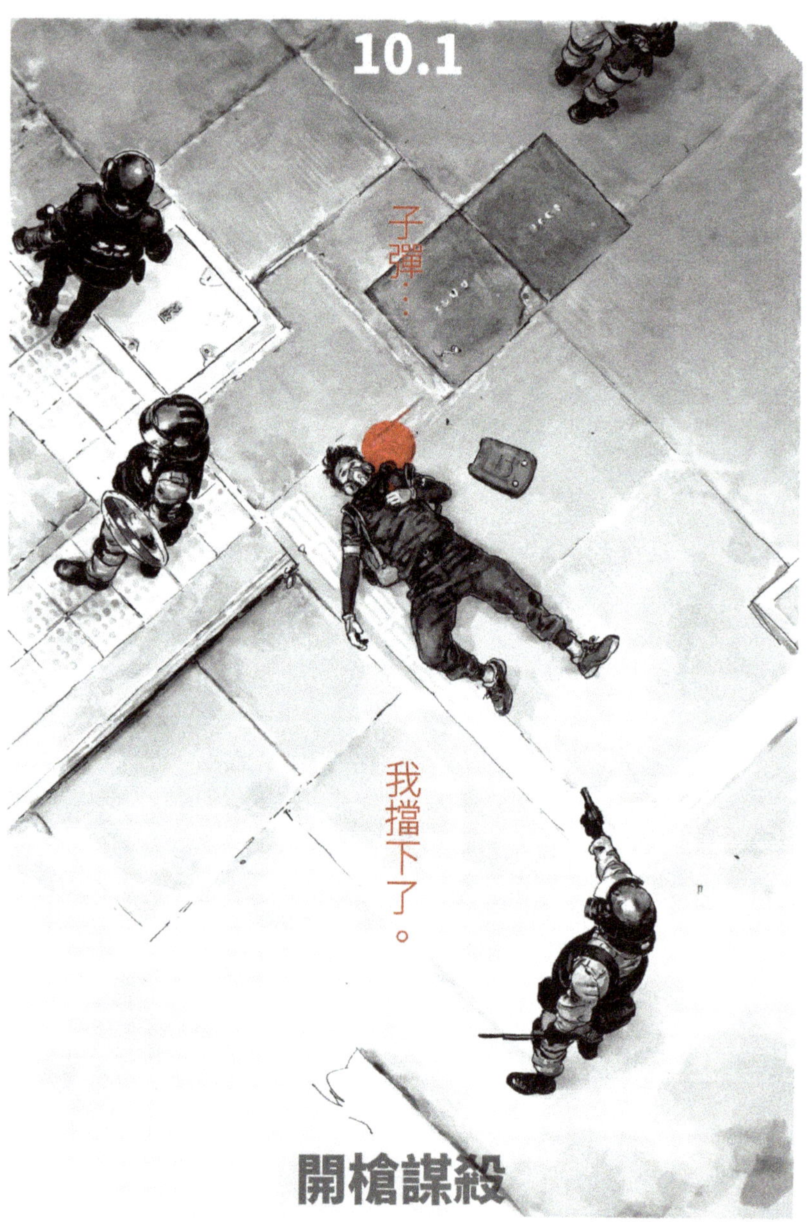

FCP (2019)
@FCP911

READS: 'HONG KONG POLICE INTEND TO MURDER STUDENTS'

BACKGROUND

For the third time since the handover of Hong Kong from British colonial rule to Chinese sovereignty, the territory exploded in mass protest in 2019. More than one million people took to the streets in a 9 June mobilisation called by the Civil Human Rights Front, a coalition of pro-democracy groups. Three days later, tens of thousands of masked protesters surrounded Hong Kong Island's Central Government Complex—comprising the Central Government Offices, the Legislative Council and the Office of the Chief Executive—to prevent lawmakers convening for a second reading of a controversial bill.

Police cleared crowds with tear gas, rubber bullets, beanbag rounds and truncheons. But protesters regrouped constantly. Residents blocked roads with cars, young people dug paving bricks from footpaths, and everywhere umbrellas blossomed. The mobilisation started early in the morning and lasted well into the evening, protesters chanting, 'Add oil, Hong Kong!'—an encouragement to persist. By mid-afternoon, Central and Admiralty districts were chaos. Police Commissioner Stephen Lo Wai-chung declared the clashes a riot sometime after 4pm. 'Such a declaration ... could have serious implications for anyone arrested,' the *South China Morning Post* reported. 'Rioting is punishable by up to ten years in prison. "It's a riot now," Lo says. "We urge people not to do anything they will regret for the rest of their lives."'

But regrets were far from participants' minds. One of the most explosive rebellions of the twenty-first century had begun. Over the next six months, an astonishing seven hundred and fifty protests took place with a cumulative attendance of thirteen million people—on average, about four mobilisations per day of seventeen thousand in a city of seven and a half million. By the end of November, the official record noted nineteen live rounds fired by police, plus fifteen thousand teargas rounds (more than eighty per day), and twelve thousand rubber bullets and bean bag rounds (seventy per day). More than six thousand people were arrested, and the number has since grown to more than nine thousand. Fifty-one percent of them were between the ages of eighteen and twenty-five; fifteen percent were minors.

'The experience—and spectacle—of tear gas came to define life in Hong Kong in 2019, whether fighting it at the frontlines,

2019 AUGUST 八月

5

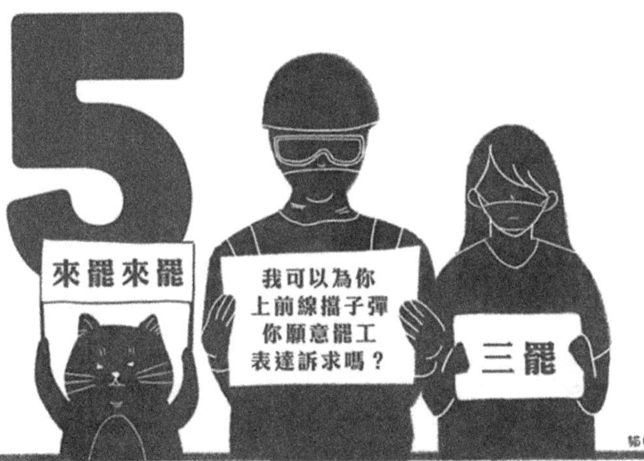

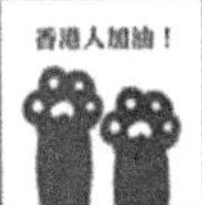

STRIKE MONDAY

罷罷罷 星期一

⊘ 不流血、不受傷、不被捕、不篤灰、不割席、不指責、不分化 ⊘

BE WATER

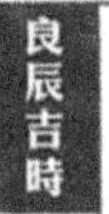

良辰吉時

下午一點正
七區集合

宜

罷工 罷課
罷市 集會

忌

返工
返學
逼地鐵
塞巴士

拒絕
白色恐佈

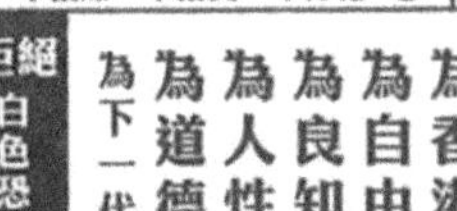

為香港
為自由
為良知
為人性
為道德
為下一代

以最和平的
勇武反抗，
向政府表達
我們的訴求

吉神方位

沙田區
百步梯

荃灣區
荃灣公園

屯門區
屯門公園

黃大仙區
黃大仙廣場

大埔區
廣福球場

旺角區
麥花臣球場

金鐘區
添馬公園

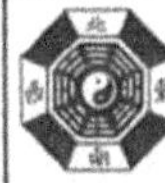

撤回修例 | 撤回暴動定性 | 釋放被捕人士 | 成立獨立調查委員會 | 真雙普選

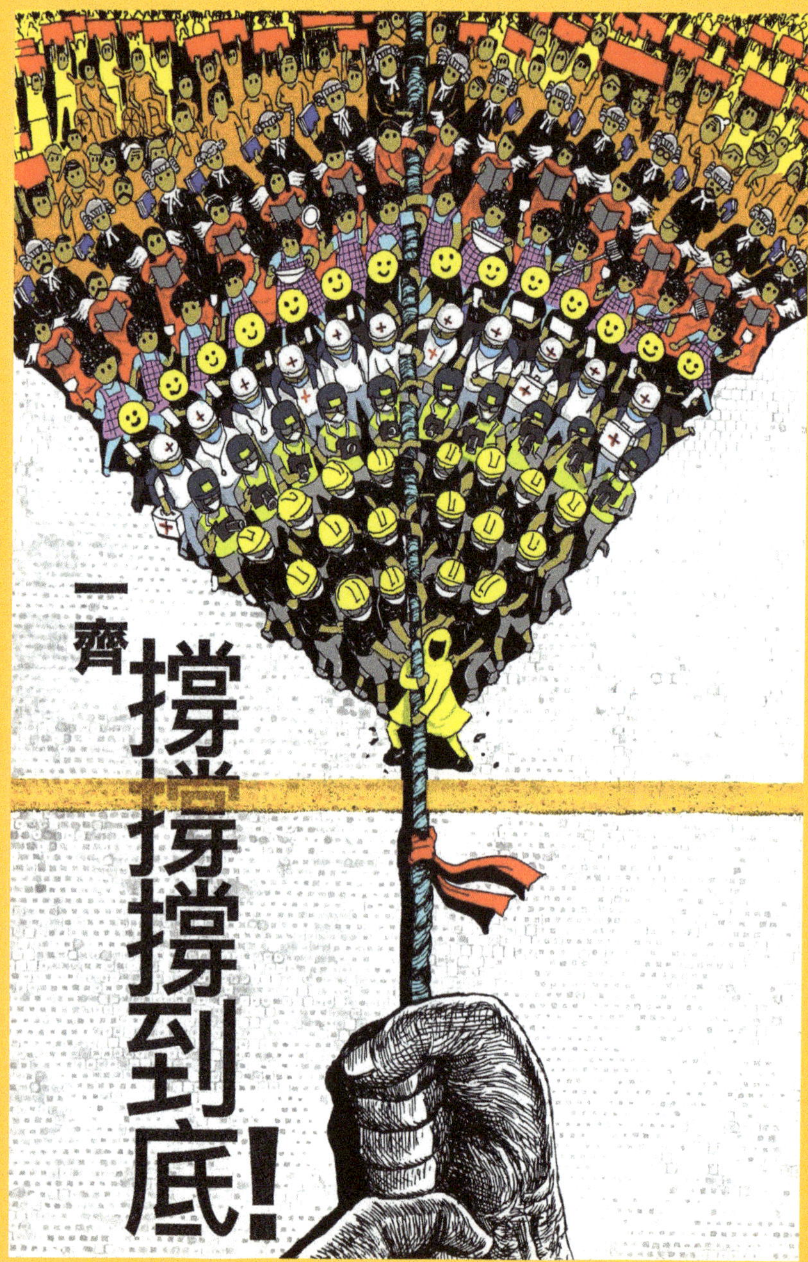
一齊
撐撐撐到底!

choking on it or dodging it while engaged in lawful protest, planning one's journeys and schedules to avoid it, watching images of it billowing on television screens, or just talking about it,' Antony Dapiran, a Hong Kong-based author and lawyer, wrote in his 2020 book *City on fire*. 'Children in Hong Kong playgrounds played "police and protesters", and talked about tear gas as casually as children elsewhere might talk about sports or computer games. After the protests of 2019, Hong Kongers have a new saying, and a new aspect to their identity: "You're not a real Hong Konger if you haven't tasted tear gas."' Behind the scenes, it wasn't a game of course. People in the movement talked about post-traumatic stress among student activists: depression, self-harm, anxiety, listlessness. They spoke of families ripped apart by the political polarisation, of unexplained or suspicious 'disappearances' believed to be police or triad murders, and unreported police violence and sexual assaults.

Yet the protesters seemingly could not be beaten into submission. They damaged or destroyed more than seven hundred sets of traffic lights. They smashed and burned hundreds of ATMs and dozens of bank branches. Across the city, students dug up pavements and used the bricks as projectiles. Footpath fencing was stripped of tonnes of metal bars, and construction sites constantly were raided for materials to build barricades. While the black-clad and masked young

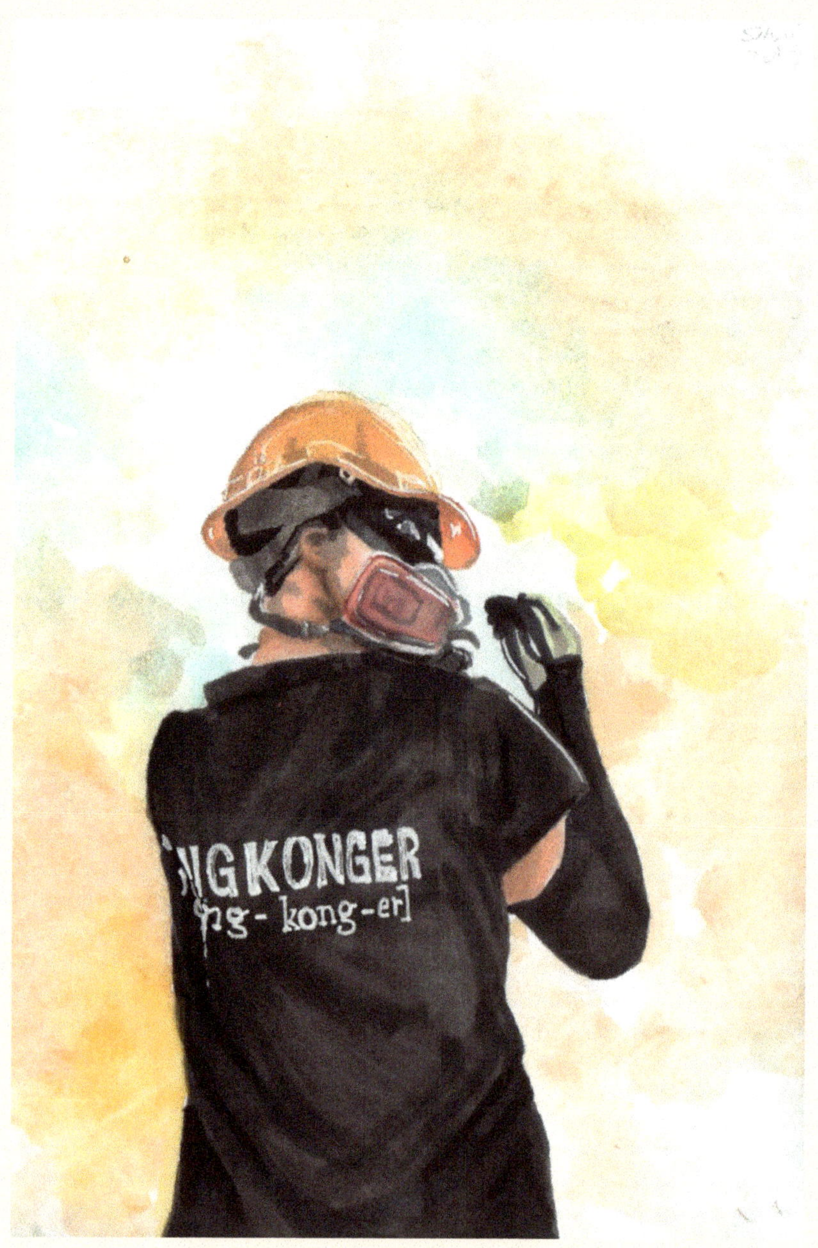

militants in the relentless street clashes numbered only thousands or tens of thousands, a mass movement stood behind them, providing food, shelter, transportation, counselling and weaponry—baseball bats, golf clubs, petrol and alcohol for bombs and thousands of umbrellas to defend against water cannons and shield militants from prying police and media cameras.

The situation peaked in November. One small incident seemed indicative of the city's mood, for this observer at least: the late-night sight of a small group of Molotov-wielding frontliners who, having doubled back along a side street parallel to Nathan Road in Mong Kok, peered around a corner, looking for an opportunity to unload and incinerate the rear-guard of riot cops who had stormed their protest, smashing barricades, firing rubber bullets and unleashing volley after volley of tear gas. It was balmy and some older locals were still going about their business and late shopping. A few people peered out of windows. From the three other corners of the intersection and a flyover walkway, maybe a dozen bystanders watched, no-one appearing the slightest bit pensive. Everyone was statue-like, all eyes trained on the kids with the petrol bombs.

The police at Nathan were far too guarded and the frontliners too far back. After a few minutes, it was clear that there would be no surprise attack. The would-be assailants

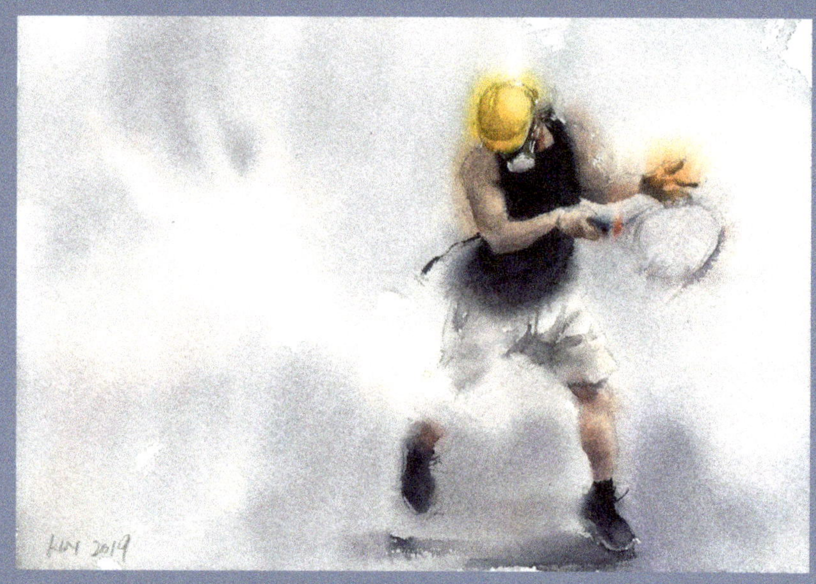

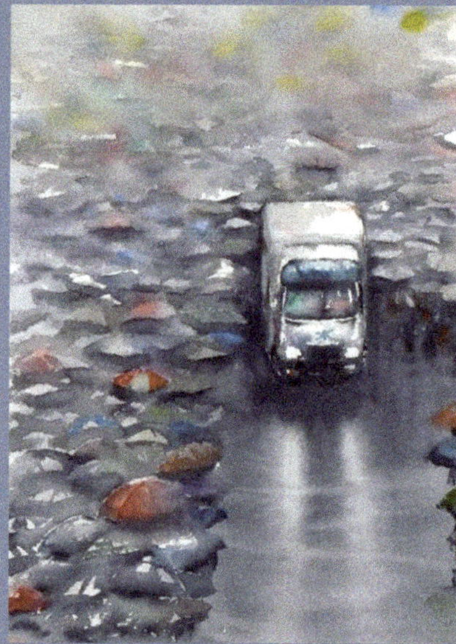

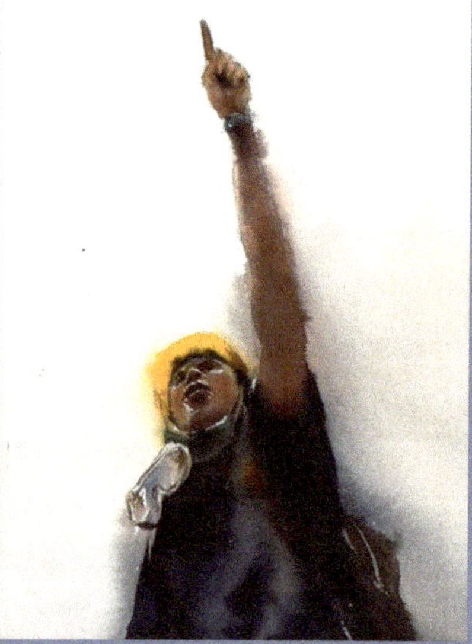

WATERCOLOUR PAINTINGS OF ICONIC PROTEST PHOTOS

FUNG KIN FAN (2019)
FACEBOOK.COM/FUNG.K.FAN

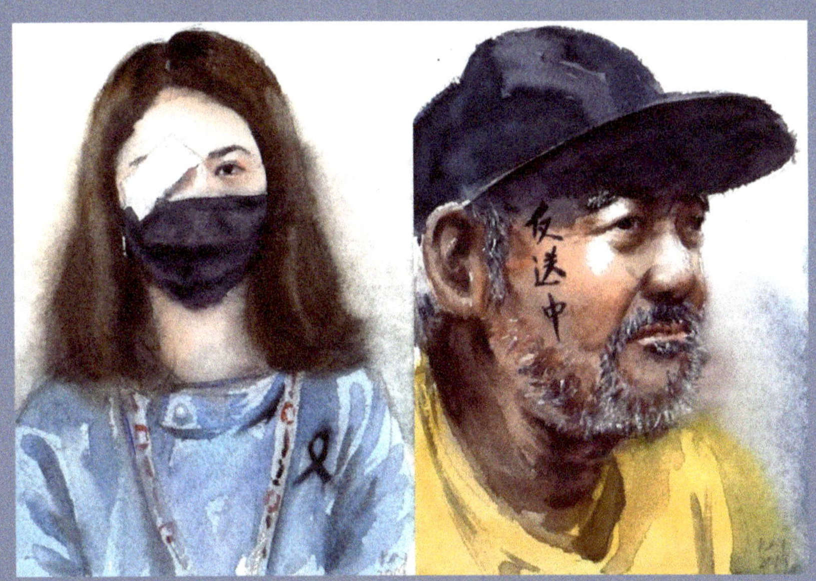

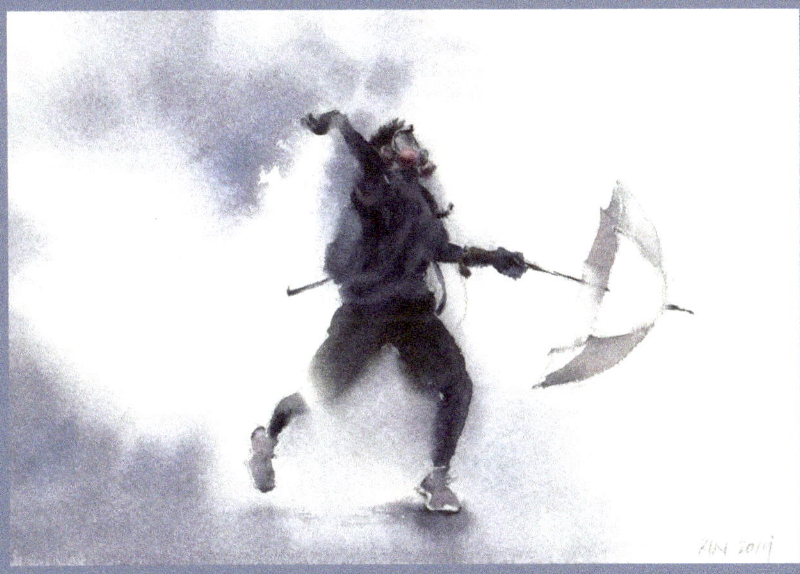

'I'M JUST AN ORDINARY CITIZEN WHO WORKS AT CONSTRUCTION SITES BY DAY AND I'M A WATERCOLOUR ENTHUSIAST BY NIGHT.'
— FUNG KIN FAN

retreated and re-joined the main demonstration. I was left temporarily stunned, though I can't remember if by elation or if it was the wretched tear gas hanging in the air. Perhaps the moment just took time to process. But one thing stuck in my head: the kids were seriously looking for an opening, and not one onlooker said a word, tried to talk them down or create a commotion to warn the officers. If it had come down to it, that night, right there, all present—admittedly a small cross-section of society, but a cross-section nonetheless—were ready to watch pigs burn. This radicalisation was real.

To outsiders, Hong Kong's explosive movement could be both absorbing and a little perplexing. A pumping heart of global finance and trade, the territory ranks fourth on the United Nations Human Development Index, has the tenth highest GDP per capita in the world (adjusted for purchasing power parity), the fourth lowest homelessness rate, a youth unemployment rate of around six percent and general unemployment of only three to four percent for a decade (and above six percent only twice in forty years). The government runs a positive budget balance, there is little public debt and nearly half of the population lives in public housing, the stock

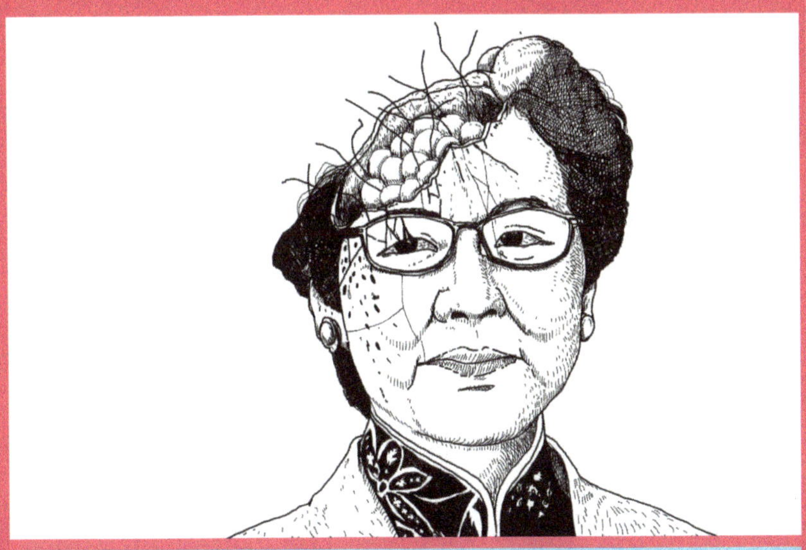

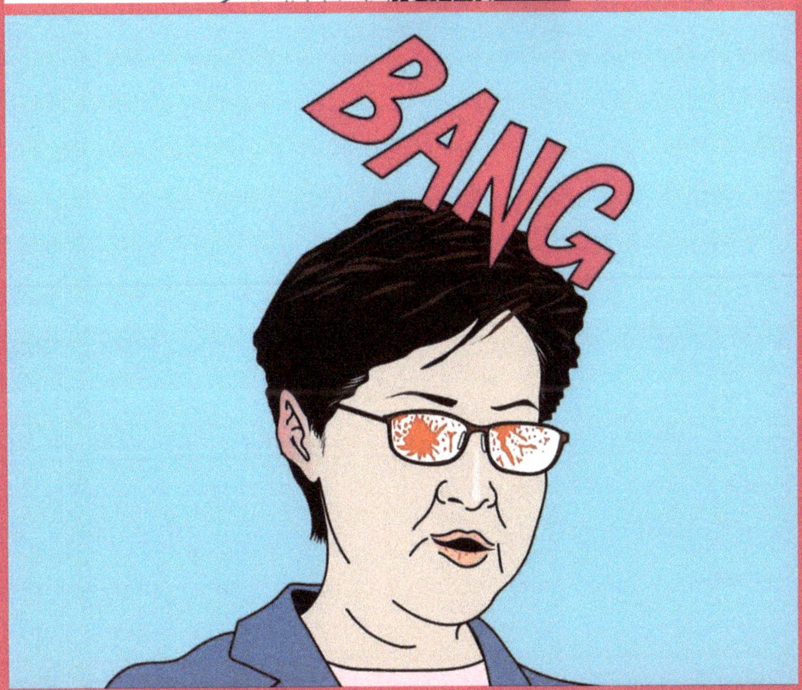

DEPICTIONS OF HONG KONG CHIEF EXECUTIVE CARRIE LAM
BY JUSTIN WONG CHIU TAT

of which continues to expand, bucking the trend for pretty much every other developed economy.

Yet, like every society, Hong Kong has its social and economic problems. Hong Kong University tracking polls showed that, by 2019, about fifty percent of the population was dissatisfied with the government's performance in improving livelihoods, and one-third was dissatisfied with its performance in maintaining economic prosperity. Incomes stagnated while dwelling prices more than tripled over the last decade, and rents increased twenty-five percent in the last six years. Subsidised public rental housing in effect halves the region's poverty rate. But even after accounting for that, it is one in ten, according to the census. And more than a quarter of a million are on the waiting list for public housing.

In the imagination of the Chinese Communist Party and its loyalists in Hong Kong, the rebellion could be explained with reference to such economic concerns, rather than political grievances. 'Economic development is the only golden key to resolving all sorts of problems facing Hong Kong today,' President Xi Jinping reportedly remarked in September, according to an essay in *Foreign Affairs*. Around the same time, China's state newspaper, the *People's Daily*, criticised property developers in the territory and urged them to release land for public projects 'instead of just

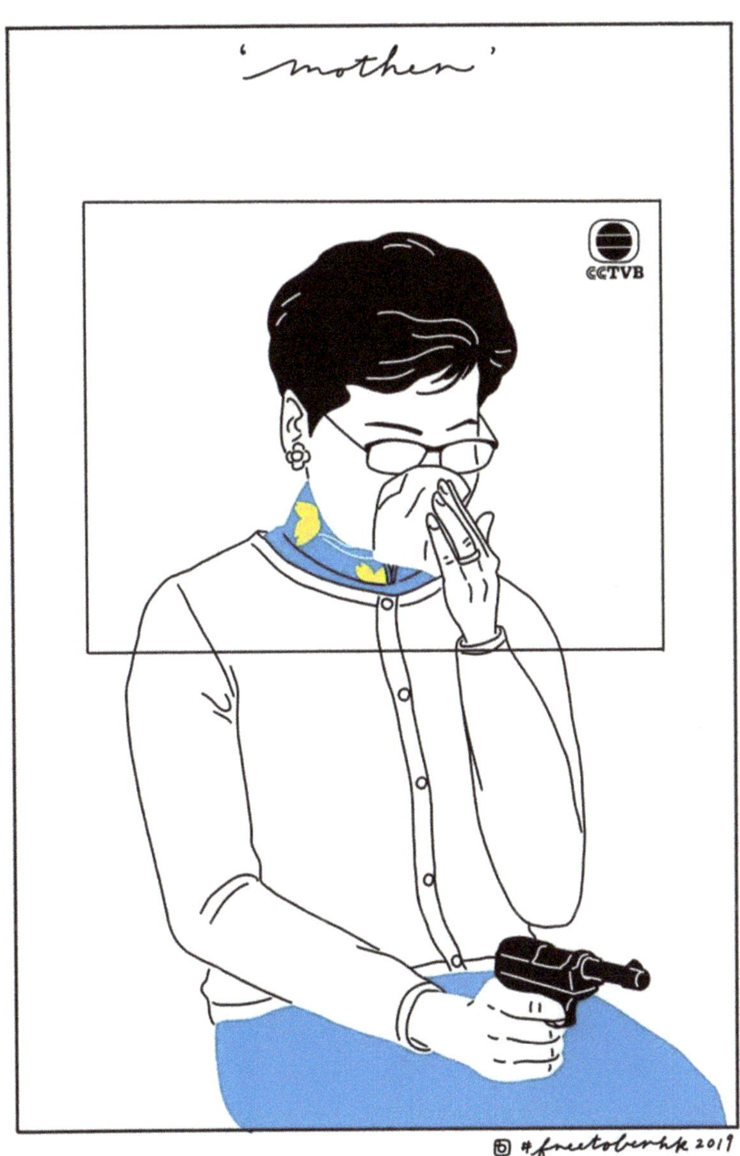

HONG KONG CHIEF EXECUTIVE
CARRIE LAM

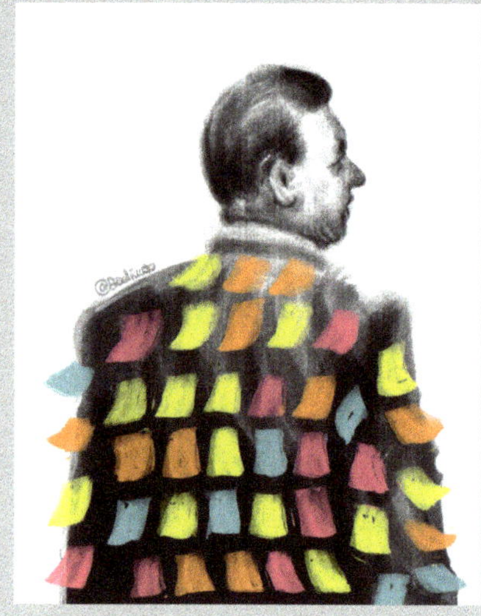

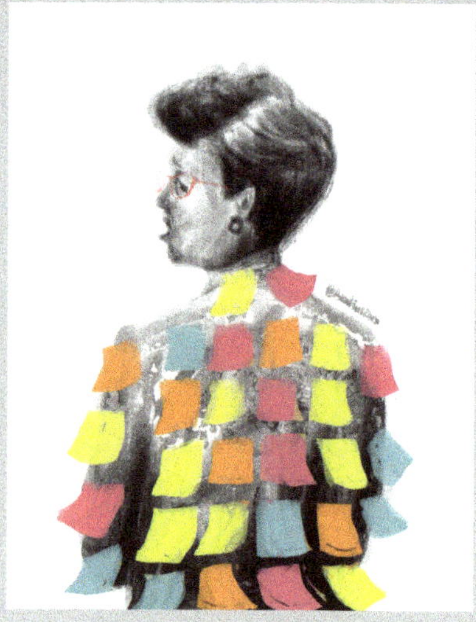

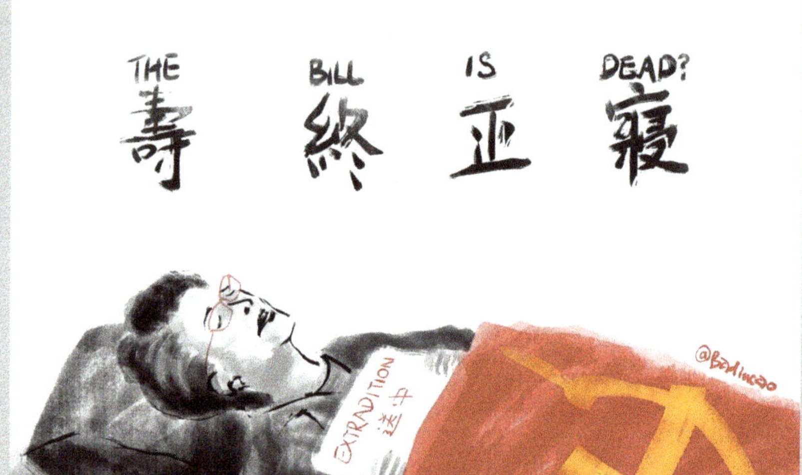

BADIUCAO (2019)
@BADIUCAO

playing their own calculations, smashing the land, earning the last copper plate'.

There's nothing exceptional about Hong Kong's economic and social problems, though. Every capitalist society is based on an unequal distribution of resources, the top one percent of the population controlling more than the bottom twenty percent or more. More notable is that Hong Kong, unlike other centres of Western finance, emerged relatively unscathed from the 2008-09 global financial crisis. There was no mass austerity, no political radicalisation expressing the underlying hostility to inequality, no Hong Kong equivalent of Bernie Sanders or Jeremy Corbyn or Alexis Tsipras. In fact, a unique aspect of Hong Kong politics seems to be that the political class consistently explains away angst among young people with reference to poor economic prospects, while young people themselves say that they are motivated by political concerns.

This was in part illustrated by the 2011 Occupy Central Movement's failure to replicate the mobilisations that took place in the United States, Spain, Greece and the United Kingdom, among other places. 'Rallying against capitalism, socioeconomic injustice and corporate greed, pitching their tents under the Hong Kong Shanghai Bank Building in Central, the number of occupiers peaked at around one hundred but averaged not more than a few dozen throughout the seven months of its existence,' Ching Kwan Lee, a professor at the University of California, wrote in *Take back our future: an eventful sociology of the Hong Kong Umbrella Movement*. 'The objective realities of economic inequality have always been a fact of life in Hong Kong, but they alone rarely fuelled collective mobilisation.'

The phenomenon was fully expressed in the groundbreaking 2014 Umbrella Movement, a seventy-nine-day protest/occupation demanding universal suffrage. One rigid pro-government narrative at the time was that there was no political problem—the demonstrators could be placated by economic development. Yet, as Samson Yuen and Edmund Cheng found when surveying participants, fewer than five percent said that they were there to demand better social policies. 'Economic matters were the least relevant to why they committed themselves,' they summarised the following year at ChinaFile. The 2019 rebellion was little different.

Beijing argues that geopolitical conspiracy also lies behind the turmoil. 'As extreme elements in Hong Kong turn more and more violent, Western forces, especially the United States, have been increasingly open in their involvement,' President Xi said in a speech to party cadre, again in September. 'Some extreme anti-China forces in the United States are trying to turn Hong Kong into the battleground for US-Chinese rivalry ... They want to turn Hong Kong's high degree of autonomy

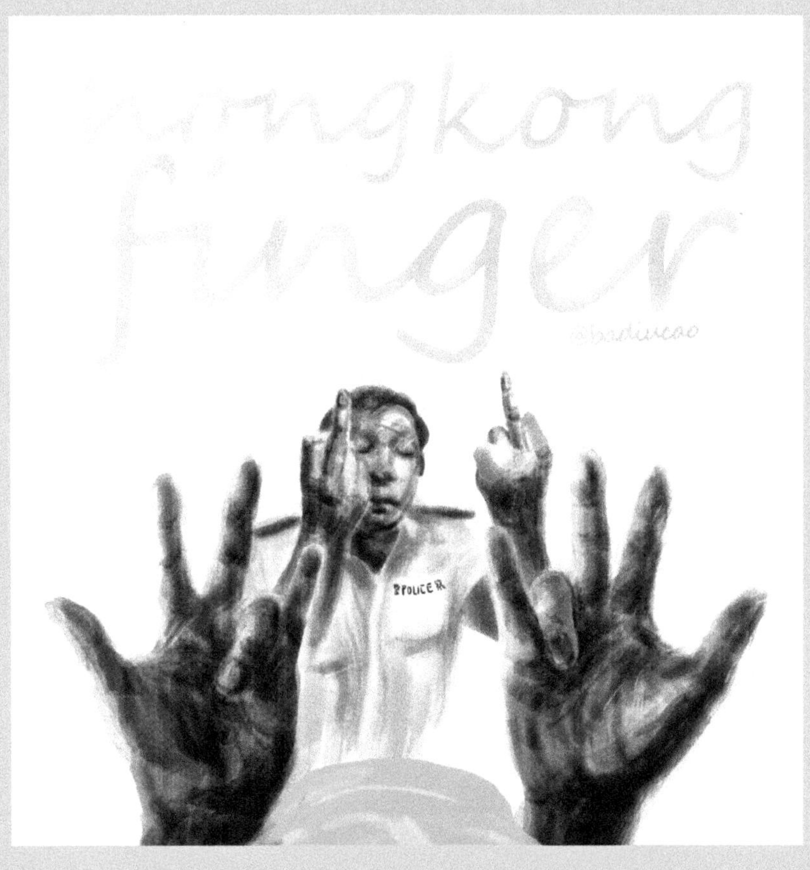

AFTER AN ACTIVIST BIT OFF A POLICE OFFICER'S FINGER, PROTESTERS ADOPTED THE 'MISSING FINGER SALUTE' TO MOCK LAW ENFORCEMENT AT SUBSEQUENT DEMONSTRATIONS

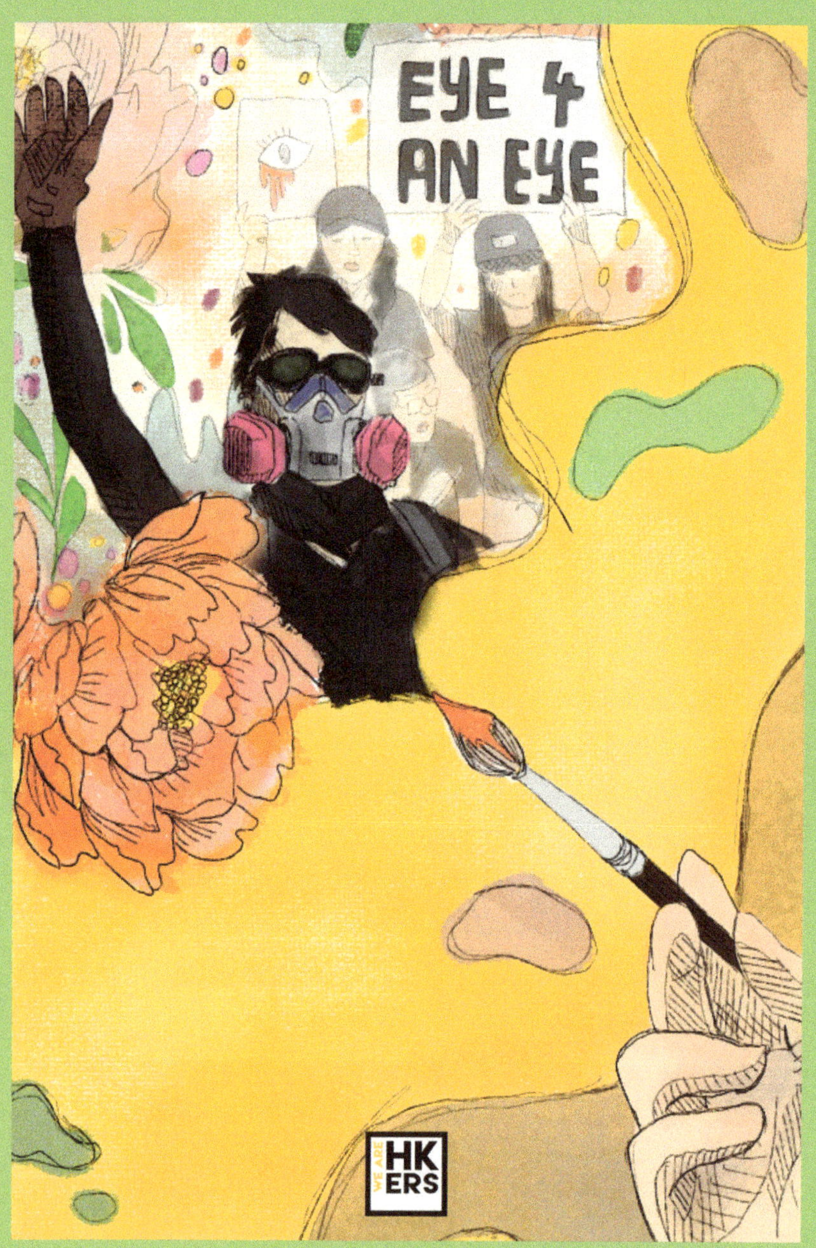
EYE 4
AN EYE
WE ARE HKERS

into de facto independence, with the ultimate objective to contain China's rise and prevent the revival of the great Chinese nation.' The US has made no secret of its hostility to China's rise, so it would be naïve to think that Washington and its proxies aren't attempting to encourage and shape the anti-Beijing resistance in Hong Kong. Indeed, a small section of the movement orients to the US and the West, which only reinforces Beijing's narrative that the city's conflict is about big power rivalry.

The Chinese Communist Party is not alone in arguing this way. Faced with one of the most explosive student radicalisations in modern history, much of the Western left has been eerily quiet. After returning from the territory in December, I interviewed WikiLeaks editor-in-chief Kristinn Hrafnsson, who asked whether 'dark forces' were at work. The gut feeling that something just isn't right with the Hong Kong rebellion has been widespread among people naturally attuned to the crimes and intrigues of US imperialism around the globe. Yet it is equally naïve to make US intrigue the frame through which developments in Hong Kong must be viewed, as though such a momentous and spontaneous outpouring of rage, sacrifice and solidarity could be engineered by the Central Intelligence Agency and other regime-change institutions. In the history of recent US interventions, you'd be hard pressed to find another episode

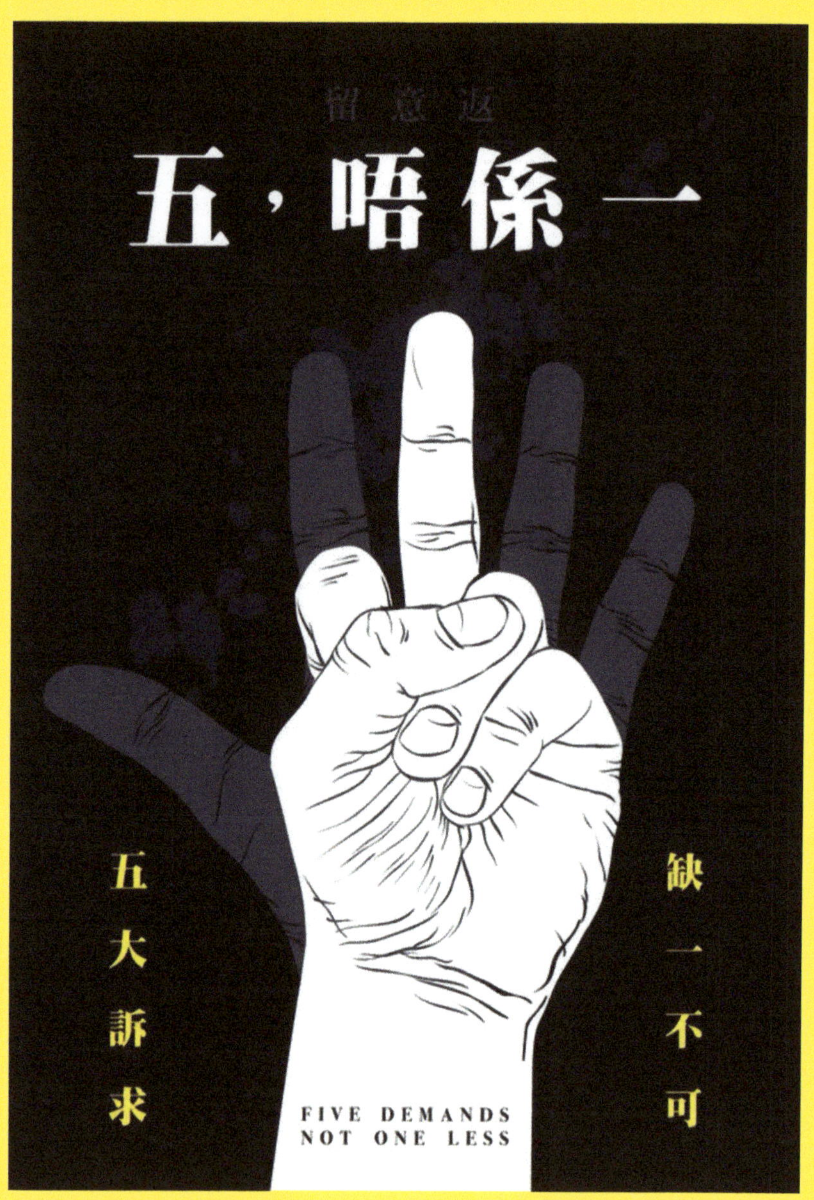
留意返
五，唔係一
五大訴求
缺一不可
FIVE DEMANDS
NOT ONE LESS

in which the empire relied on school children and university students—armed with bricks, umbrellas and medieval weaponry such as bows and arrows and home-made bamboo catapults—to take on cops armed with AR-15s. Yet those in agreement with the Communist Party's line are left holding onto this flimsy proposition. Beyond an attack on reason, it's an insult to the tenacity of the territory's young people, not to mention the CIA—which is a lot of things, but not so thoroughly inept. More broadly, thinking that so many could be duped, or bribed with a few dollars, into rising so forcefully for a foreign power indicates a deplorable view of the human condition.

History will record that the trigger for the uprising came in February, when the Hong Kong government tabled an extradition bill that, if enacted, would have allowed Hong Kong residents to face trial in mainland China. It was this bill's imminent passing that drew millions into the streets in June, led tens of thousands to lay siege to the Central Government Complex and resulted in the moniker 'anti-ELAB protests' (ELAB being the acronym for 'extradition law amendment bill'). But the movement, under severe repression, soon

STAND WITH

HONG

1 Full withdrawal of the extradition bill

2 Independent commission of inquiry into alleged police brutality

3 Retracting the classification of protesters as "rioters"

4 Amnesty for arrested protesters

5 Dual universal suffrage

FIVE DEMANDS
NOT ONE LESS

KONG

morphed into an open fight for democratic rights with five demands at its heart:

1. Withdraw the extradition bill
2. Retract Commissioner Lo's characterisation of the 12 June demonstration as a 'riot'
3. Release and exonerate arrested protesters
4. Establish an independent commission of inquiry into the police
5. Implement universal suffrage

The final demand is both the most radical and the most desired. The chief executive, Hong Kong's equivalent of a president, is selected by a twelve-hundred-member Election Committee and vetted by the Chinese Communist Party—not elected by residents. The Legislative Council, the city's parliament, cannot introduce bills, only scrutinise those tabled by the executive. Half of its seats are filled by representatives from 'functional constituencies', mostly appointees from industry bodies. So the political decision-making institutions are anti-majoritarian and under the sway of the central government in Beijing. One result of this is a high level of political alienation; popular grievances in the territory, having few outlets, tend to build up and explode in protest, which is one reason that 2019 was prefigured by 2014 and 2003 (for

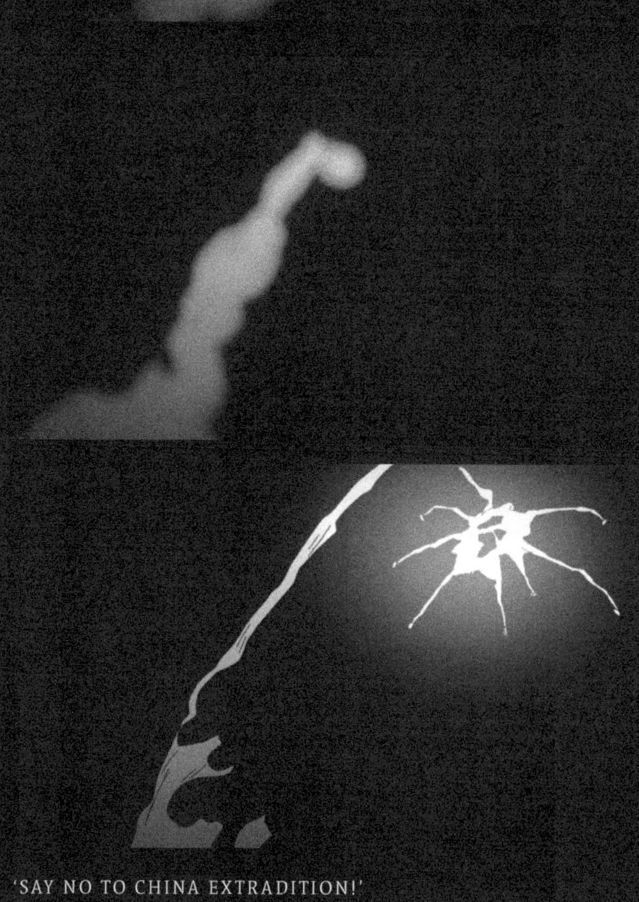

'SAY NO TO CHINA EXTRADITION!'

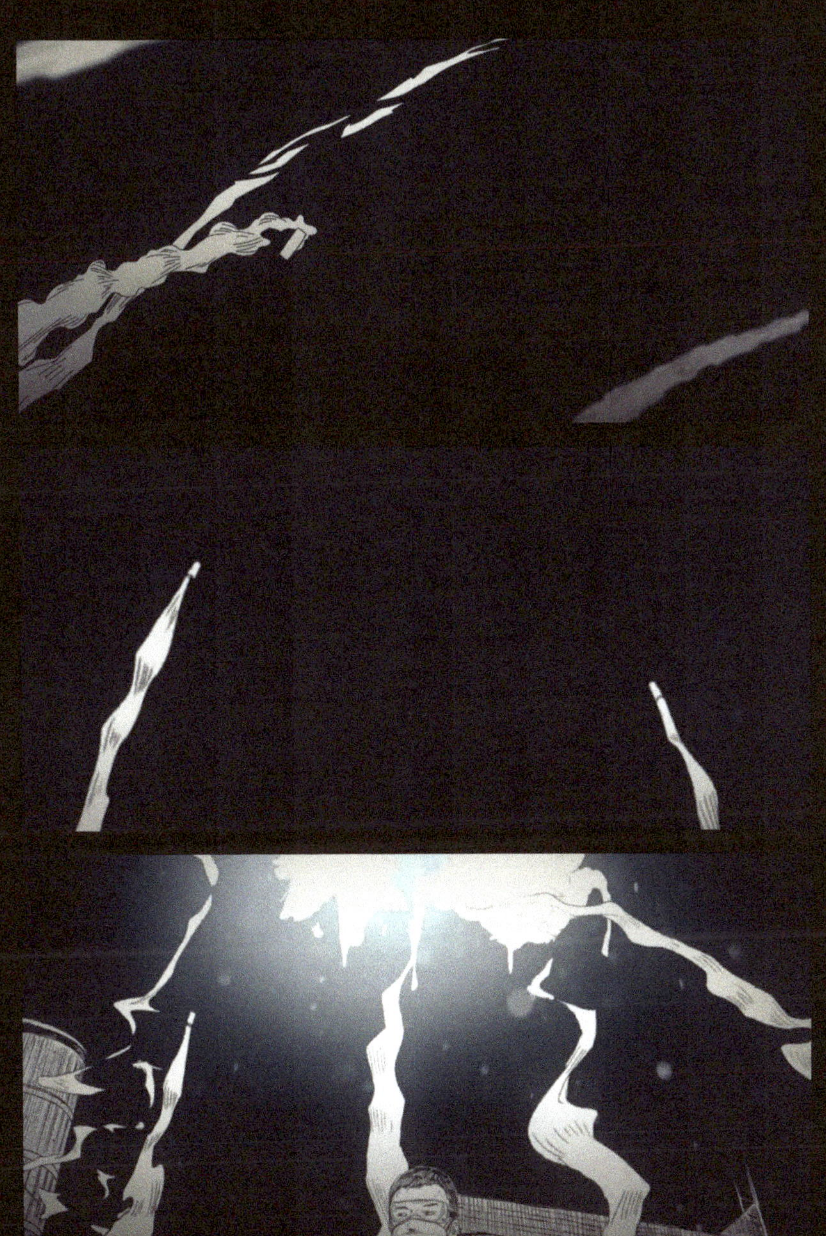

YOUTUBE.COM/WATCH?V=RXAHYWPLAD8

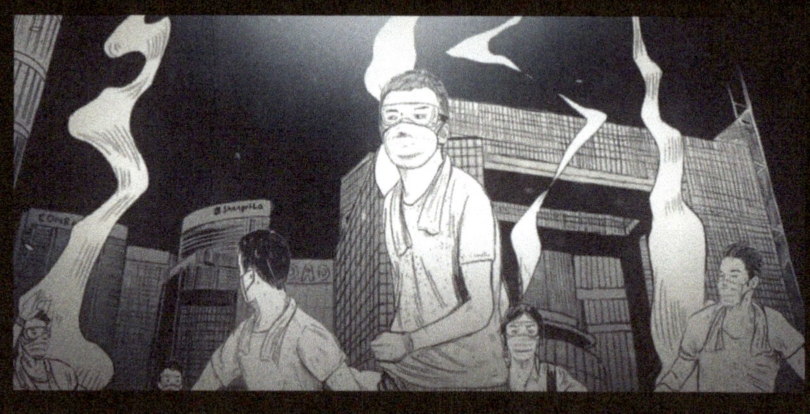

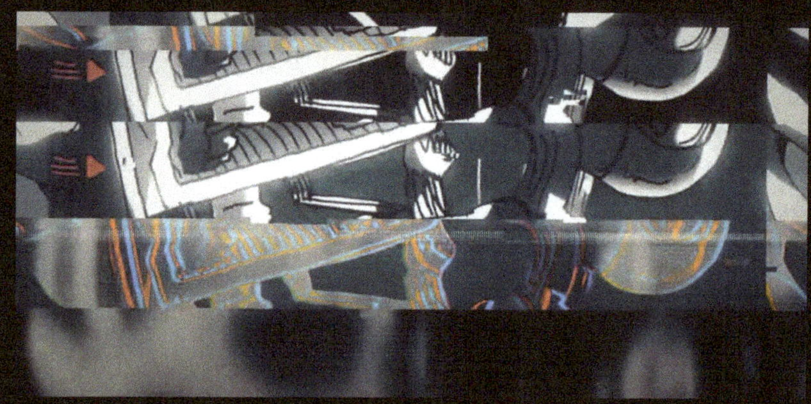

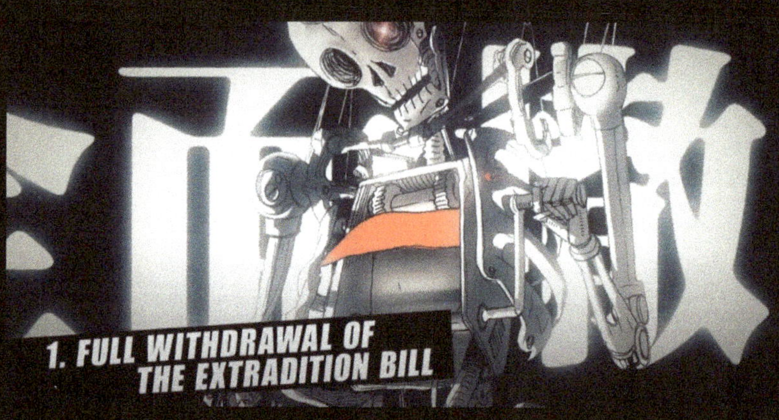
1. FULL WITHDRAWAL OF
THE EXTRADITION BILL

2. RETRACTION OF THE "RIOT" CHARACTERISATION

不是暴動

3. RELEASE OF ALL ARRESTED PROTESTORS

釋放 爭者

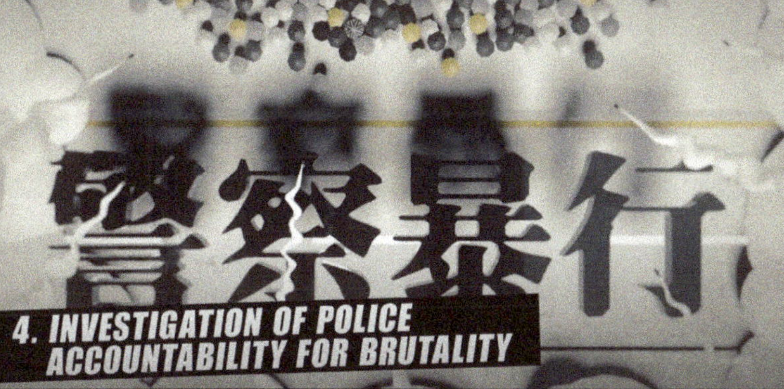

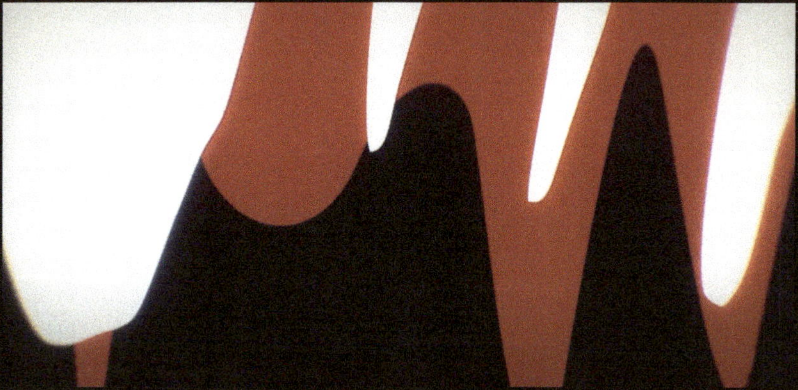

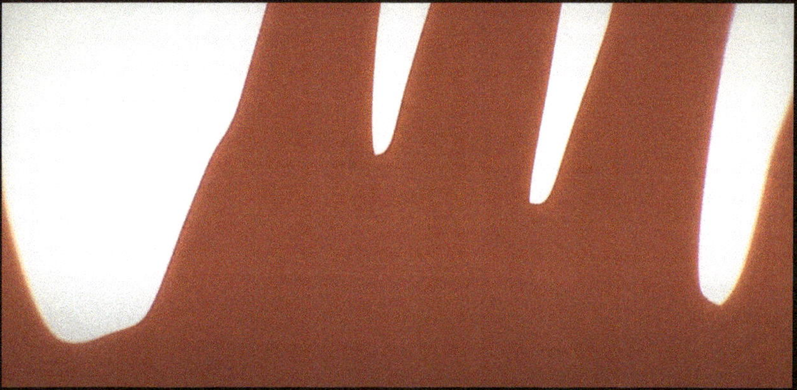

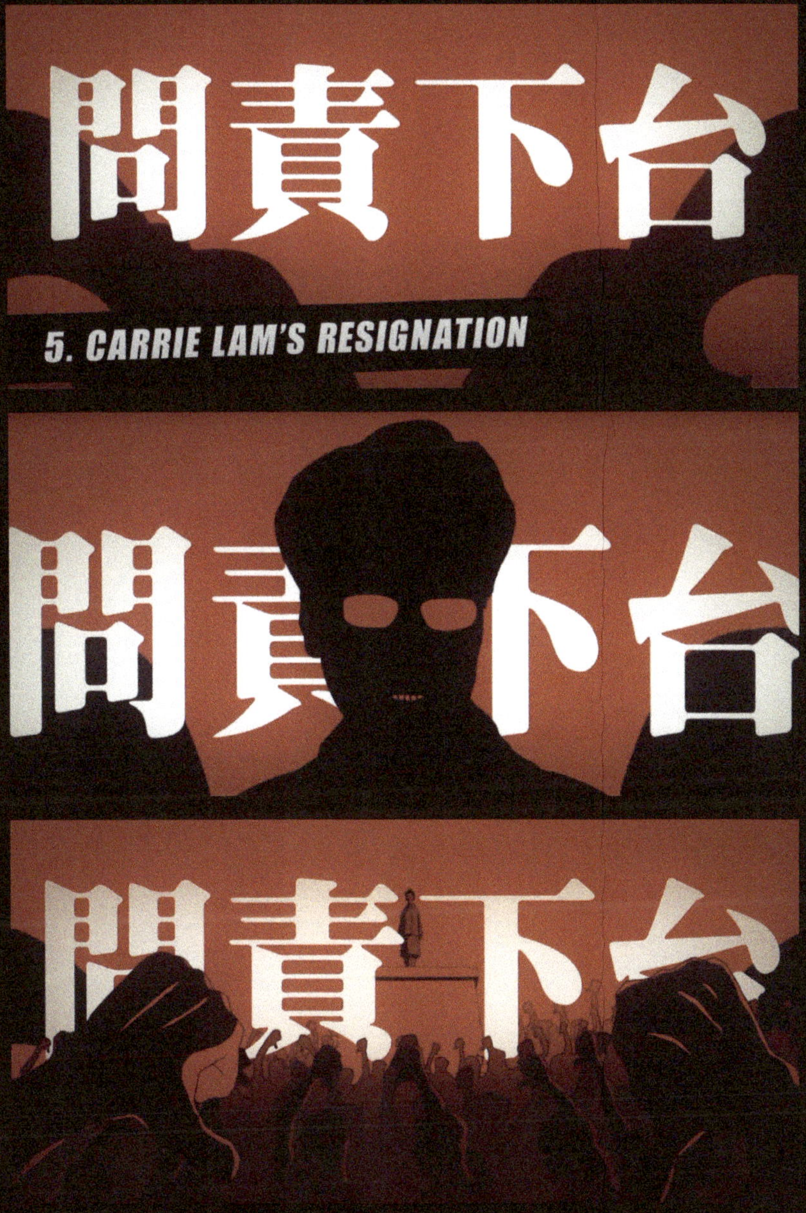

問責下台

5. CARRIE LAM'S RESIGNATION

問責下台

問責下台

N.O
EXTADITION
LAW

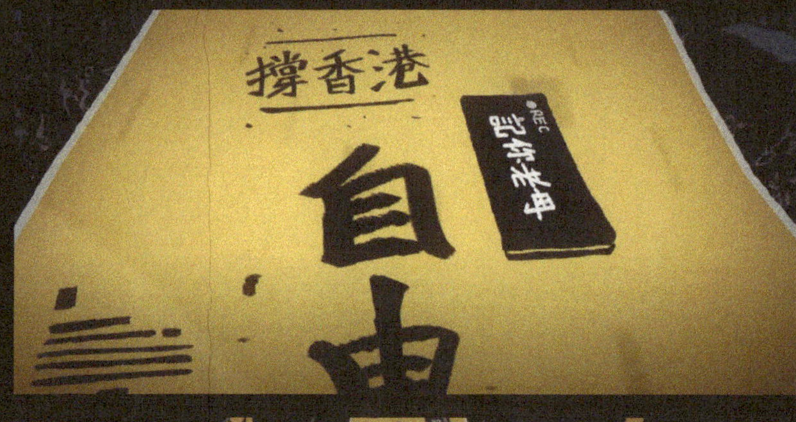

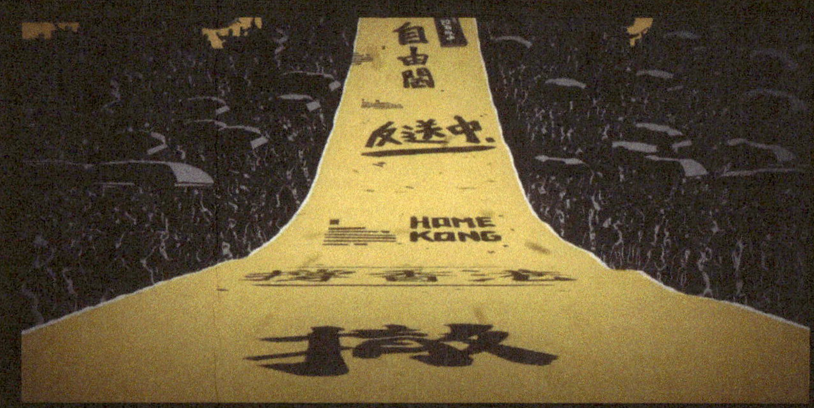

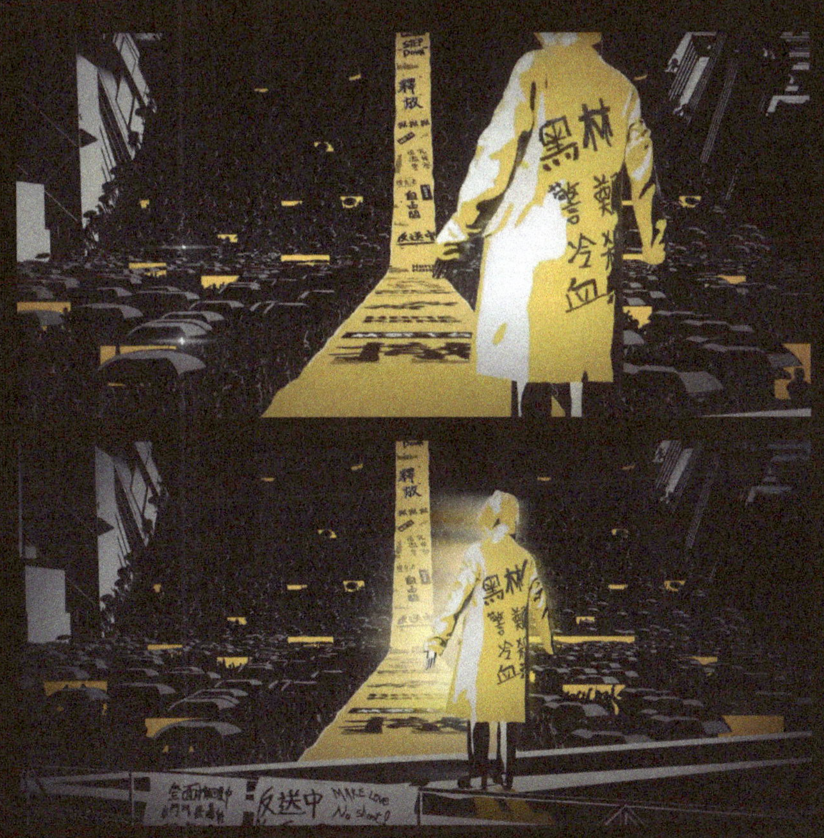

不撤·不散

WE WILL NOT BACK DOWN
UNTIL ALL OUR DEMANDS ARE MET

more on this history, see the 'further reading' section at the end of the book).

Despite the extradition bill being formally withdrawn on 23 October, the mobilisations not only continued but became more confrontational. 'The extradition bill exposed that China wants to finish off Hong Kong autonomy once and for all,' Au Loong Yu, author of *Hong Kong in revolt: the protest movement and the future of China*, said at the time. 'Why do you think even all the old people like me are yelling? We are known to be very calm here in Hong Kong. But the fight to defend our autonomy overrides everything.'

The people of Hong Kong had little say over their future when the territory was transferred from British colonialism to Chinese rule in 1997, but the arrangement agreed by London and Beijing, 'one country, two systems', was amenable to most residents. It stipulated that, for a transition period of fifty years, the territory would retain a 'high degree of autonomy', with its own laws, some limited political freedoms absent on the mainland and its own education system, among other things. It also promised universal suffrage—but every time the issue was raised, the Communist Party seemed to demur. As time passed, 'one country' was overwhelming 'two systems'. Ching Kwan Lee wrote of a recolonisation encapsulating three processes: 'political disenfranchisement, colonisation of the life world and economic

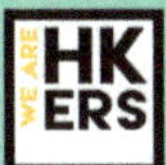

"As a paper lover,

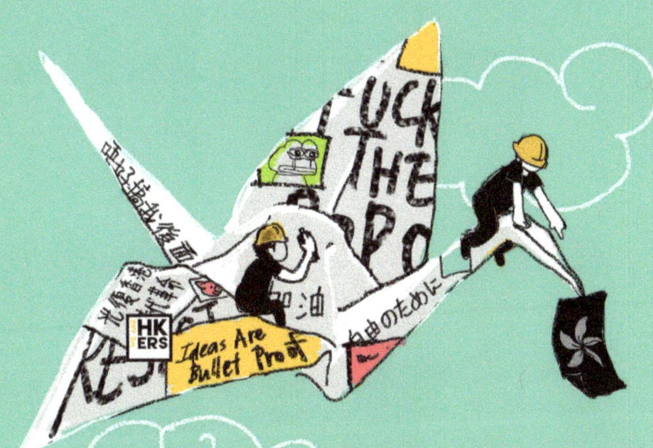

I love how Hong Kong people go back to paper for communication and promotion."

www.wearehkers.com
Wallpapers @ our IG @hkersweare

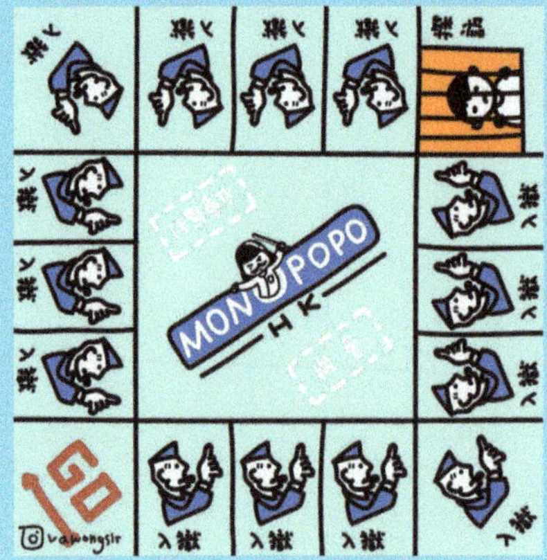
入獄
入獄
入獄
入獄
入獄
入獄
入獄
入獄
入獄
入獄
入獄
入獄
入獄
入獄
MONOPOPO
HK
GO
vawongsir

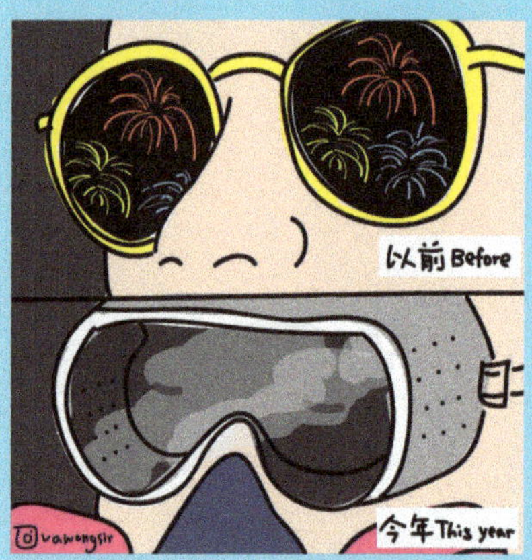
以前 Before
今年 This year
vawongsir

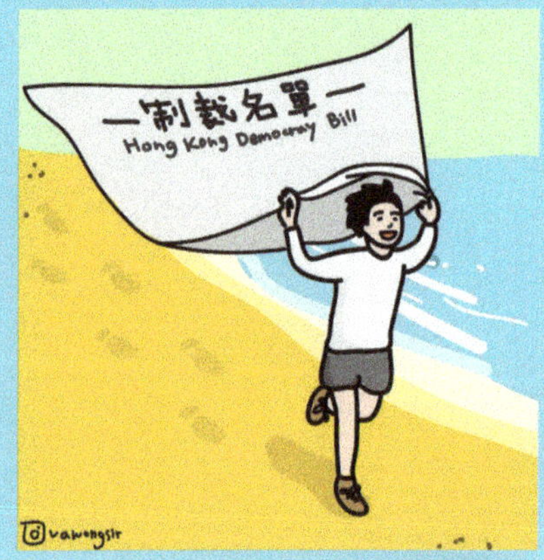
—制裁名單—
Hong Kong Democracy Bill
vawongsir

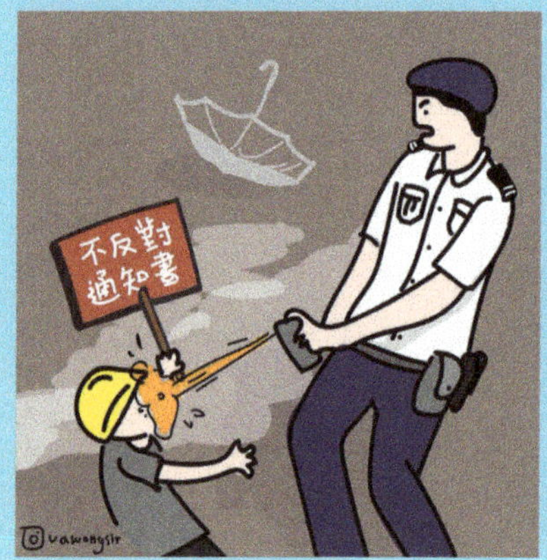
不反對
通知書
vawongsir

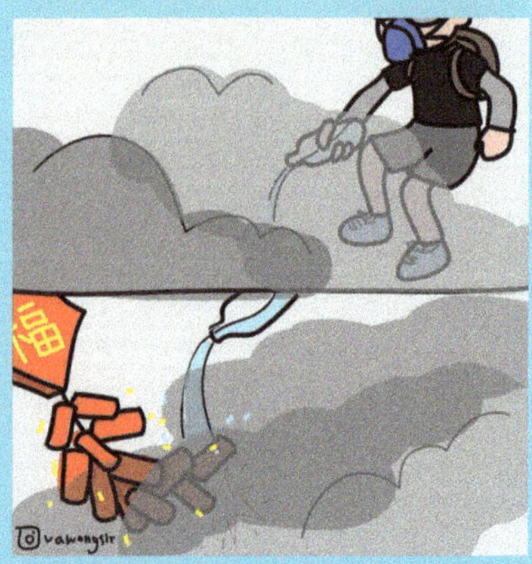
福
vawongsir

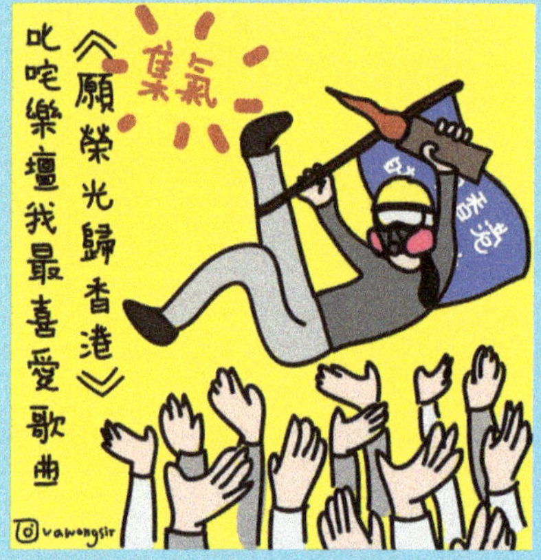
集氣
《願榮光歸香港》
叱咤樂壇我最喜愛歌曲
vawongsir

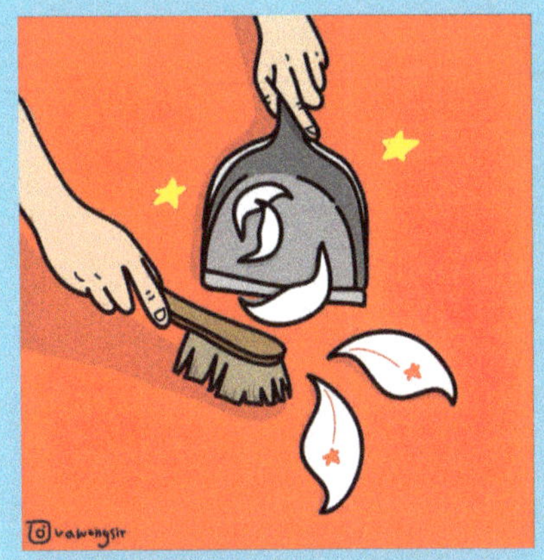

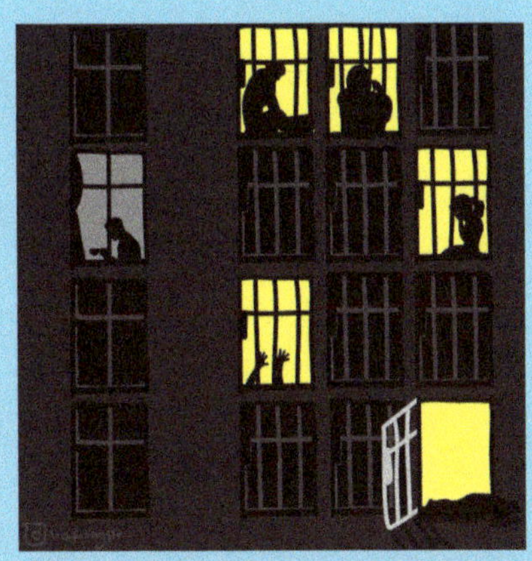

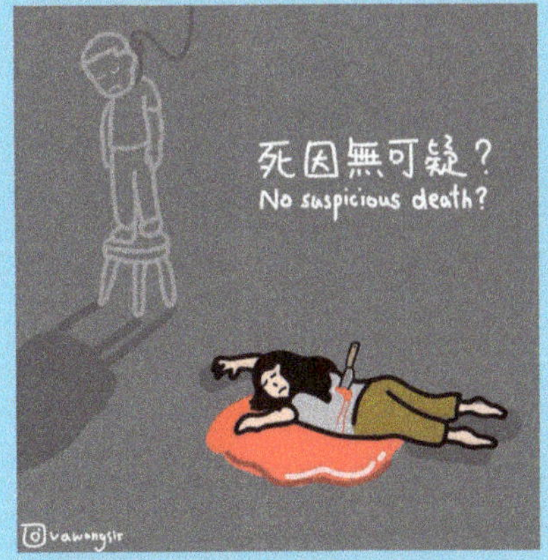

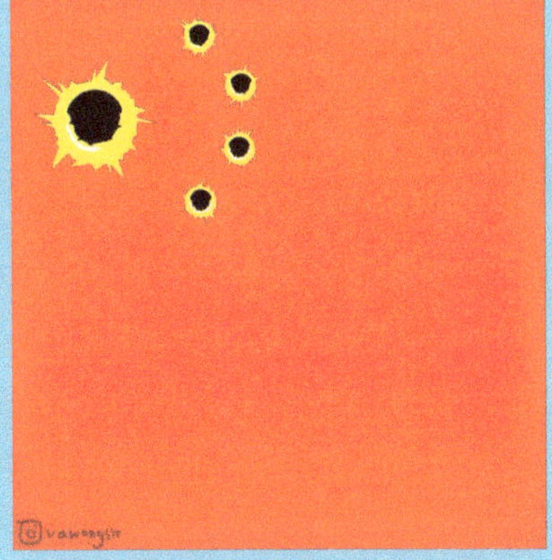

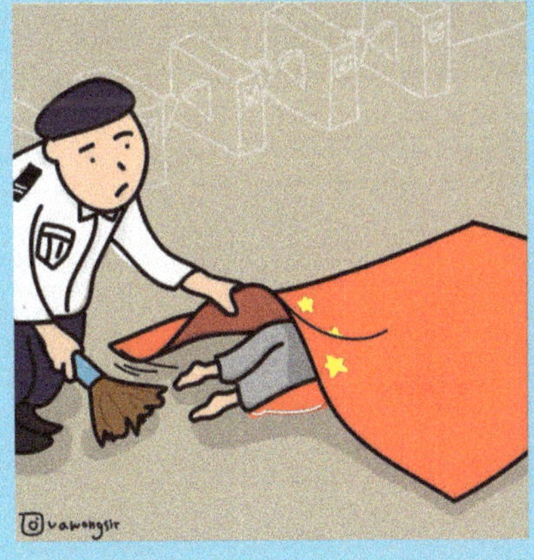

VAWONGSIR (2019-20)
FACEBOOK.COM/VAWONGSIR

subsumption'. Under the authoritarian rule of President Xi, these processes deepened.

Yet Beijing's attempts to erase the many lines of distinction between the territory and the mainland not only raised the ire of Honk Kong residents; it generated a political movement based on their perceived unique identity, an emerging 'peripheral nationalism'. In 1997, forty-seven percent of respondents to Hong Kong University's tracking polls identified as 'proud' citizens of China. By June 2019, before the rebellion fully developed, the figure had dropped to twenty-seven percent. Seventy-six percent identified as Hong Kongers; only twenty-three percent identified as Chinese. The aversion to direct Chinese rule is acute among young people, born into a city that, according to the Basic Law (the territory's mini-constitution), will be subsumed under Beijing's dictatorship no later than 2047. Ninety percent of those aged eighteen to twenty-nine said they were not proud to be citizens of China.

This broad shift, and the depth of feeling in the street, are key to understanding contemporary politics in Hong Kong, and why a significant current now talks not simply of autonomy but of self-determination. It is worth quoting from a 2015 essay written by eighteen-year-old Joshua Wong, one of the leading figures of the previous year's Umbrella Movement. Kong Tsung-gan, a resident author and a contributor to *Hong*

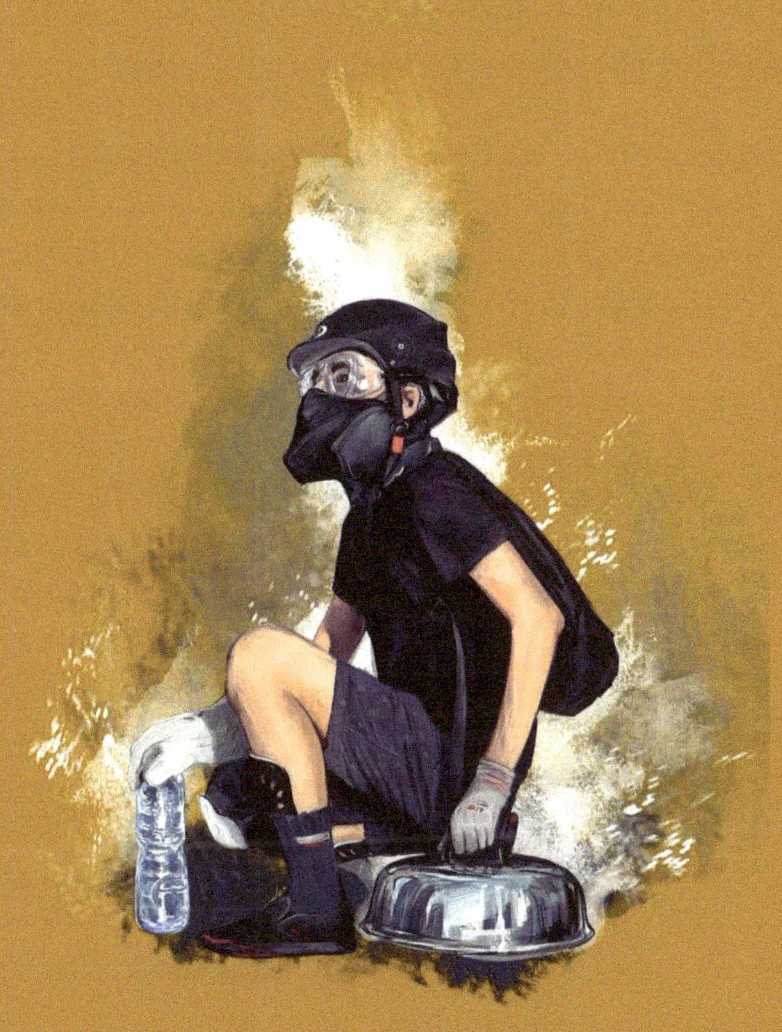

Kong Free Press, at the time called Wong's contribution 'the most substantial vision yet presented by a prominent democracy movement leader in Hong Kong on the future':

'In this post-reform period, while the localists [Hong Kong nationalists, for want of a better term—BH] have not gained mainstream support, they have put forward an agenda for self-governance or independence and provided a solution to the democracy movement in Hong Kong. The pan-democrats [the establishment, and generally liberal, pro-democratic forces] ought to understand that a "democratic return to Chinese sovereignty" is futile ...

'The fundamental problem is that the demand for reform has no foundation ... Many of our friends continue to repeat "I want real universal suffrage" without revising their strategy to avoid endless argument over political reform. It is therefore unsurprising that the number of people on the streets has not swayed those in power. Any movement for democracy is a long-term struggle. Yet many retain the threadbare fixation on gaining seats in Legislative Council or the Election Committee or champion joining hands with civil society as if they have discovered the New World ...

'If Beijing had not welched in 2004 and had allowed universal suffrage in 2007 according to the principle of "a democratic return to Chinese sovereignty", perhaps today's radicals would not be so rapidly proliferating on the internet

... The recent burgeoning of localist discourse is largely the result of young people's reaction to the authoritarian politics of the Chinese Communist Party and their belief that Hong Kong cannot practice self-governance under the rule of China. Thus, Beijing's noncompliance in 2004 has been the catalyst for the tendencies among young people towards independence and separatism ...

'What the democrats have learned in this period of political reform is that facilitating mutual trust with Beijing is an unrequited desire, that implementing universal suffrage according to the existing framework for political reform is a pipe dream, and that the regime's policy on Hong Kong is changing. "One country" is interpreted as primary to "two systems"; a high level of autonomy is equated with Beijing retaining control of governance at all levels; the separation of powers misunderstood as the collusion of powers. This all demonstrates that Hong Kong faces the grave possibility of becoming no different from Shenzhen ...

'If we hope to continue along the path of democratic self-governance in Hong Kong and successfully address the "second question of the future" [i.e. the post-2047 arrangement], we must show the will and vision for sustainable self-governance in this age of democratic bankruptcy. Our goal in struggling for self-governance is self-determination, which means that the Hong Kong people have the right to

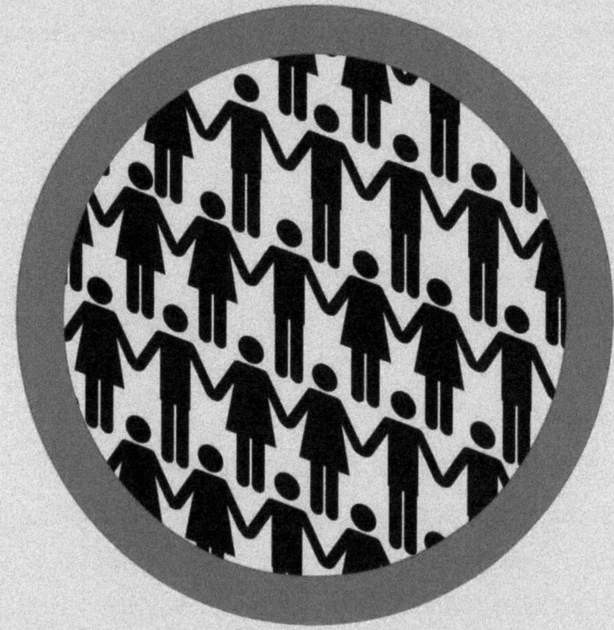

PHESTI
@PHESTI_HKER

decide Hong Kong's future, and which also establishes a Hong Kong subjectivity.'

Self-determination does not necessarily mean independence. A survey conducted for Reuters in December 2019 found that only one in five is opposed to "one country, two systems" and that just seventeen percent support a total break from Chinese sovereignty. Broadly, the movement is not 'anti-China', although the sentiment exists. It is driven by Beijing's overreach and compounded by the passage of time bringing totalitarianism ever closer. While 'localism' as an organised current remains somewhat marginal, national or localist consciousness (whatever it may be called) has become a highly influential political and cultural phenomenon. Self-determination is now a central question in the city—only by grasping this can the 2019 rebellion be understood.

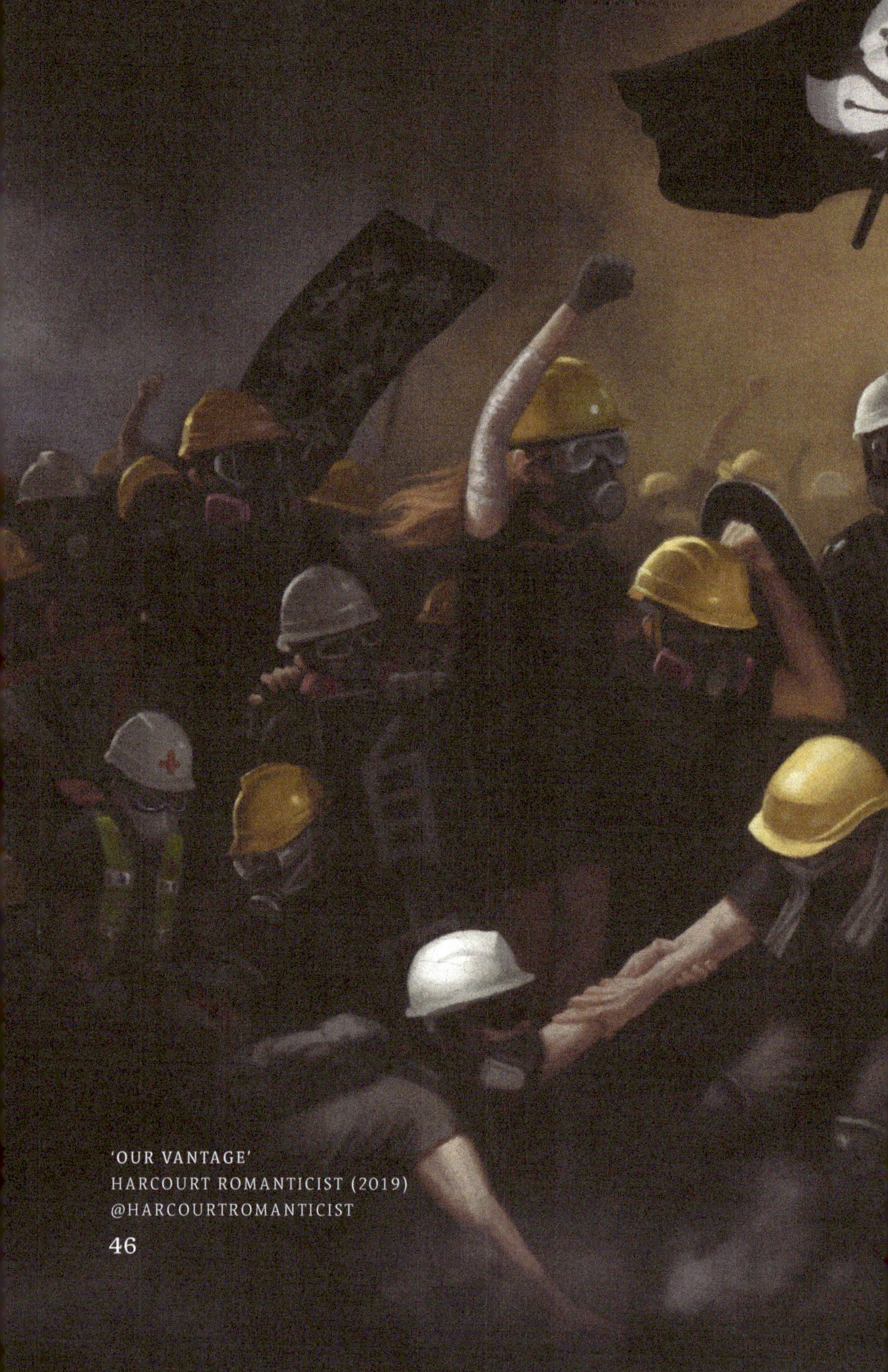

'OUR VANTAGE'
HARCOURT ROMANTICIST (2019)
@HARCOURTROMANTICIST

NOVEMBER

NOVEMBER

BATTLE FOR THE STREETS

TUESDAY 12 NOVEMBER | Barricades and fires are everywhere along Nathan Road and in adjacent streets in Mong Kok. Masked students are digging up bricks from the footpath, smashing them and littering the place to stop vehicles getting through. Others smash shop fronts, CCTV cameras and traffic lights. The signal boxes are being torn open and set ablaze, before exploding.

'Every night there is something. Tonight, the scale is bigger,' says a young protester. 'Police are attacking the university tonight—so we fight here to spread their manpower thin. When we had the peaceful demonstrations in the day, the government would shut down the trains and then the cops would stop and search the buses, taking people away to the police station. Now we are getting smarter; we are learning

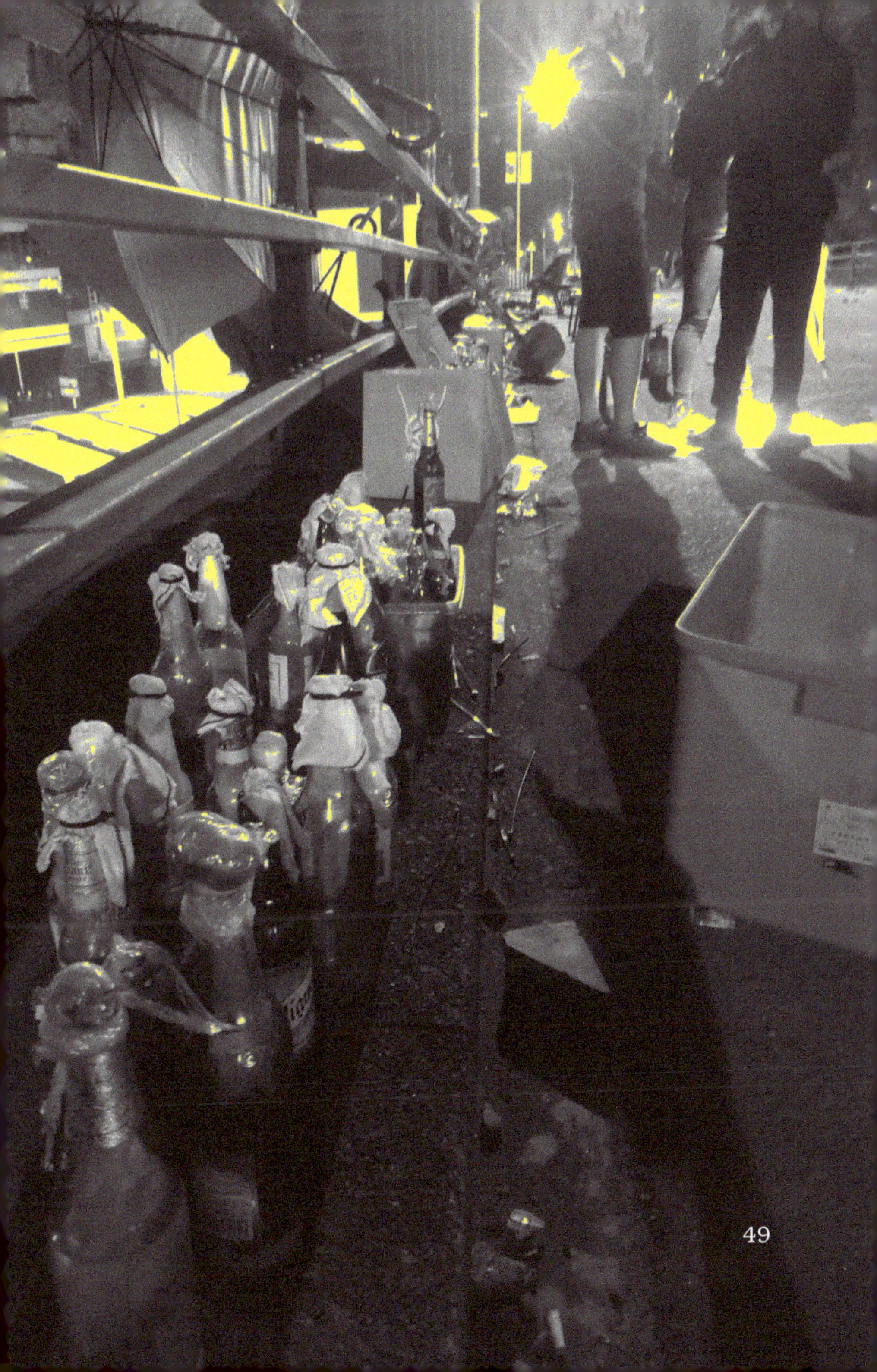

from our mistakes. Now we fight in our neighbourhoods. We fight everywhere.'

Thirty districts have been shaken by protests. The *South China Morning Post* reports that yesterday almost three hundred people were arrested. One was shot with a live round. Two hundred and fifty-five canisters of tear gas, two hundred and four rubber bullets, forty-five beanbag rounds and ninety-six sponge grenades were also fired. Protesters say that organised crime groups are being used as hired thugs as well.

At the Chinese University across town, police are again firing rubber bullets and trying to take the campus. But word has it that they are facing stiff resistance. The police have shut the eastern metro line only to trigger absolute carnage in this part of town. Busloads of riot police move in, firing volley after volley of tear gas. The protesters blow whistles and disperse. 'Be like water,' they say. The cops advance several hundred metres south along Nathan, firing teargas in all directions. A water cannon hits a few people who stayed too close. For a time, it seems as though police have secured the road. Wrong.

When they move back toward their HQ, bricks fly from a side street. The students have doubled back, almost in a pincer move. It felt like there were hundreds. But now they are swarming everywhere. There are thousands of them. Busting into construction sites, they dismantle scaffolding and use it

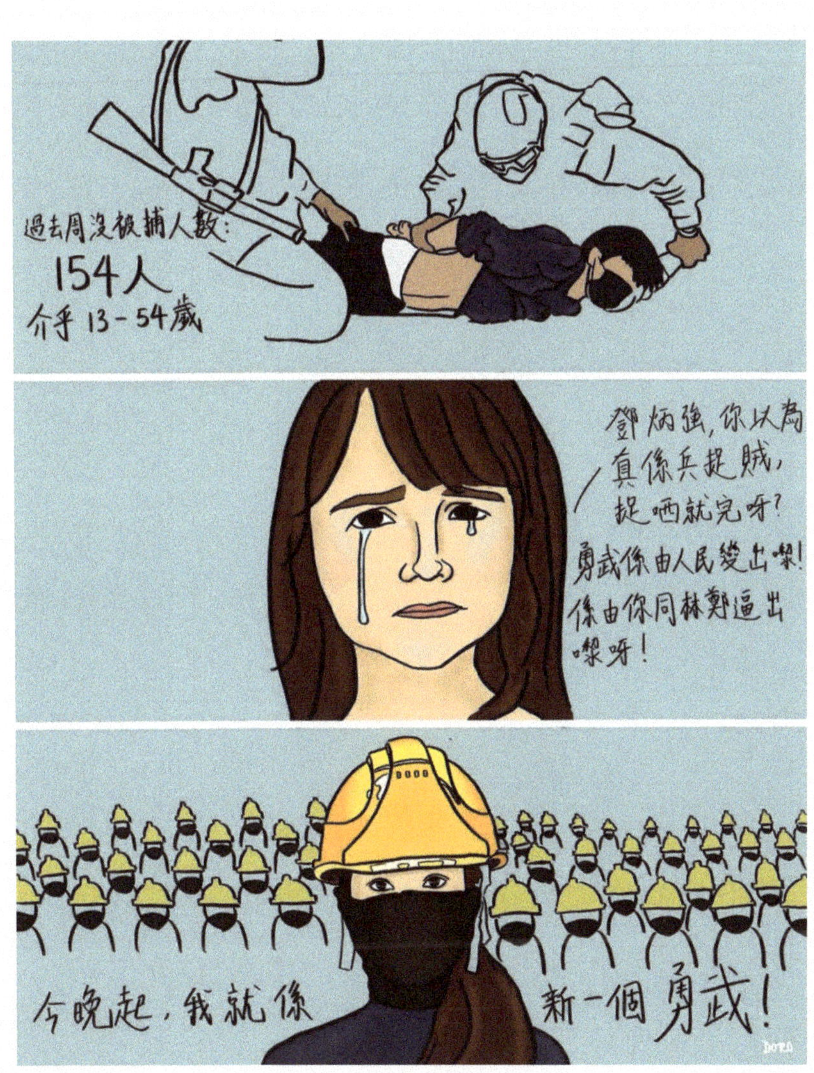

LAIFEII
@LAIFEILLUSTRATION

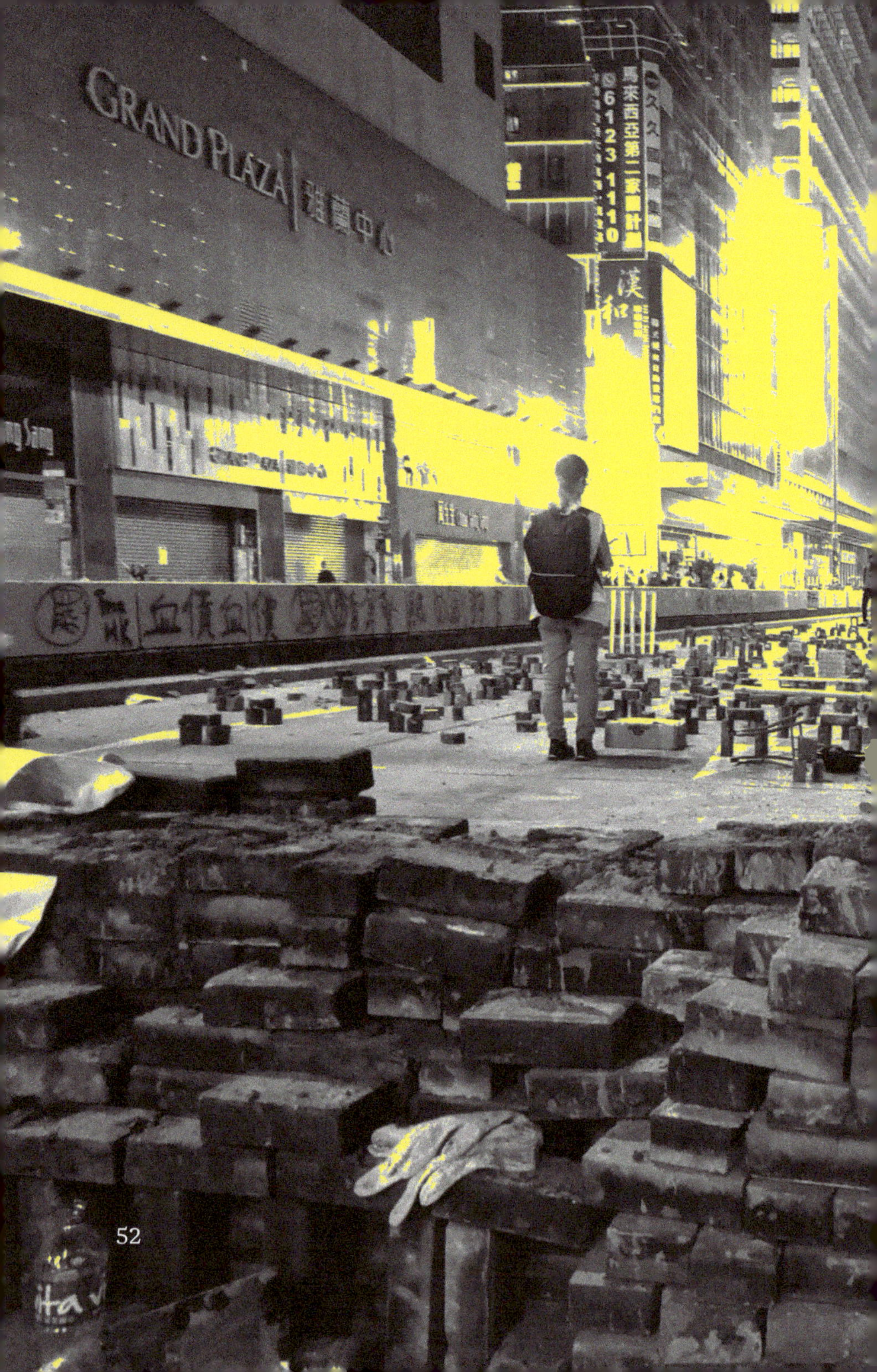
GRAND PLAZA
6123 1110
血債血償

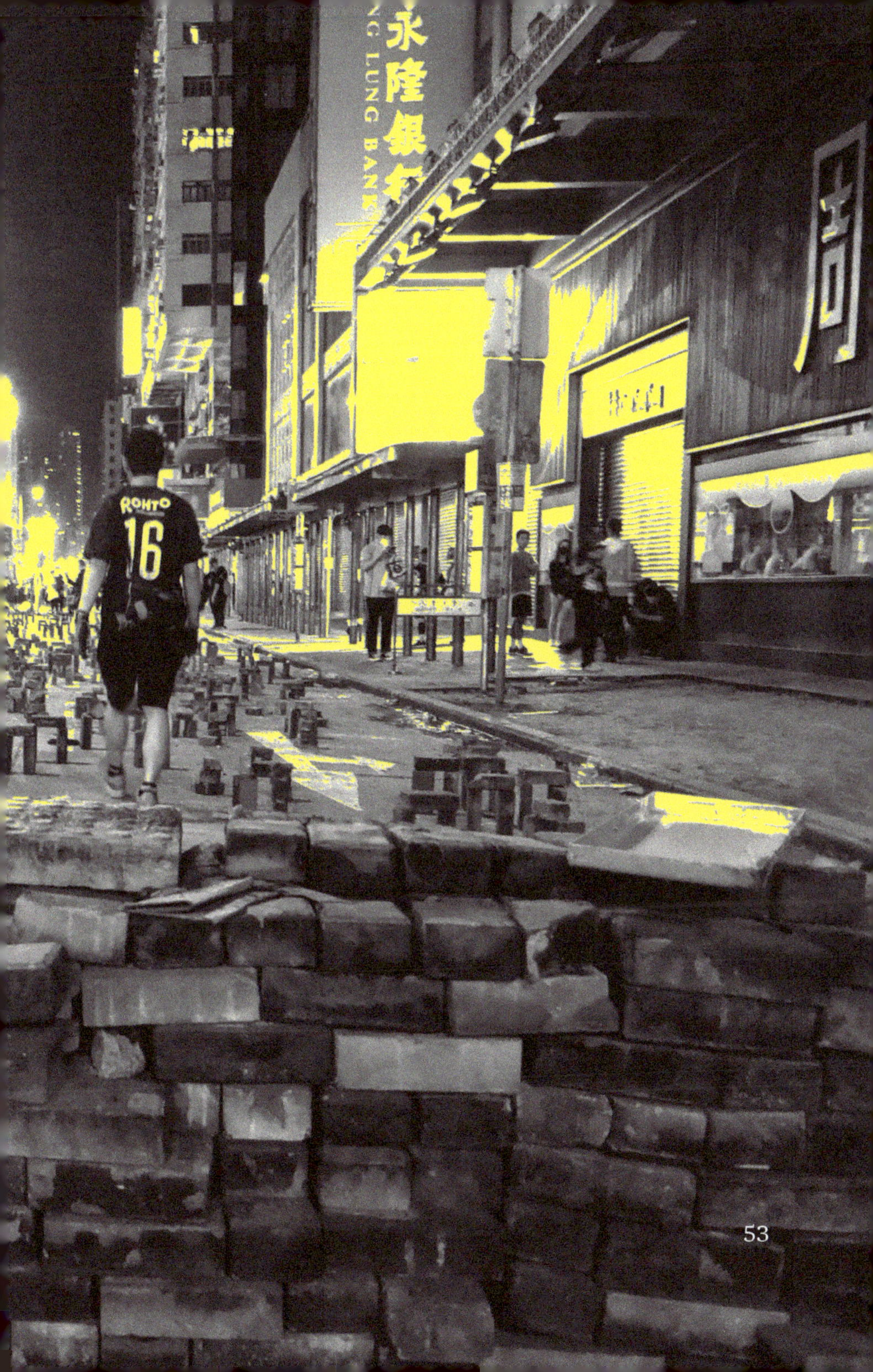
永隆銀
NG LUNG BANK
ROHTO
16

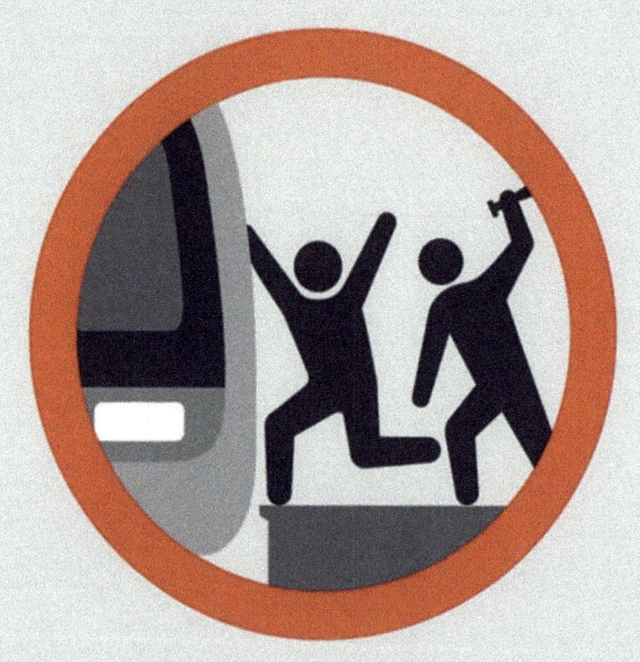

請小心元朗暴徒

Please mind the thug

to reinforce the barricades. They grab anything they can get their hands on—long bars of reinforced steel, bags of rubbish, bamboo poles, plastic wrapping—then spray the whole thing with whatever sticky or gluey substance they can find. The sidewalk is being torn apart and brick after brick is thrown onto the roads.

'CCP [Chinese Communist Party] and the government have the power to stop this,' a young woman says. 'There should be universal suffrage so we can choose for ourselves how to live.' This is one of the key issues at stake. Hong Kong's Basic Law, drawn up before the territory was reincorporated into Chinese sovereignty in 1997 following more than one hundred years of British colonial administration, noted universal suffrage as an 'ultimate aim'. However, growing hostility to CCP authoritarianism means fewer and fewer people in Hong Kong identify as Chinese.

In 2014, the Chinese government clarified that giving everyone the vote is definitely the aim. But candidates for chief executive must be 'patriots'—'a person who loves the country [China]'—chosen by a nominating committee chosen by the government. And while Hong Kongers continue to have more rights than mainlanders under the Basic Law, the territory will be fully incorporated no later than 2047. The people on the street don't like this one bit.

Protesters yell at the cops constantly. What are they

saying? Murderers! 'We want to piss them off, make them angry,' says another protester. 'We have to engage them. Keep them here. We have to save the university.' To the side, a dozen squat, holding open umbrellas to conceal themselves. They're making Molotov cocktails. Another group, using the same method of concealment, are trying to break through a bank roller shutter. It's impossible to make out the politics of the hardcore blocs (within the broader protest, there are at least a dozen different groups ranging in size from six to twenty participants). Graffiti everywhere—literally everywhere—attacks the 'PoPo' (police). There's also 'Freedom or death', 'We are the future', 'Catalunya independence', and a riff on Che Guevara's famous quote: 'Injustice (CCP China) anywhere is a threat to justice everywhere'. Some carry metal bars and hammers to smash anything and everything.

'Where am I, Syria?!' says an older man, visibly shaking as he points to the attempted bank break-in. He doesn't support the students? 'I support the students, of course! All the violence is from the police. This was inevitable. The police take their orders from China. The government takes its orders from China. To me [Hong Kong Chief Executive] Carrie Lam is the devil woman. To go to hell ten times is not enough!'

No-one has a megaphone. The protesters rely on collective mustering, shouts starting at one position and filtering down to give directions, make appeals or warn of police movements.

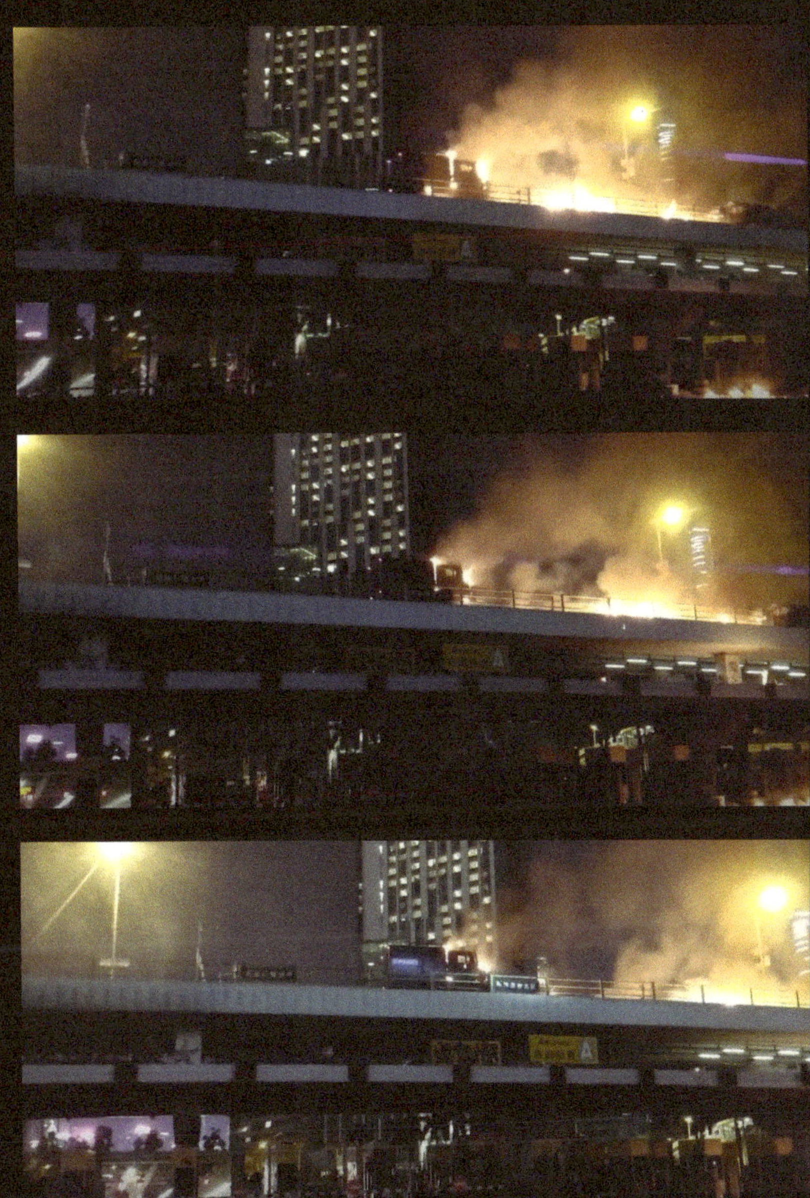

AN ARMOURED VEHICLE ON FIRE AND RETREATING NEAR THE POLYTECHNIC UNIVERSITY, 17 NOVEMBER

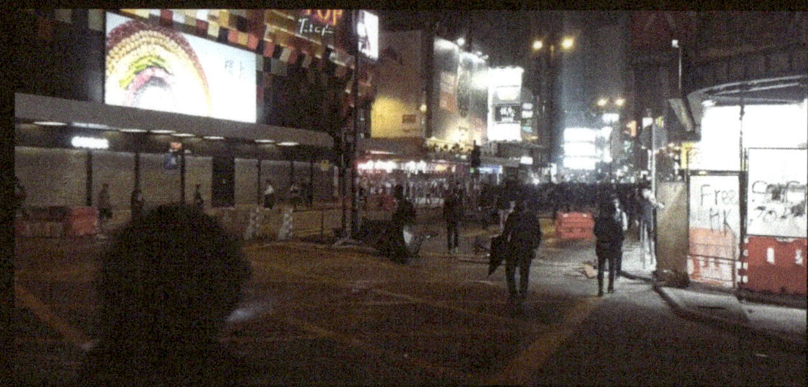

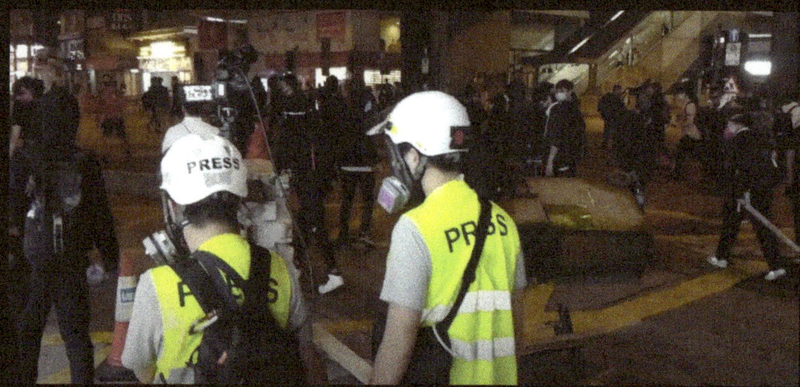

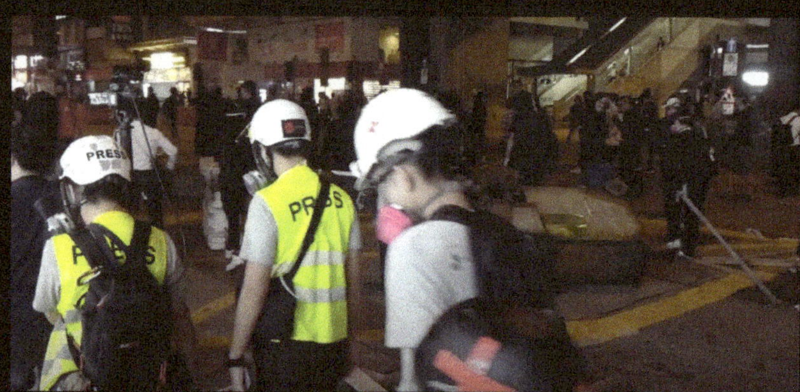

MAKING BARRICADES AT MONG KOK

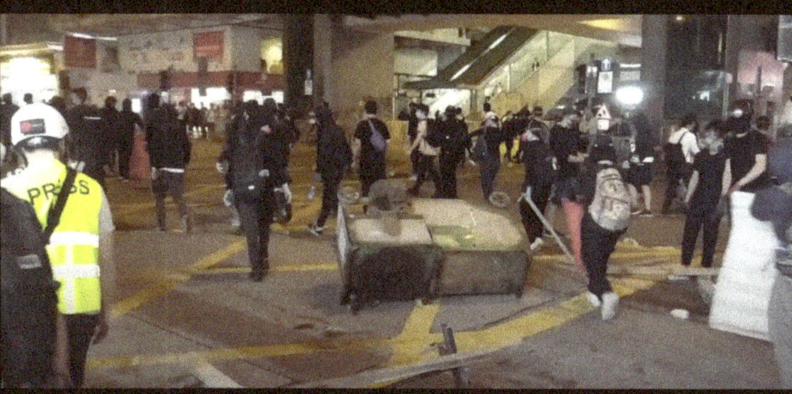
PRESS

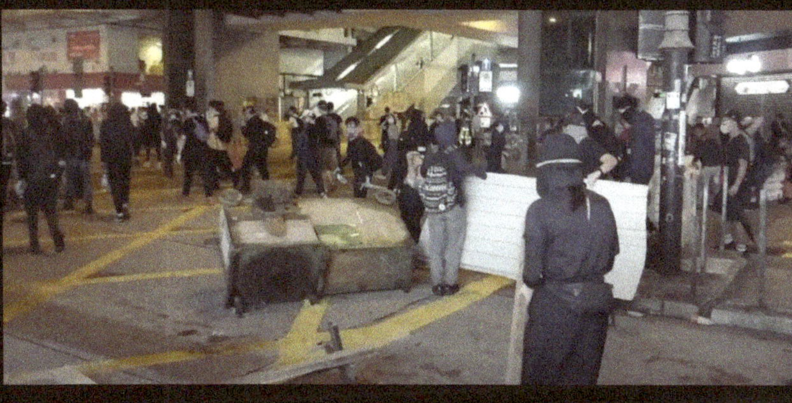

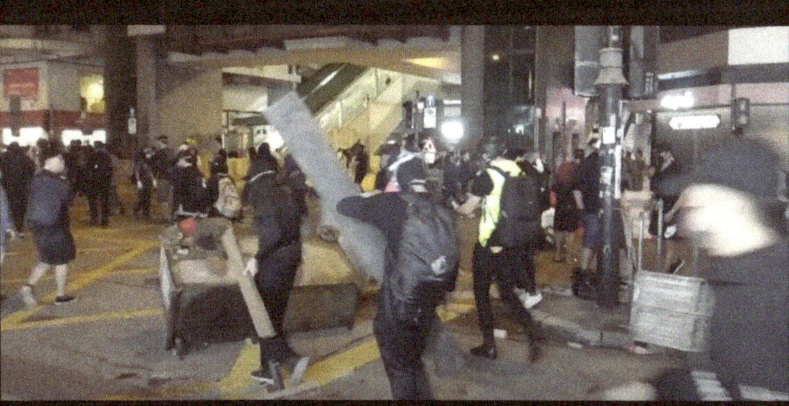

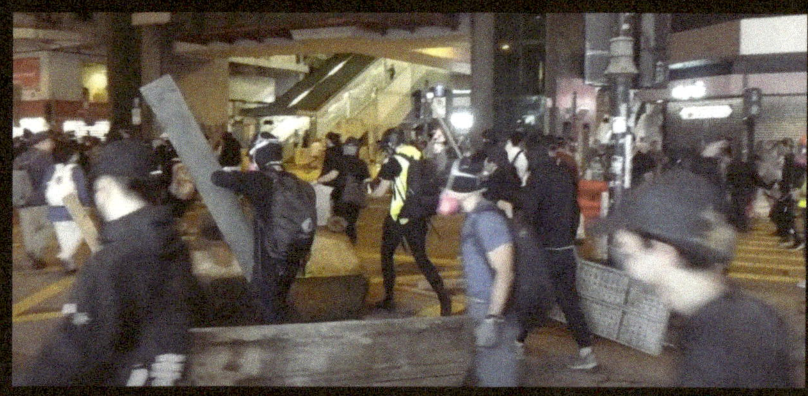

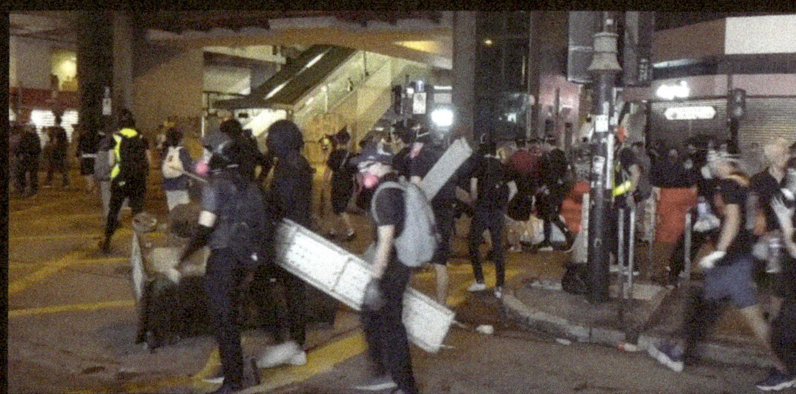

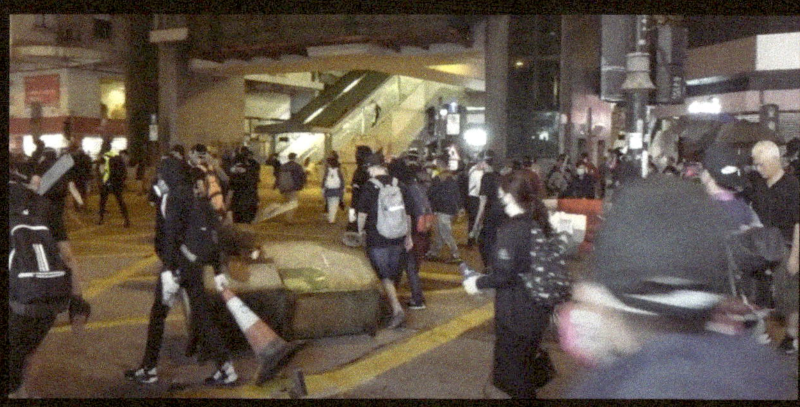

MAKING BARRICADES AT MONG KOK

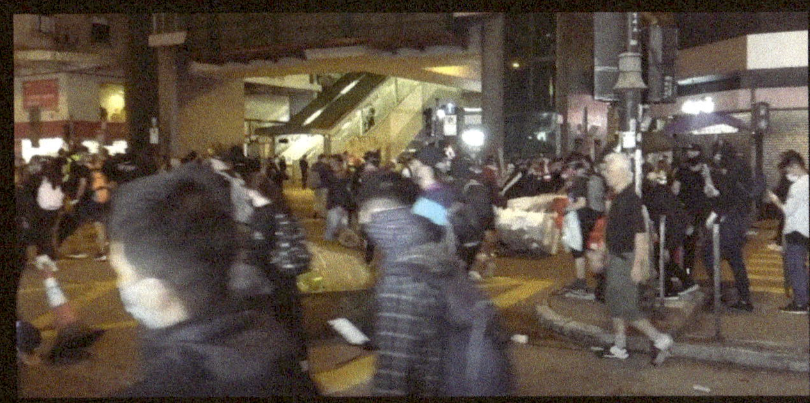

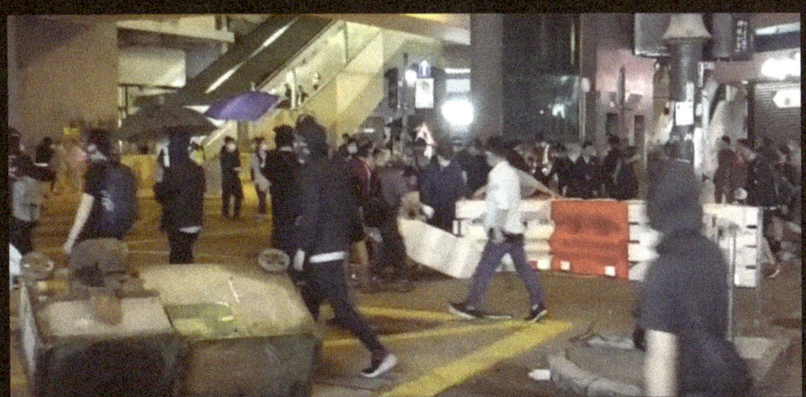

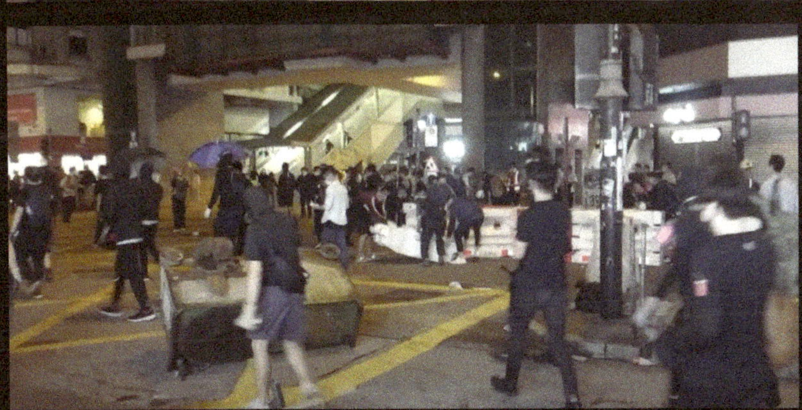

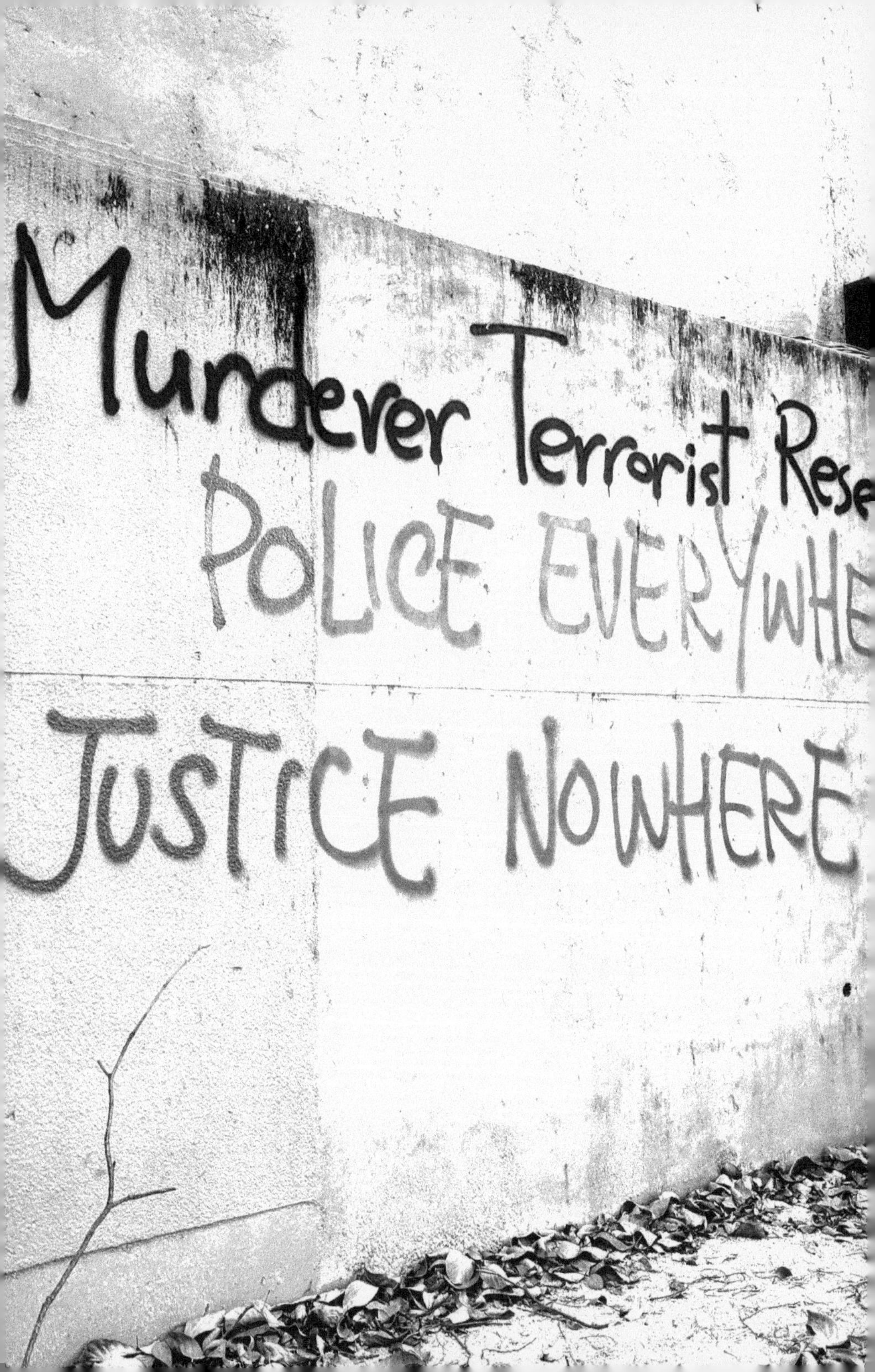

Murderer Terrorist Rese

POLICE EVERYWHE

JUSTICE NOWHERE

It is a constant back-and-forth. Cops move forward, fire tear gas. Protesters retreat, then move forward again. Just after midnight, a human chain about two hundred metres long forms along Nathan Road. They pass umbrellas and bottles to the front. The Molotov operation is quite collective.

Some shine lasers and high-powered torches on figures at the top of a nearby building. It's the district police station and the commander is on the roof, surveying the situation. The cops have left the street and fortified their position in the building. The complex's loudspeaker airs repeated calls to disperse. But the frontline umbrella group advances anyway, only to be belted with tear gas. While many protesters have gas masks, most don't. They retreat. But as soon as the gas clears, people push forward again. Several dozen police storm out, firing yet more gas. Another retreat followed by another advance. It is unrelenting.

The cops fire rubber bullets. One student is hit in the leg. A bullet glances off another's jaw. They are rushed to a side street by the student medics. But no-one will let up. The umbrella group again moves forward, throwing Molotovs. One is dropped by a rubber bullet to the leg. Another's little finger is left gashed. Calls ring out left and right for the medics, who race to every injury.

A middle-aged man in a suit jacket walks through the crowd handing out umbrellas. 'There're not from me, they're from my neighbour. She is old and didn't want to come down. But she wanted to help,' he says. Another man walks around with a shopping bag full of small tissue packets. After 1am, the cops come out in force again. Bricks and Molotovs fly in retaliation, but now they are just gestures. Everyone has been driven back and into the side streets by a barrage of tear gas cannisters. The air is thick with it and smoke from everything else burning. In the middle of it all, an old street stall vendor continues selling away. He's nonchalantly sitting there in a gas mask doing a vigorous trade in drinks, completely unperturbed.

Police progress several blocks and there is a lull. When they retreat at about 2:30am, the protest has diminished in size. Again, the students move forward and reassemble the damaged barricades. It will be on again tomorrow.

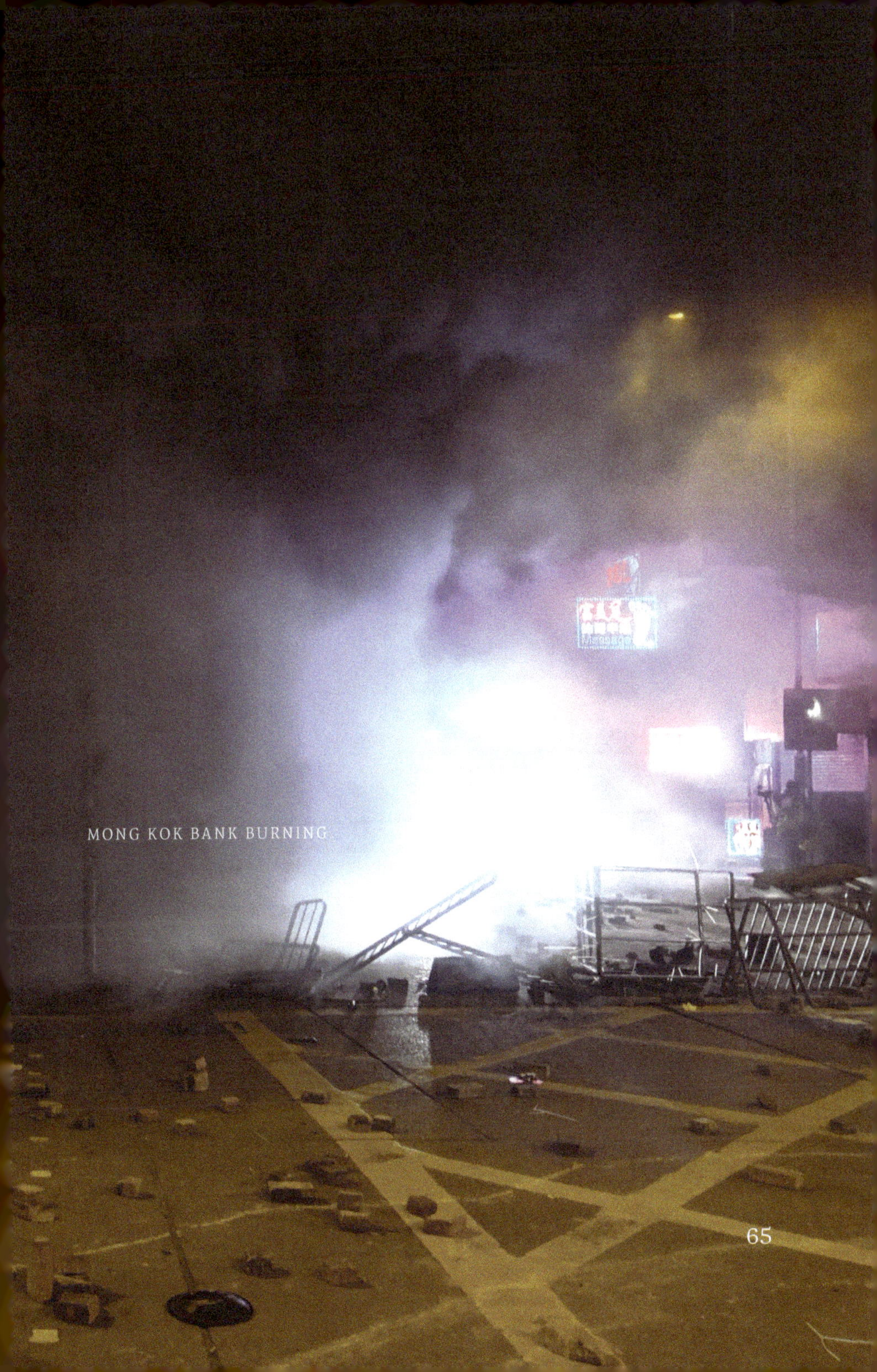

MONG KOK BANK BURNING

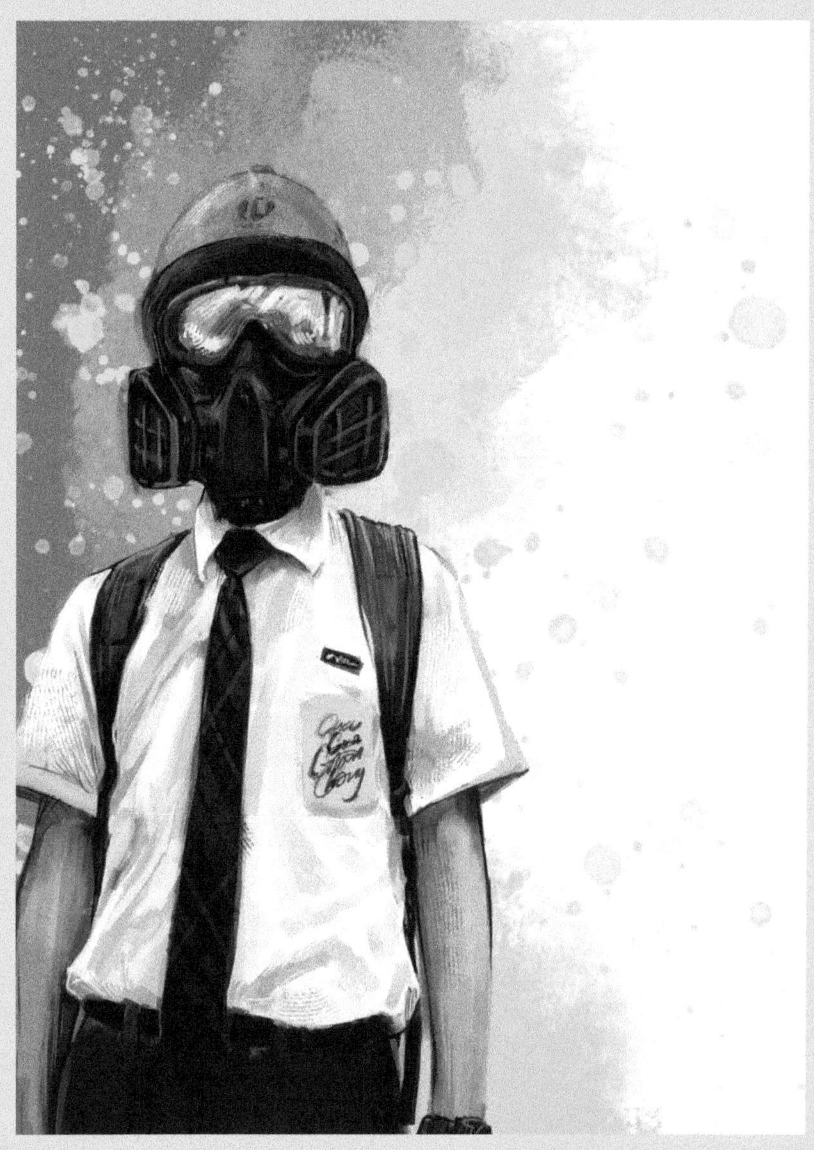

EYEWITNESS TO THE CLASHES AT THE CHINESE UNIVERSITY

LOKMAN TSUI IS AN ASSISTANT PROFESSOR AT THE SCHOOL OF JOURNALISM AND COMMUNICATION AT THE CHINESE UNIVERSITY OF HONG KONG (CUHK). THIS IS AN EDITED VERSION OF A POST PUBLISHED BY LOKMAN ON FACEBOOK, AND LATER AT GLOBALVOICES.ORG, DETAILING THE CLASHES BETWEEN STUDENT ACTIVISTS AND POLICE ON TUESDAY 12 NOVEMBER. IT HAS BEEN INCLUDED HERE TO GIVE CONTEXT TO THE EVENING PROTESTS IN MONG KOK, DESCRIBED ABOVE.

As I write this, I am sitting in my office. It's 9am Hong Kong time on 13 November. I've just brushed my teeth, washed my face and got myself some tea. Yes, I slept in my office, on the couch. My body feels a bit stiff and tired, and it reminds me of the days I'd go out clubbing until sunrise—except of course I am not that young anymore, nor was I exactly dancing last night. I shouldn't complain, because at least I had a couch to sleep on. I don't know how many students slept outside last night, but by the time I left, around 3am, many were still outside working the supply lines, literally holding down the fort.

The day of 12 November was completely nuts. It started with the 11am press conference in which I participated. In 'normal' times, taking the Department of Justice to court over an injunction seeking to censor online speech would be newsworthy. But yesterday, only a sprinkling of journalists were present. The conference was live streamed on the news portal HK01, and it got coverage from Apple, RTHK radio, Unwire and some others. But on a day like yesterday, this was not news—and understandably so, with everything else that was happening.

After the press conference, which was held in the Legislative Council Building, I looked for a place to sit down and calm my nerves. I was walking towards Central district. It was almost lunch hour; for the second day in a row, office workers were coming out to protest against the Hong Kong government and the police. In front of Louis Vuitton, people wearing suits and high heels were trying to occupy the road, shouting slogans. Some were kneeling to leverage bricks so we could use them as roadblocks. Others stood on the sky

DEAR TRAVELER

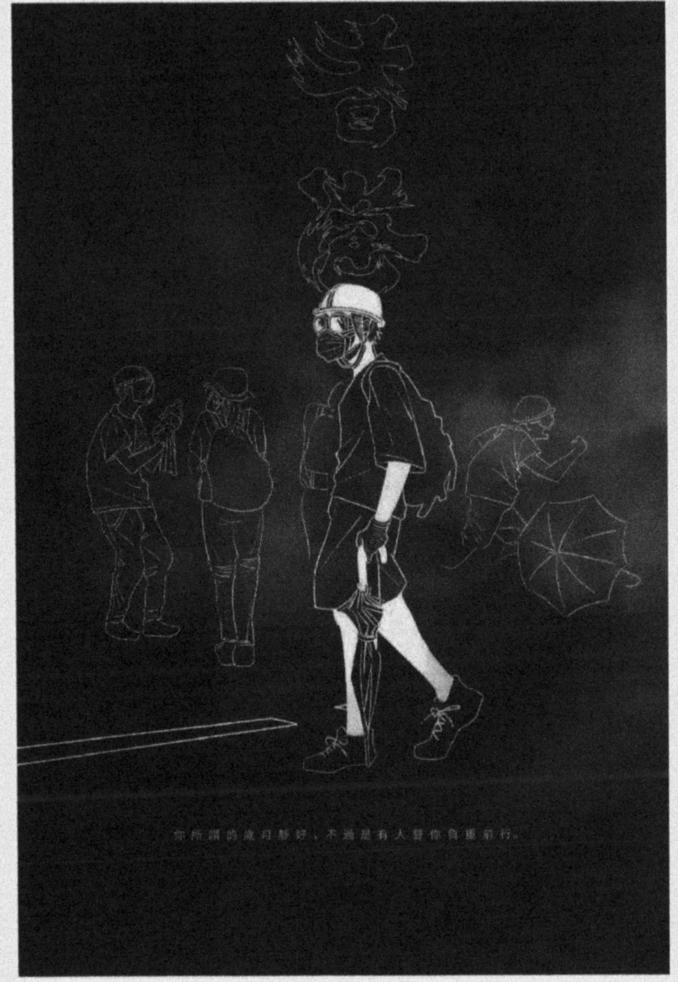

HAVE A NICE TRIP.

bridge looking down at us, and many were yelling at them to come down and join us, that this is not a movie.

At some point, five high school girls showed up, visibly excited. They started shouting slogans and the rest of the crowd followed suit. Then members of the press started photographing the high-schoolers—inappropriately, as such a record could haunt them later. The girls giggled with embarrassment at first, then moved away; but the photographers followed them. In the end, several of us took out our umbrellas and shielded the girls. We held our umbrellas up for a while until my arm started getting sore. I told the girls to remember not to neglect their studies (when did I become this person?), and we went our own way. As 2pm neared, people began retreating. The lunch hour was over. Only moments before, we'd been standing strong, facing down the police, then abruptly 'reality' kicks in, and it is time to go back to the office. I got myself some food and headed home.

That was when I began seeing footage of the scenes at CUHK—the university where I teach. Some of my students were tweeting things like 'where is the university president, where is the management, where are the teachers?!' I felt terrible. As I responded to friends who were asking me if I was okay, I decided, fuck it—I'm going to campus. But how? I'm in Sheung San, Hong Kong Island, and my university is in Shatin in the New Territories, some distance away. Traffic is

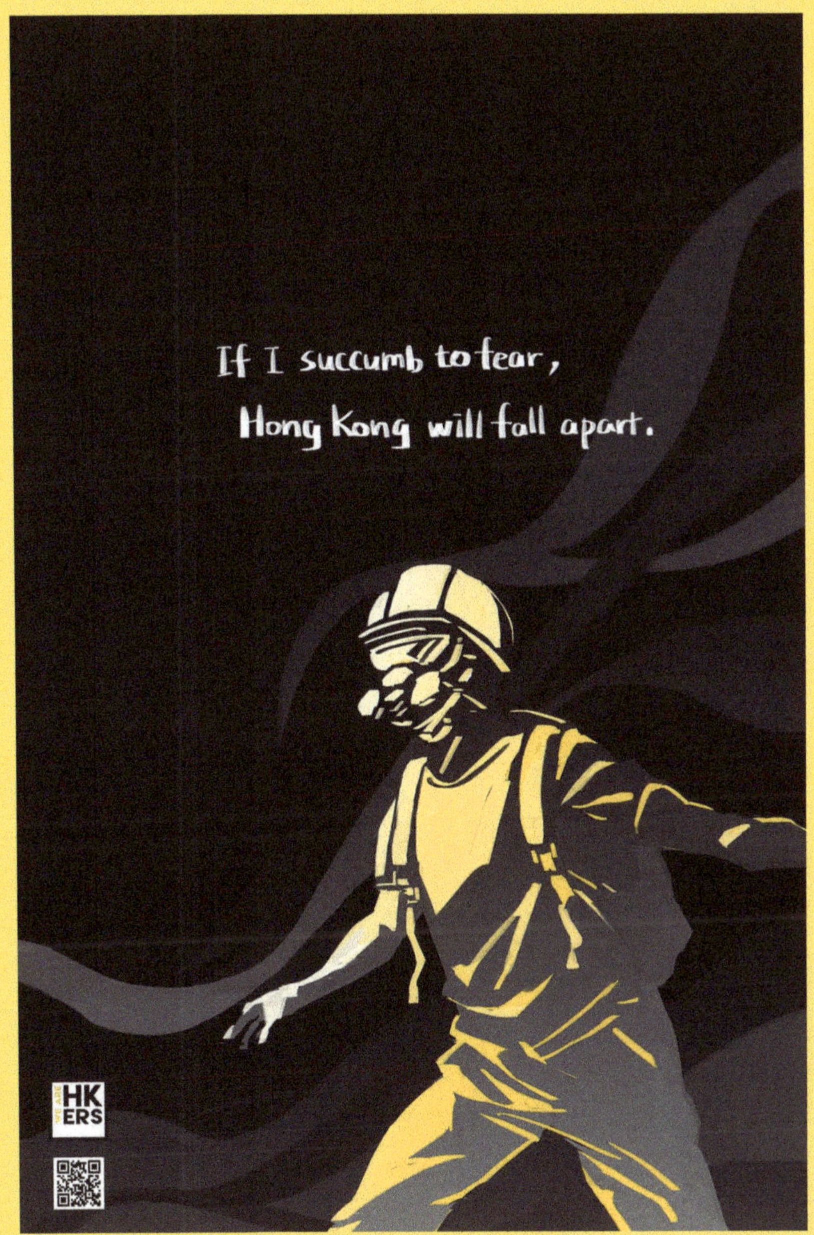
If I succumb to fear,
Hong Kong will fall apart.
HK ERS

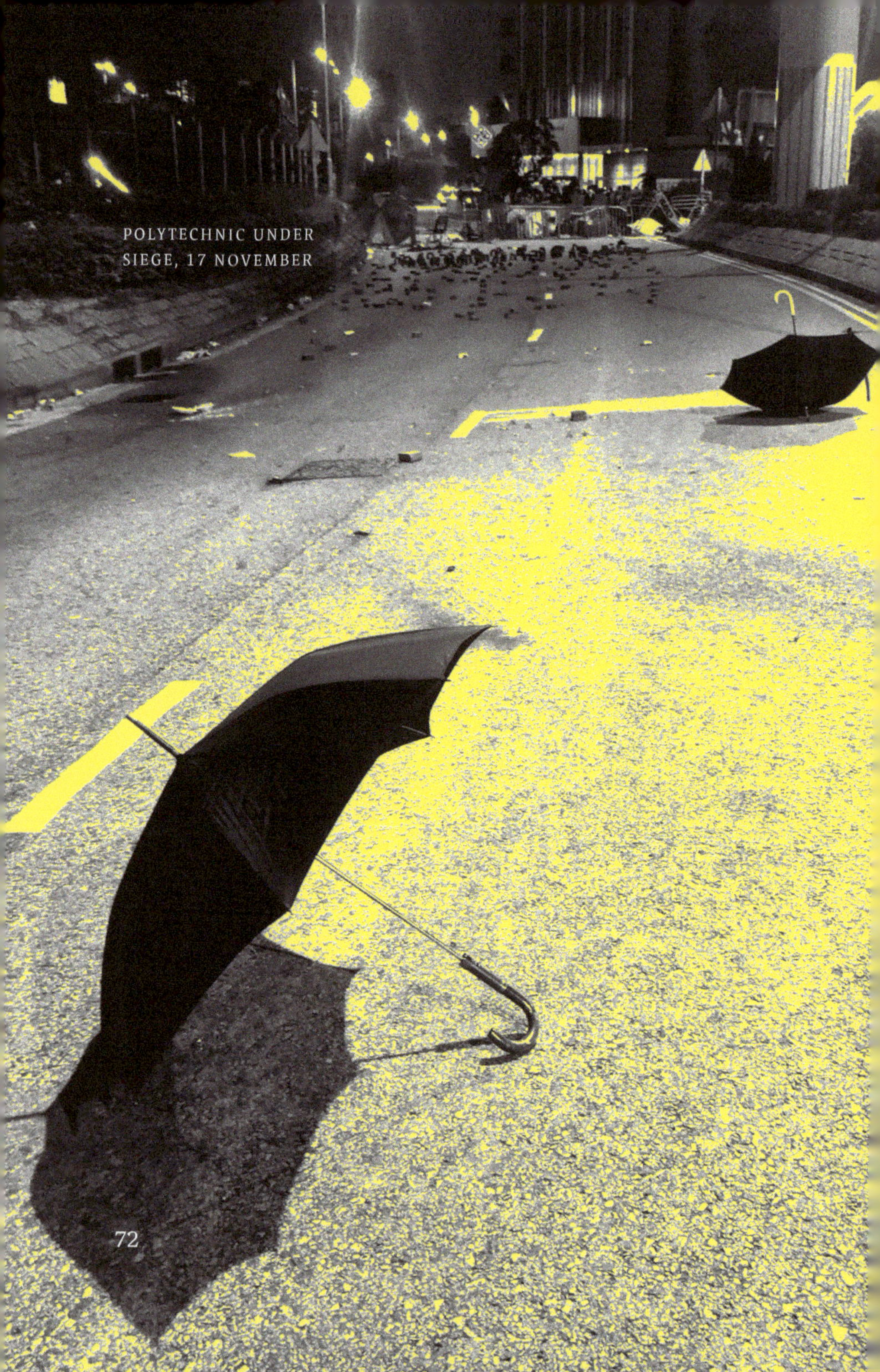

POLYTECHNIC UNDER SIEGE, 17 NOVEMBER

disrupted. Then a friend offers me a ride. We pick up several others along the way, and, with the car loaded, we are off on our way to CUHK, talking along the way about the people we know who have been arrested.

The traffic jam is huge, partly because of roadblocks by protesters or police, and partly because it seems like a massive part of Hong Kong is mobilising to go to CUHK to help out. At a certain point we cannot drive any further as the road is blocked by people and cars all trying to unload and distribute materials, helmets, water, etc. 'Please help move stuff, this shit is heavy!' someone yells. I volunteer. I'm handed a big box containing hard hats.

When I go to the university by car it usually takes maybe a few minutes via the Tai Po public road. The road is much longer if you have to walk it, and it feels even longer if you are carrying a big box of hard hats. When I finally reach a supply point, I hand over my box, relieved. Where to now? I know the campus, but the updates on the situation are changing fast. I start walking towards where I think most people would be. Everything after that, the rest of the night, is a bit of a blur.

I remember seeing some friends who recognised me in spite of my helmet, goggles and face mask. Moments like these are really important. Where we say to each other, *yes I am here too, yes, we are in this together*. You feel the solidarity so vividly and so deeply. We are here in body. We use our hands

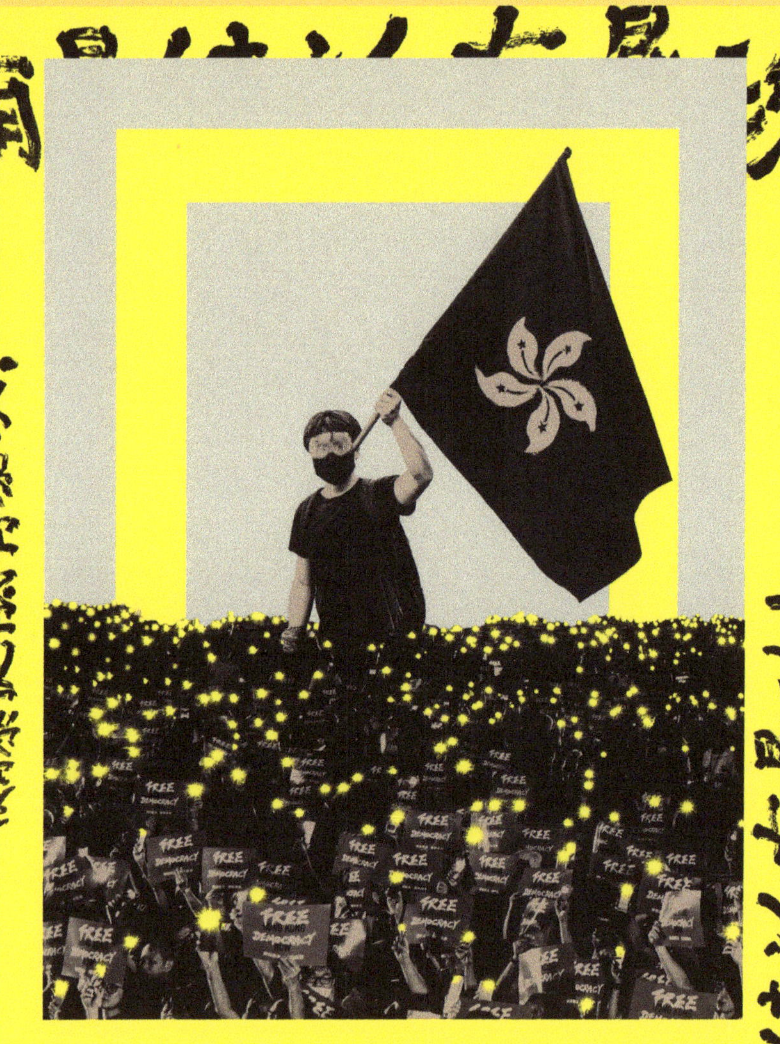
FREE
DEMOCRACY

and arms and feet to help each other. Students were busy distributing food. Some were working on the supply line. Others were reporting, and yet others trying to mediate between the different parties. In the midst of all this, I am helping to move stuff, while trying to check in on friends to make sure they're okay. And all the while my iPhone is being bombarded with messages from friends near and far. I am comfortable telling the closest friends where I am, but I try to not say too much, lest they worry.

I don't like telling people where I am going and what I am doing at the protests. I am just one of the people. I am just doing my bit to help, and I often feel I don't do enough. I'm also careful about who I share this information with, because this stuff is sensitive, especially these days in Hong Kong. But I also want my students to know I am there for them. I grew up in a family where emotional abuse was rife and I am still coming to terms with that. Part of that abuse had to do with emotional (and physical) absence. This is a longer story, of course, but it helps explain why it's important to me that my students know I am there for them. A few more moments that stood out for me:

As the water cannon hits the frontline, many have to retreat, take off their clothes and recover. 'Water' cannon is not quite accurate: the 'water' is not only dyed but also laced with some toxic chemical (probably tear gas) that makes your skin feel like it's on fire. I am taking a break at the stadium, as the students turn on the sprinkler and a massive water party breaks out. It's a brief moment in which you're reminded that these are kids, after all. In the midst of it, the first aid crew is yelling for t-shirts and towels. I'd brought two t-shirts with me, and some towels, and hand them all over.

Douglas Adams wrote in his most famous novel that a towel is one of the most useful things you can keep on your person, and it's true. With a wet towel held against your mouth, you can protect yourself against tear gas. A towel will keep you warm on a cold evening, and you can use it as a blanket when you go to sleep. You can wash with it, or fold it and use it as a pillow. And wave it to signal to someone that you are here and not there. Towels are love, towels are life. Towels are highly underrated.

Another moment that left an impression on me: I'm standing on bridge two, where the majority of the action took place earlier that day, watching the university leadership, together with two legislators, negotiate a deal with the students. The university leadership is suggesting they retreat, saying that the police promised they would not return, and that the university security team would protect the bridge.

What gives me some hope is that the students repeatedly give the leadership opportunities to speak, and they listen. But of course, the advice to retreat is not exactly persuasive and the police have already broken several promises that day alone. And can they really depend on the security team that has disappeared over the last two days? (Though to be fair to them, I don't think they signed up for this).

When you look at media reports you mostly see the violence, the vandalism, the unrest. Rarely the solidarity, or that we are here to protect our home and protect each other. That we refuse to back down in the face of repression and brutality. That we might not always get things right, but that we at least try. And that so far, we have been learning from our mistakes. And that we hope the rest of the world doesn't make the same mistakes but learns from our experience.

In 2017, I wrote about why I wanted to stay in Hong Kong. 'Is there a future here?' Well, let's not forget the future is open. It is not set in stone. We don't know what will happen. And because of this, there is hope. As Leonard Cohen said, 'There is a crack in everything, that's how the light gets in.' I am grateful Hong Kong is (still relatively) free. I will fight to make sure Hong Kong stays free, becomes more free. I also believe there is much we can learn from Hong Kong, that Hong Kong plays a critical part in the larger struggle for freedom globally. That is why I am in Hong Kong. That is why I want to stay here.

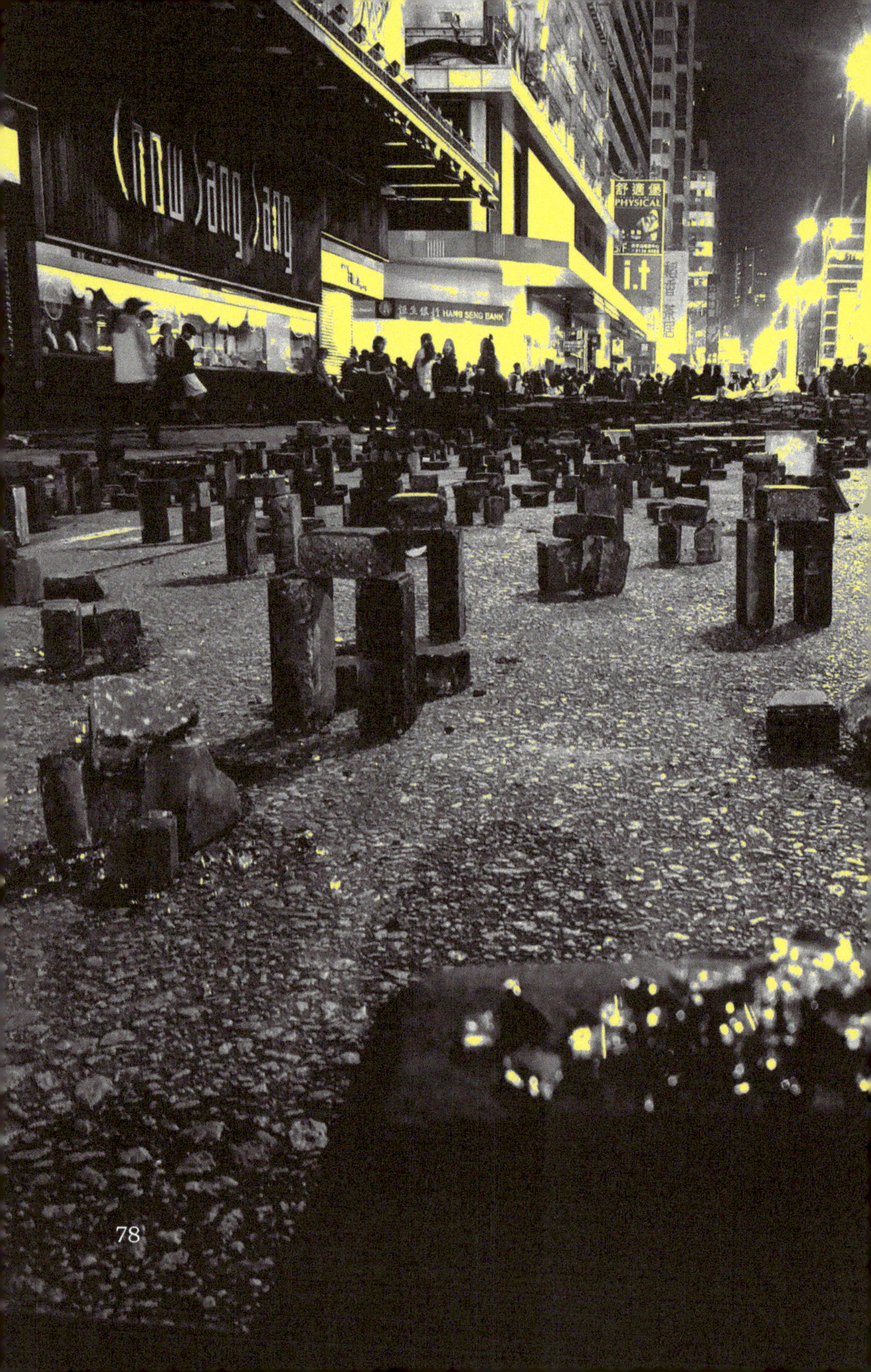
Chow Sang Sang
恒生銀行 HANG SENG BANK
舒適堡
PHYSICAL
i.t

LIBERTY OR DEATH

WEDNESDAY | Hong Kong Polytechnic is calm, the barricades enormous and the graffiti ubiquitous. Among the slogans are 'Liberty or death', 'Kill someone, pay the price' and 'If your family member were killed, would you still go to work?' The last is an exhortation for the city's workers to strike over the death of twenty-two-year-old Chow Tsz-lok last week. Police say he fell from a car park. Students don't believe it.

Several buildings have been smashed up, including the ground floor of the Registrar's Office. Masked students chat in a coffee shop amid shattered glass. Others spray slogans on the ground outside the student union and on walls not already covered. Two more drive seconded maintenance vehicles about. On the roof, a lookout keeps watch. They are nervous, one student says, about another police offensive,

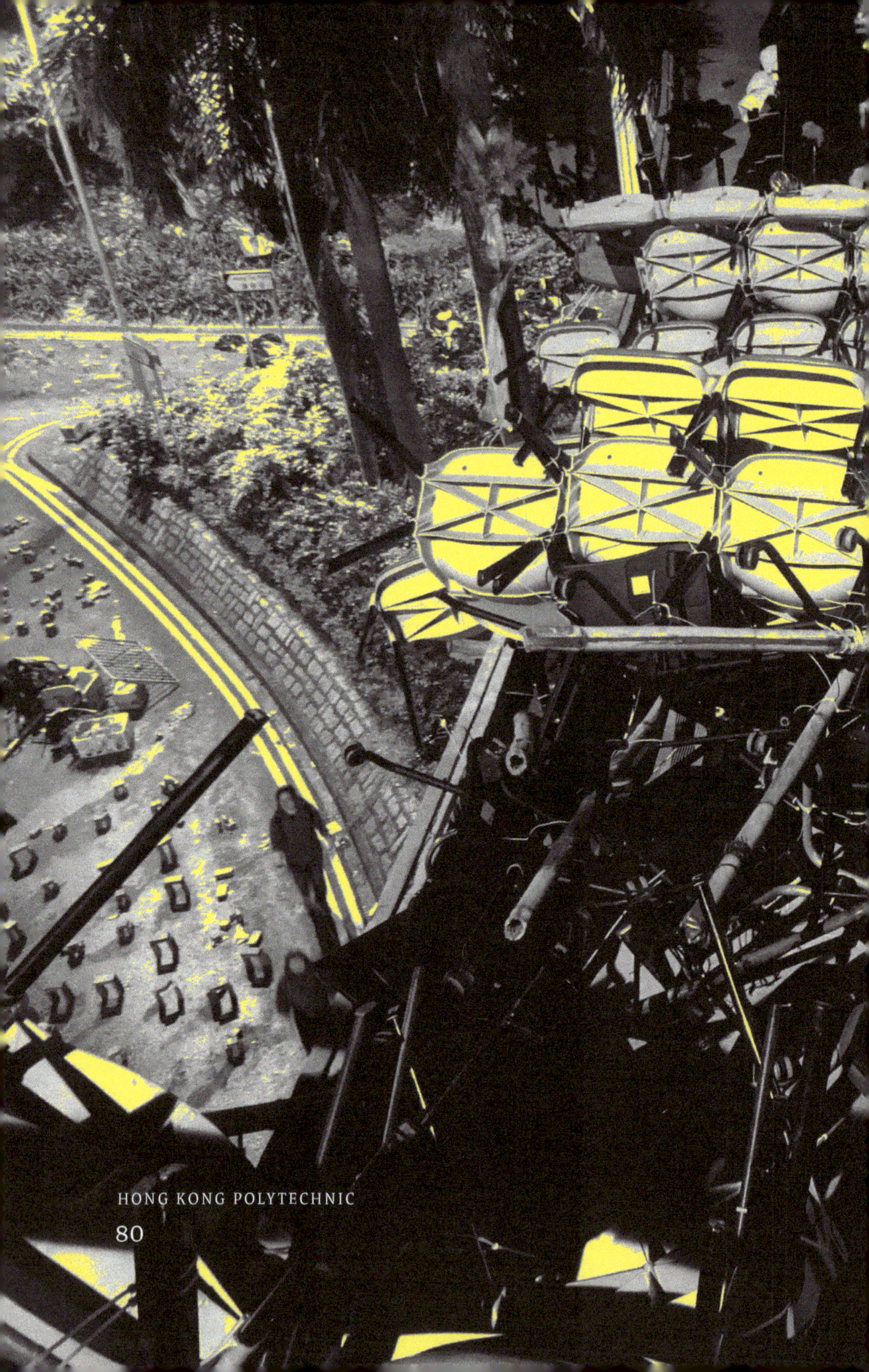

HONG KONG POLYTECHNIC

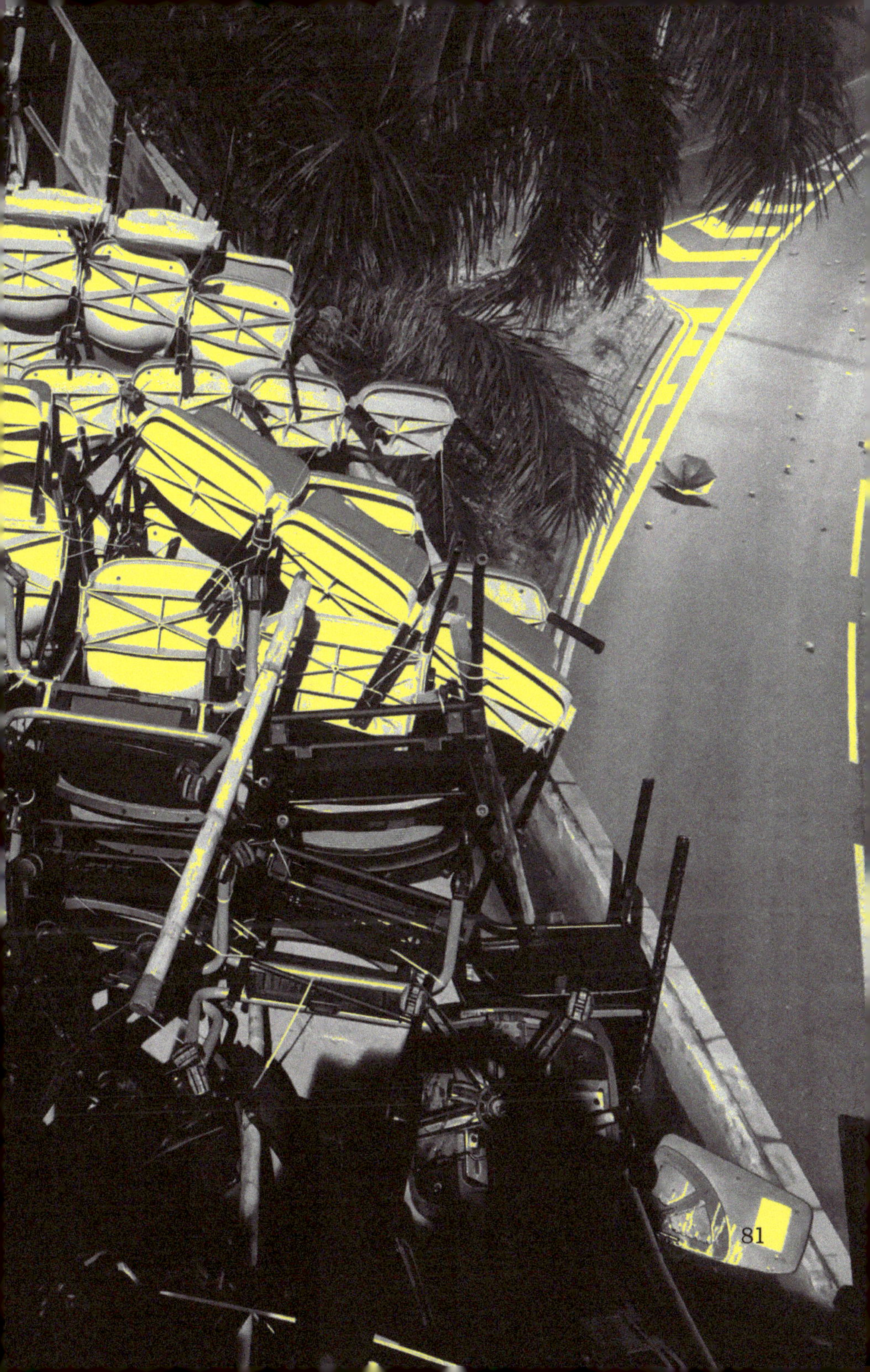

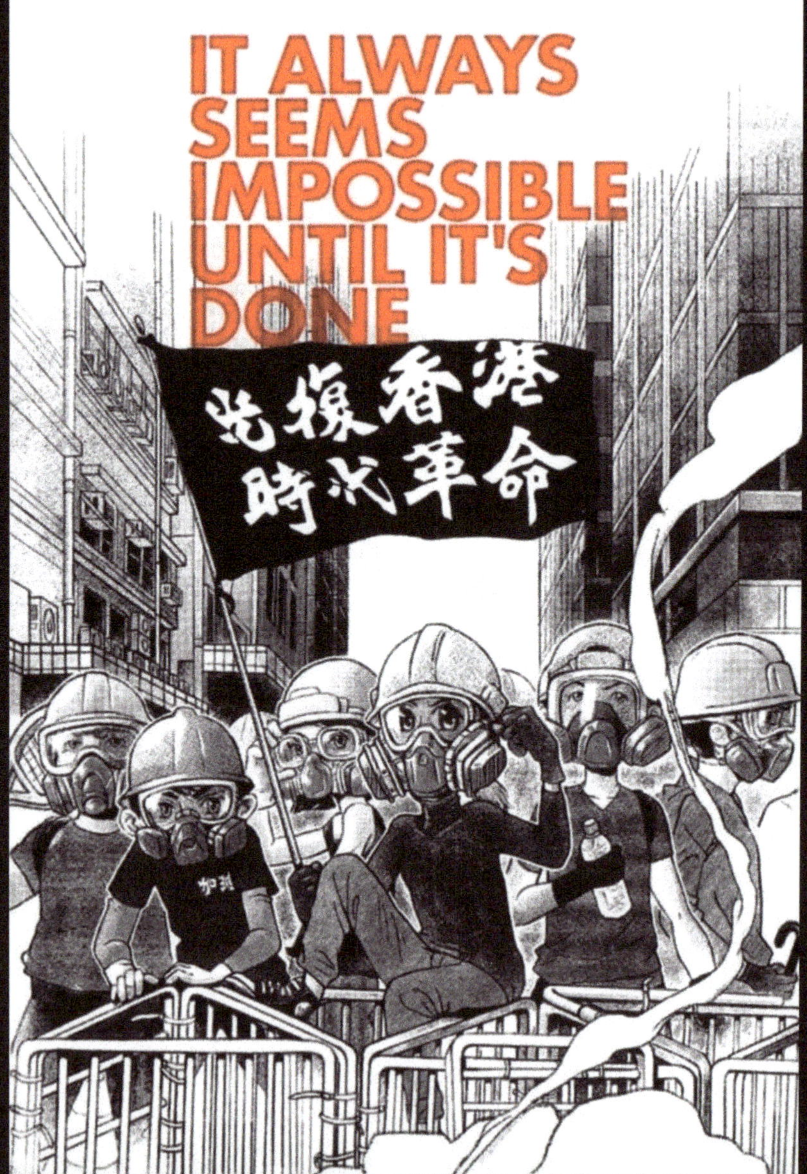
IT ALWAYS SEEMS IMPOSSIBLE UNTIL IT'S DONE
光復香港
時代革命

like that at the Chinese University yesterday.

CUHK is under siege. The train line to it has been shut and, being in the outer east of the region, you can get there only by car. But police have set roadblocks to control who goes into the area. The university has cancelled all classes until the end of the year and is telling resident students to leave. It is an ominous development that will isolate the activists on campus and open them to a perhaps more ferocious attack. At least sixty people were injured when police invaded the campus on Tuesday, firing rubber bullets and tear gas. It wasn't just current students. Many alumni rushed to the university to help. The university president and other officials came to negotiate with police. They were tear gassed as well.

The university has historically been one of the centres of student activism in Hong Kong. And it has been at the forefront of opposition to the now-shelved 'extradition bill'—a catalyst for the current upheaval because it would have allowed Hong Kongers to be extradited to the mainland for trial and imprisonment. 'These students have been very active,' Au Loong Yu, a veteran activist and author, says in his office on the other side of town. 'CUHK got the moniker "Riot University" from pro-Beijing netizens and it has been taken up by many people. They and the police say the dorms are factories for producing Molotov cocktails and that the university encourages it.' CUHK militants certainly are tough. After yesterday's assault, today students tested a catapult they built to launch petrol bombs at police when they next try to take the campus. There is consensus here that CUHK is the most important centre of university activism and—depending on which side you are on—that it must be defended or be crushed.

Barricades protect several universities across Hong Kong as the situation escalates. The movement has five demands. First is the complete withdrawal of the extradition bill. Second is that the government retract its labelling as riots the mass protests that happened on 12 June. Third is the release and exoneration of arrested protesters. Fourth is the establishment of an independent commission of inquiry into the police. Fifth is the resignation of Chief Executive Carrie Lam and the granting of universal suffrage. They have won only the first demand. It's not enough.

'The extradition bill exposed that China wants to finish off Hong Kong autonomy once and for all—not in thirty years, not in ten years, but in one or two years. Not officially—that would not be good for them economically—but in practice,' Au says. 'Why do you think even all the old people like me are yelling? We are known to be very calm here in Hong Kong. But the fight to defend our autonomy overrides everything.'

The students know they have mass support. And they know they can't win by themselves. But right now they are fighting alone, desperately trying to provoke a general strike

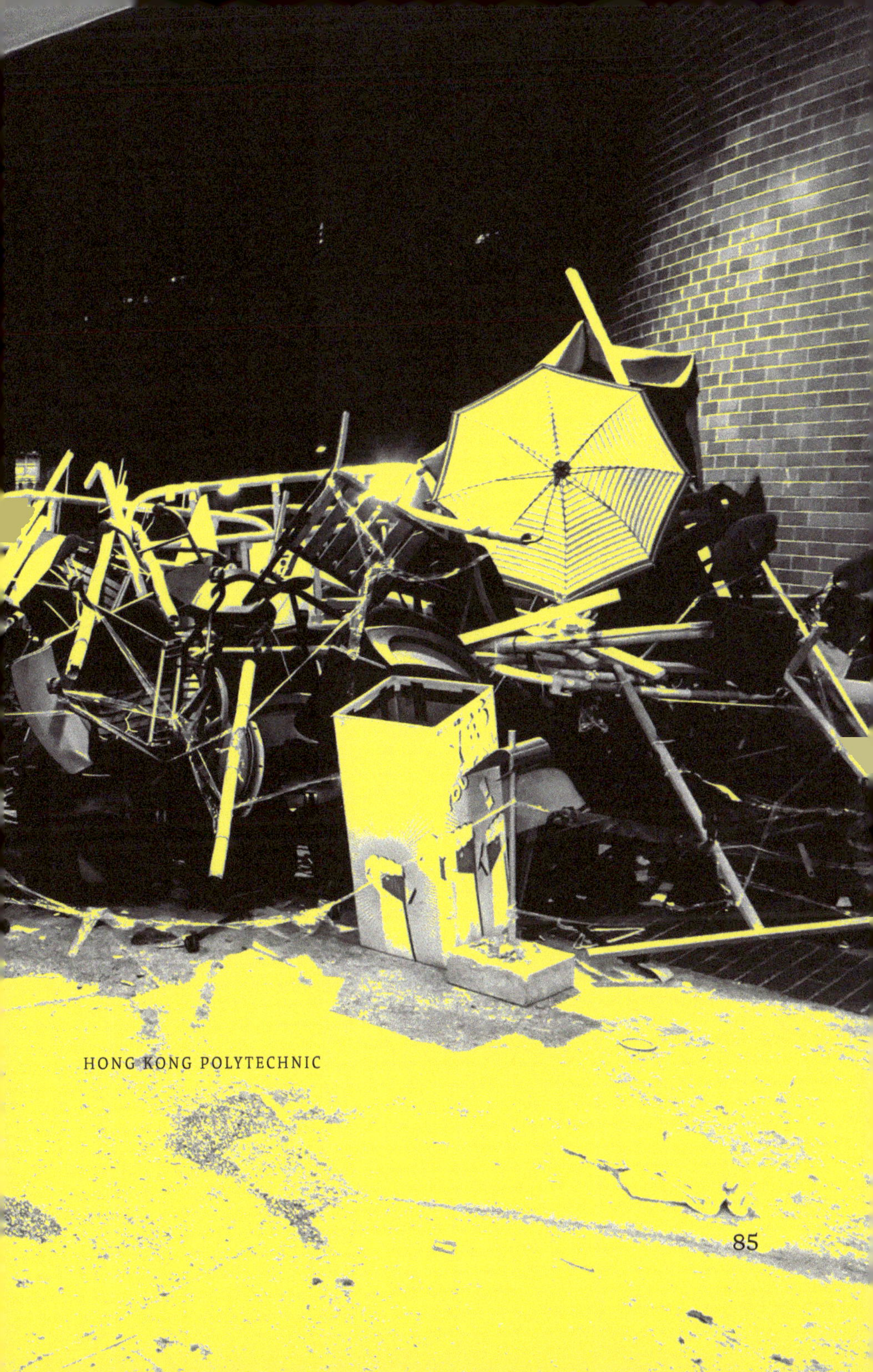

HONG KONG POLYTECHNIC

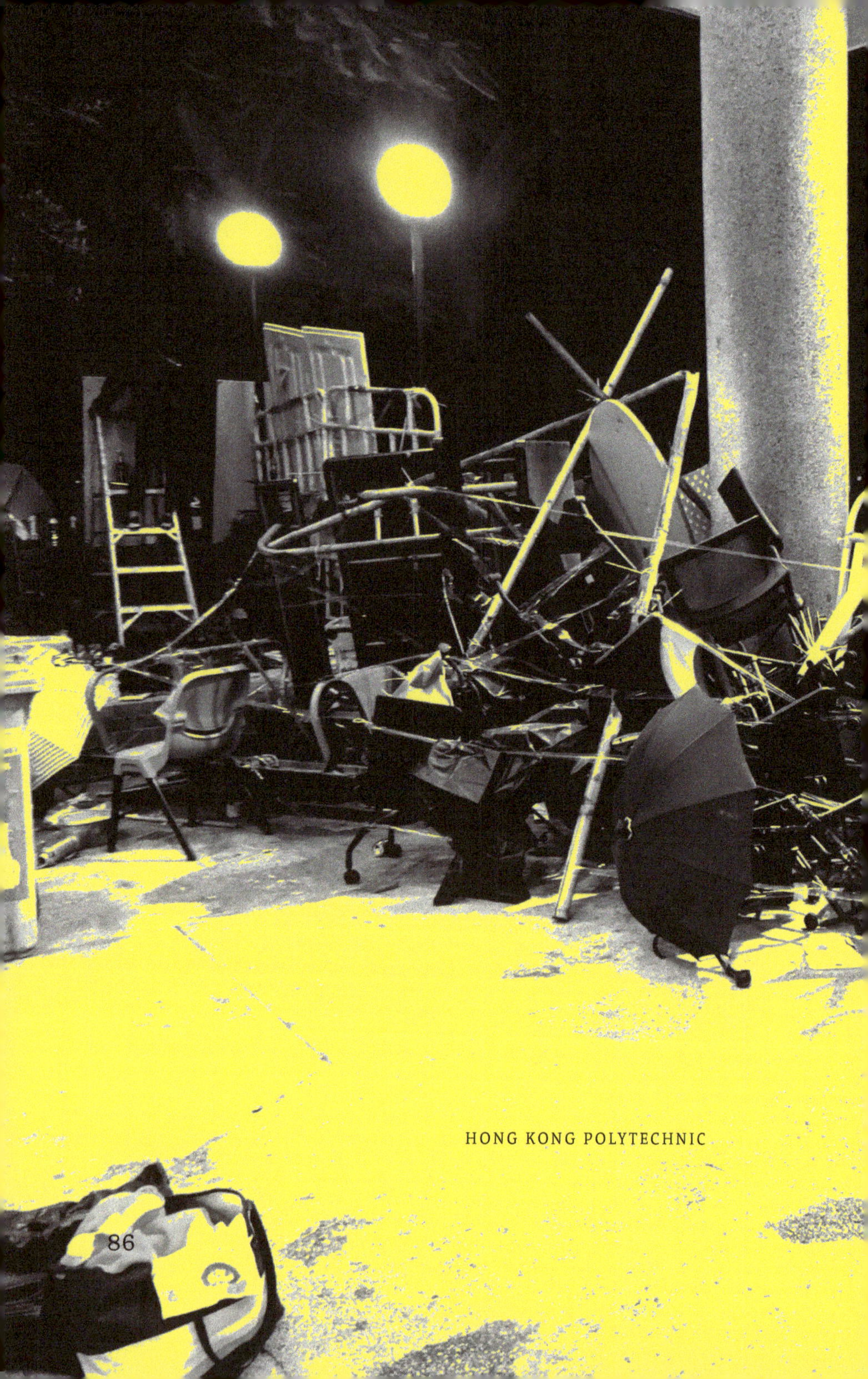

HONG KONG POLYTECHNIC

by causing mayhem wherever they can. They are left to substitute themselves for a working class which seems happy enough to be disrupted for the cause, but whose leaders are incapable, or unwilling to call them out to defend the students.

Near the Polytechnic in Hung Hom, a barricade has gone up, in both the 'construction' and the 'in flames' senses, at the entrance to a road tunnel to Hong Kong Island. Today is chaos—sabotage, firebombs, roadblocks, protests and confrontations across the city. The metro intermittently shuts down lines and stations to stop people coming to the flash points in solidarity. In a metropolis reliant on the train system, it is an effective weapon in the hands of the authorities. But the greater the number of lines and stations closed, the more pressure there is on the roads, which makes student roadblocks even more effective.

Behind the scenes, the protesters seem to have a high level of coordination; actions in different parts of the city are complementary. But there are also differences. 'It's not a unified movement; it's a multi-tendency movement,' Au says. There are the 'localists'—those who want full independence and tend towards xenophobic, anti-Chinese nationalism. They influence the movement through propaganda and social media, 'but they have no organisational muscle'. Most actions are coordinated via messenger services. They are just young people fighting for their future. At the Polytechnic, this feels confirmed.

What about the militant core of masked groups—how many are anarchists and how many are the far right? Is it possible to tell? Au bristles at the use of the term 'black bloc' to describe these students. Not because some of them are provocateurs from the Hong Kong police, the Chinese police and the mafia, but because politically, he says, it is misleading. He gives a short history lesson. While the Chinese University has been important, it was never anything like the Western universities where various currents of Marxism and anarchism flourished at different times. One of the university colleges was founded by Chinese liberals in the late 1960s. It was less elitist than Hong Kong University, the main establishment campus. But there is no legacy of deep radicalisation. The students today are still of this general progressive ilk. There is no indication, he says, that there is a radical left developing—layers of students reading Marx or Bakunin for example. So, by Au's estimation, the 'masking up' by protesters is purely tactical and has very little, if any, ideological content. Everyone is doing it to protect themselves.

Under the circumstances, it is probably wise. The stakes here are extremely high. China is demanding that the government crack down. The Liaison Office, Beijing's directorate in Hong Kong, says the city is 'sliding into the abyss of terrorism'. And the local administration promises retaliation against activists. One minister warned protesters that there will be 'no place to hide' when they start identifying people. The words have no effect. In the evening, Mong Kok is in another confrontation. So too Yuen Long, Kwai Chung Estate, Tai Po and Sheung Shui. Smaller actions of sabotage are happening all over. There is concern that another serious police offensive against CUHK is getting closer, so, again, the students are 'blossoming everywhere' to spread police resources thin.

The young protesters seem like an unstoppable force. But in Beijing, they face an immovable object. It can't keep going on like this for much longer.

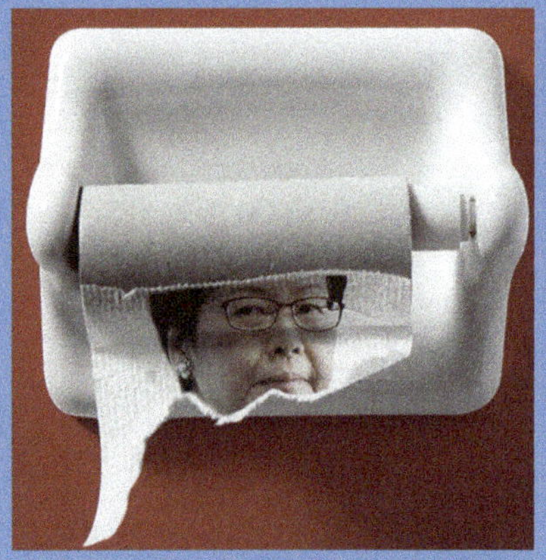

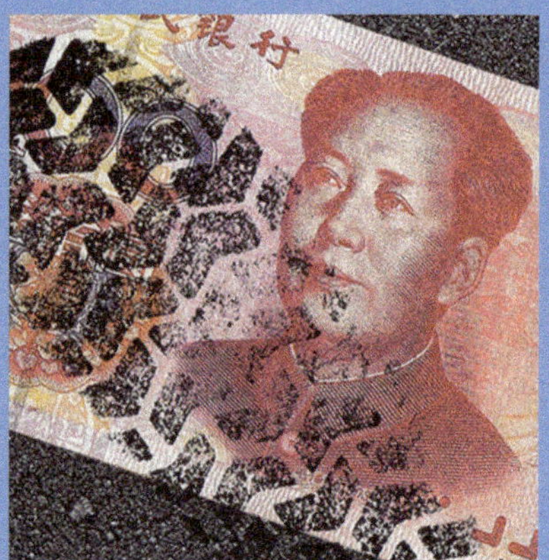

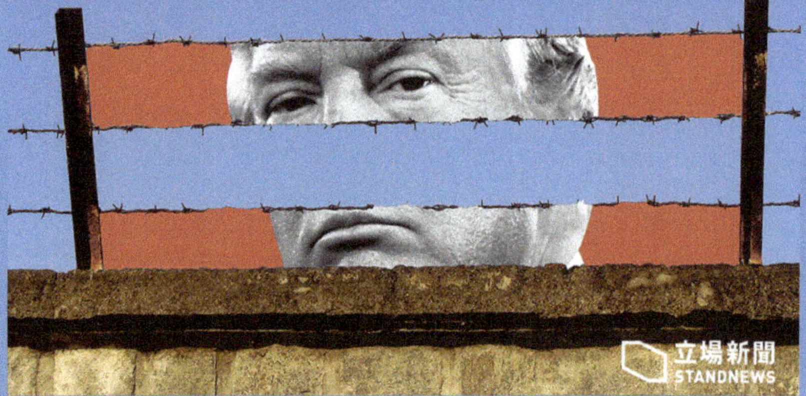
立場新聞
STANDNEWS

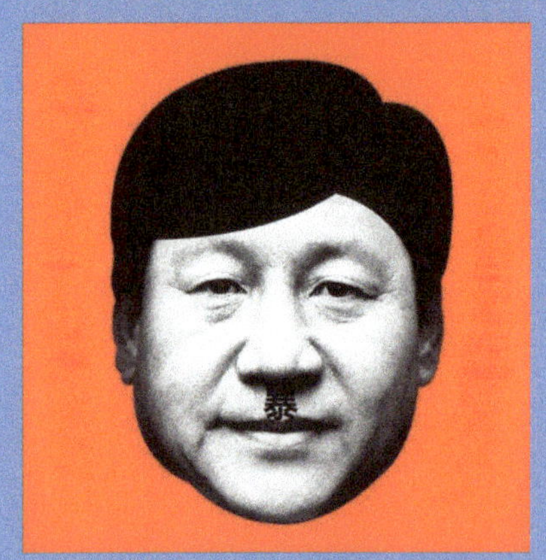

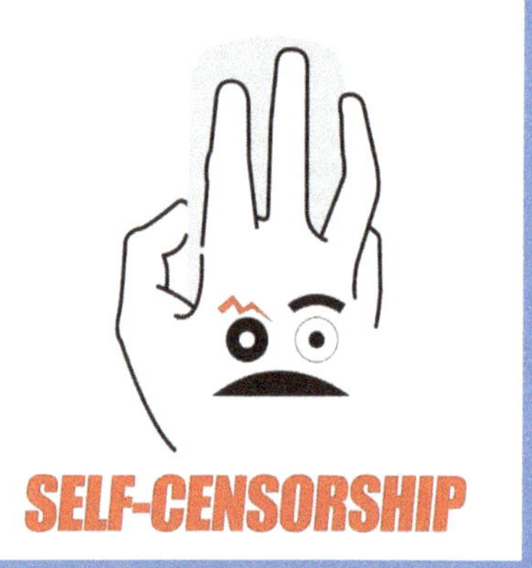
SELF-CENSORSHIP

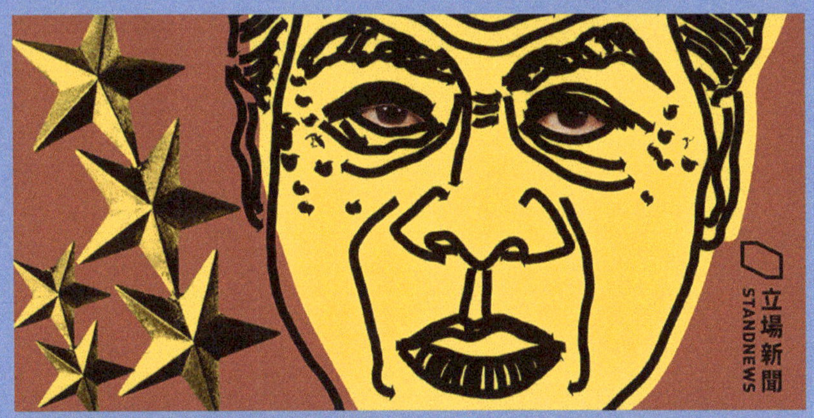

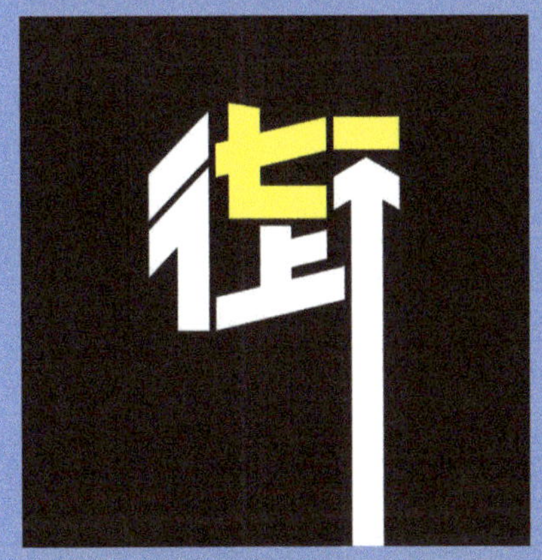

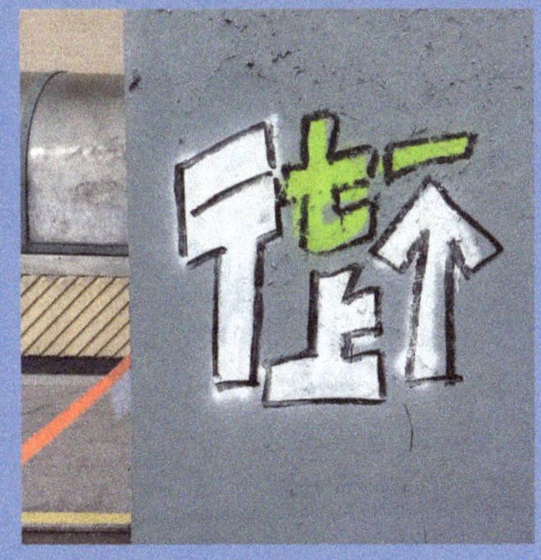

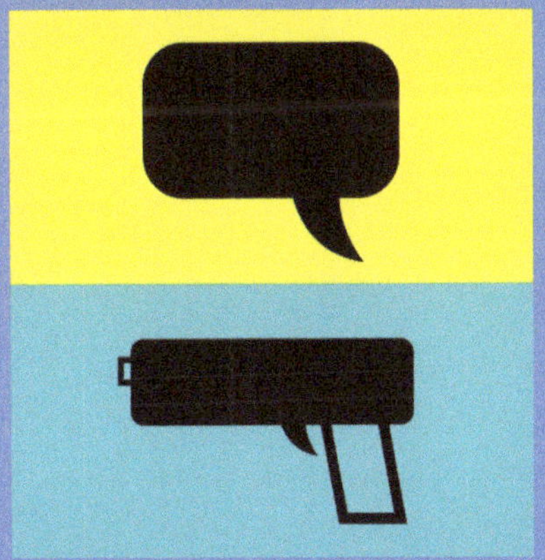

SEEN IN THE STREETS—THE DESIGN ABOVE IS A COMBINATION OF FOUR CHARACTERS MEANING 'TAKE TO THE STREETS ON JULY 1'

LAU YAN-HIN (2019-20)
@LAUYANHIN

INSIDE THE CUHK OCCUPATION

THURSDAY | 'I saw them on TV cook just sausage with rice. I thought this is not good, so I came to help.' Chef Suzie* is standing next to the kitchen in one of the Chinese University canteens. The campus is under student control; a small experiment in self-government. This place has been the site of the most vicious confrontations in the city's student rebellion. For now, however, there is a lull, and the young people have a chance to regroup. Susie is not a student. But, like many others, she wants to do whatever she can to contribute to their struggle. Three canteens across this sprawling campus are feeding an immense occupation. They need cooks and Suzie stepped up because, well, she thought their fighting was good, but their culinary skills were shit. And good fighters need good food.

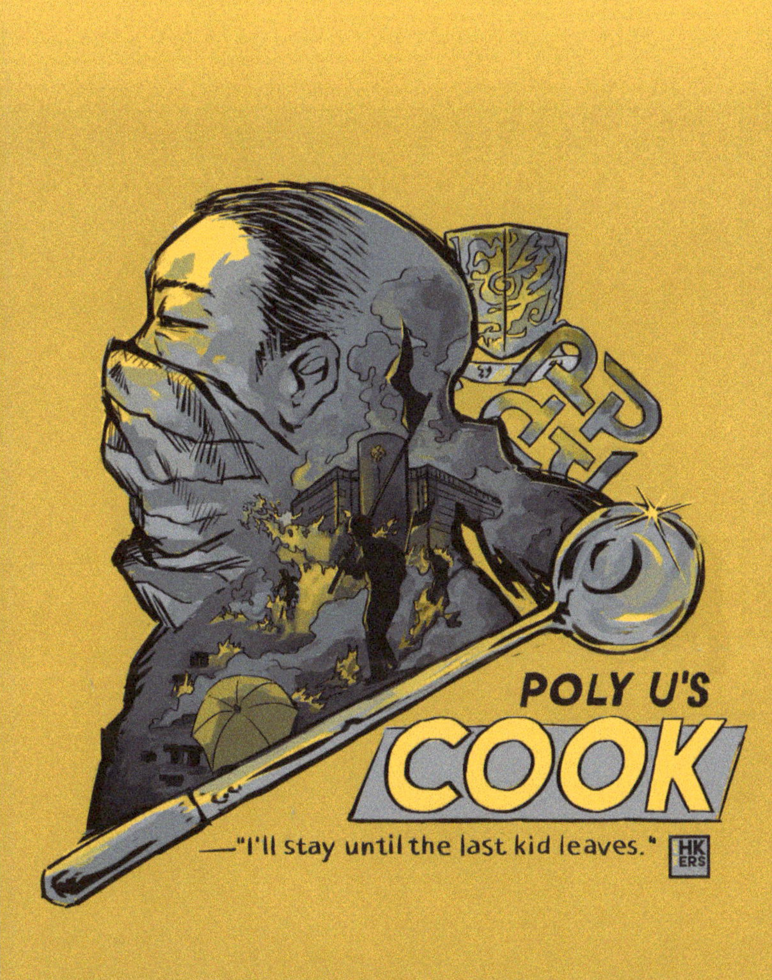
POLY U'S
COOK
—"I'll stay until the last kid leaves."
HK
ERS

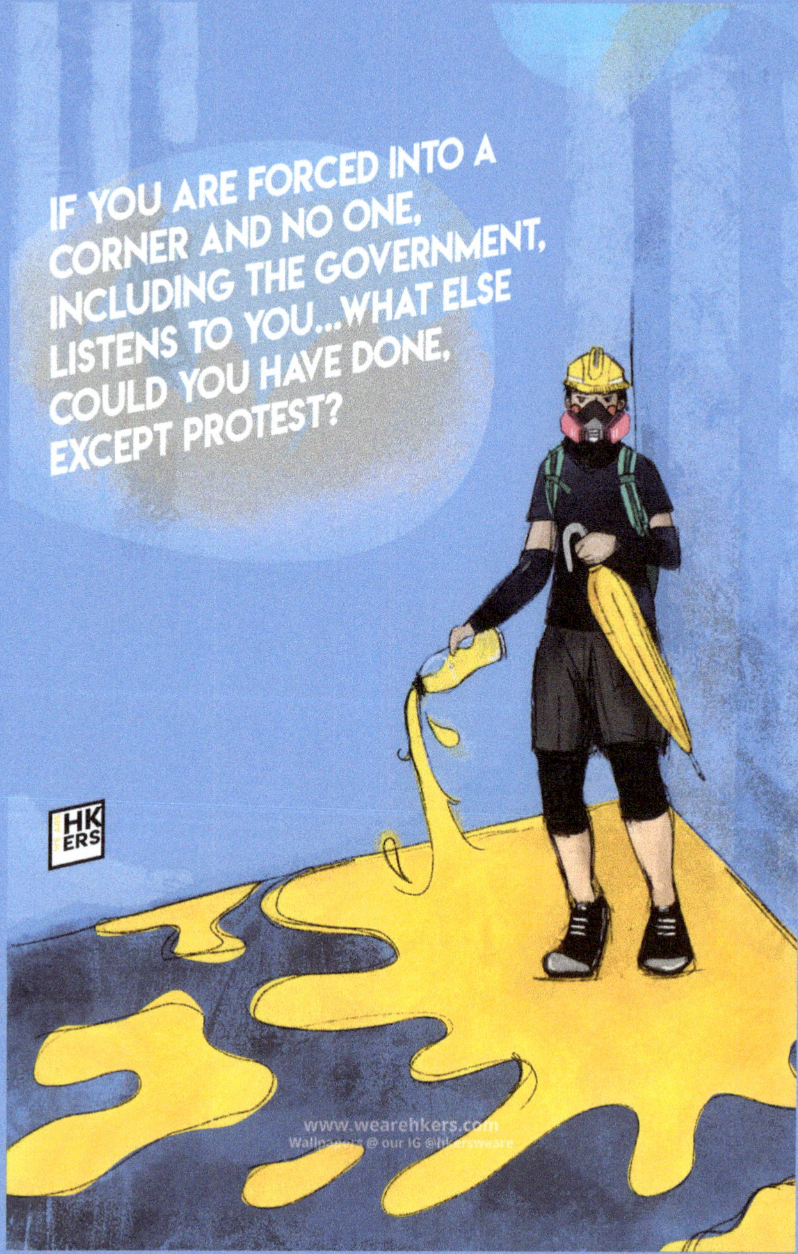
IF YOU ARE FORCED INTO A CORNER AND NO ONE, INCLUDING THE GOVERNMENT, LISTENS TO YOU...WHAT ELSE COULD YOU HAVE DONE, EXCEPT PROTEST?
HK ERS
www.wearehkers.com

Che's not a student either. He graduated from a different university last year and now has a job. Like Suzie, he watched footage of riot police invading the campus on Tuesday, laying people out with rubber bullets and choking them with tear gas. More importantly, he watched the students hold their ground. So now he is here—not out of pity, which never helped a soul, but out of respect and a desire to be part of the ferocious collective power that the activists have put on display. 'I just make sure they have enough food and drink and rest and energy to fight,' he says. 'That's my job today.'

Two young men sit at the cash register desk, which has become a donation station. A wad of notes is in front of them, collected from the open box on the counter. Where does the money come from? 'Mainly the locals just come in to help out.' Is watching the donations their job here? 'Now, yes. But we rotate jobs. We just ask someone to swap. As long as the money is always watched, we can do other jobs. I have been doing cleaning before this.' Outside, six students walk along the pavement picking up rubbish with tongs. 'This is our home and we want it to look nice,' says one. 'And be hygienic!' Were they assigned, or is this spontaneous? 'We do it ourselves,' says another. 'Like our support just comes from the public—it just happens. So we make it happen. No-one tells us.'

Locals are donating or loaning whatever they can to back the occupation. Hundreds of umbrellas—which Hong Kongers have made one of the greatest mass-defence urban conflict instruments of the twenty-first century—hang from railings everywhere. Students load onto trolleys crates of vegetables delivered by sympathisers. People turn up with their cars volunteering to be couriers. 'Locals come with food, tools, first-aid kits—even bikes and motorbikes for us to use,' says Ed, a young linguistics student.

Maintenance and security workers have gone, and all vehicles have been seconded. There are at least six buses now graffitied with slogans such as 'HKPF, how do u like our big black bloc?', 'FUCK POPO' (police), 'Ideas are bulletproof' and insignia from the 2005 film *V for Vendetta*. There is also a bunch of vans and god knows how many scooters to go with the ones on loan from locals. People drive around constantly in the vans, moving materials to reinforce barricades. 'We don't have all the keys, so they have been hotwired. Students have put their skills to very good use,' Ed says, showing me how on a nearby vehicle. 'We move people and all sorts of things quickly with these.' Staring at the ground for a moment, he changes register:

'It is stupid, but a lot of us feel like we are learning more from this than we do from [university] lessons. It's not what we want, but so it is. Cooperation, helping each other, cooking—even driving! Some students don't have a licence, but they are learning how to drive a bus to get people around

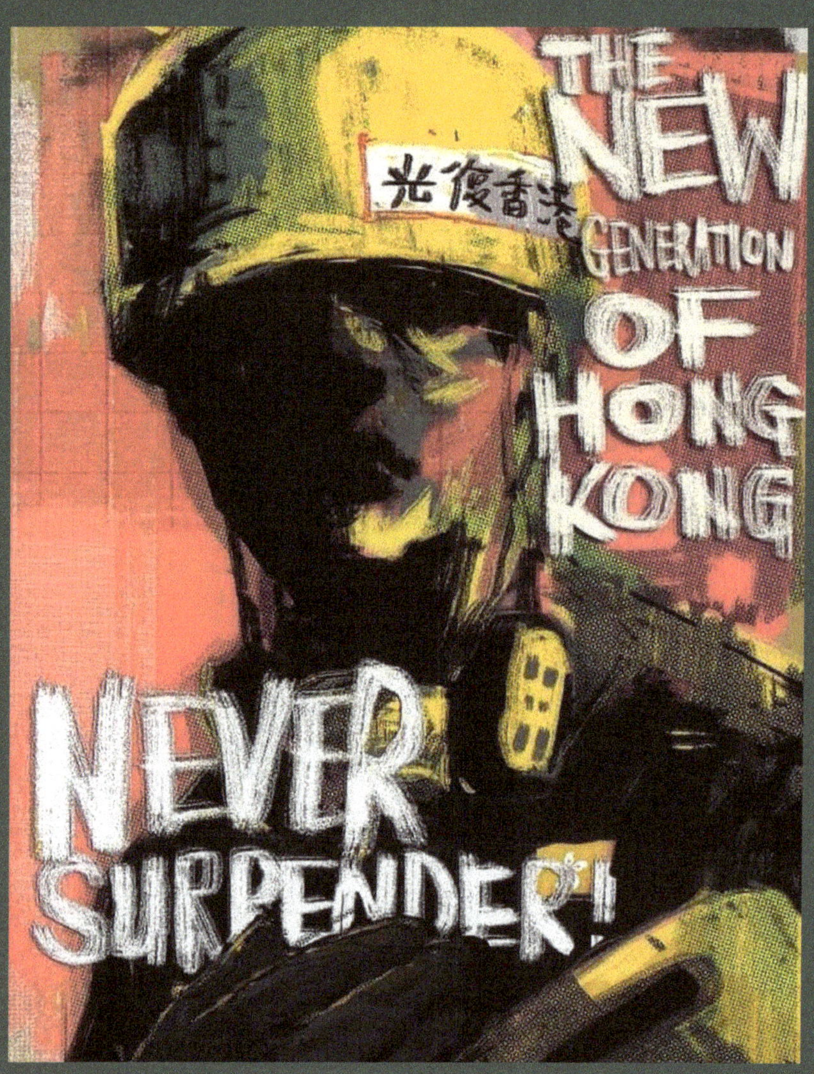
光復香港
THE NEW GENERATION OF HONG KONG
NEVER SURRENDER!

campus quickly when we need them. I have cried several nights because I am touched by the sense of unity. The whole thing is built on trust; all the Hong Kongers helping. I don't know him. I don't know her. [He's pointing at passing students, voice breaking.] But we are working together ... We don't know each other personally, but we are allies.'

Piles of paving bricks have been turned into mortared walls across the entrance down from Tai Po Road. 'Because the war stopped yesterday, we wanted to build something strong before it starts again,' Fiona says. She has come from Hong Kong University. Many students are shifting campuses temporarily to help here. Some stay several hours, others several days. Everyone says stay safe.

At one of the round-a-bouts, an alumnus, an undergraduate in the 1990s and now an English teacher, relates how at this spot yesterday there were twenty activists making Molotov cocktails. He wasn't a happy unionist: 'They were not thinking about safety. The equipment was poor—and someone was smoking a cigarette ten metres away! I said be careful! Be careful!'

Away from the canteen and the middle of campus, the mood is slightly different. The police roadblocks have been down for maybe twenty-four hours. So the students have set up their own. The four main entrances are heavily barricaded. One is University train station. I wrote yesterday that the eastern line, which services this station, was shut down to stop supporters getting here. That's not true. The students destroyed the station. Before that, from the overpass they threw whatever they could onto the tracks and torched the train that is still sitting. They wanted to make the line inoperable. 'No work, no study, no shopping—the city must be shut down,' an activist says.

At the intersection of Lai Ping and Tai Po roads, masked students check bags and IDs to keep state operatives out. 'No police, there's peace,' Ed says. Activists here are referred to as the frontline. People choose their own role in the movement. If you want to clean, you clean. If you want to drive, you drive. If you want to make posters, you make posters. If you want to fight, you join the frontline. A few are wearing body armour almost indistinguishable from riot cops—but for the track pants and runners. Two medics are dressed in army fatigues with knee and shin pads. Everyone is so young and polite. All bags are checked for weapons and everyone is questioned as they file through a gap in the barricade. The security detail bow with respect once they confirm you're clean. At the entrance to Chung Chi College, further up Tai Po, another very polite young man holding a baseball bat asks for ID. More respectful bows follow.

The number two bridge on the other side of campus is, along with the train station, the most important piece of real

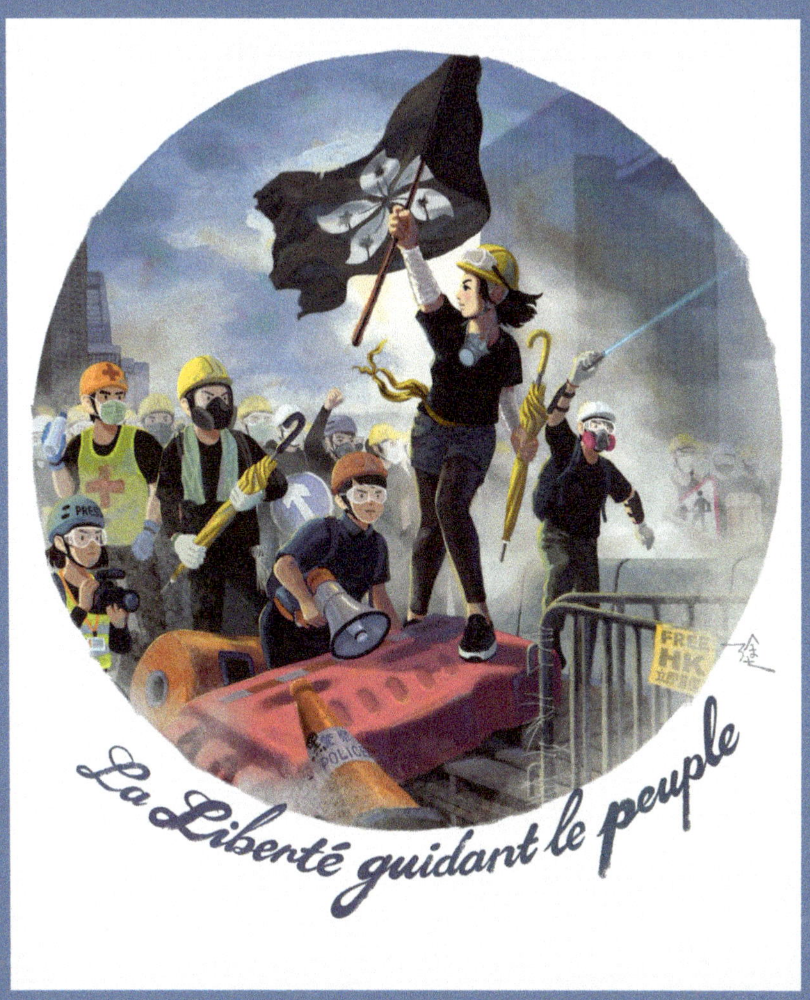
La Liberté guidant le peuple
FREE
HK

estate. This is where the police broke through on Tuesday and it is heavily guarded. The bridge spans the eight-lane Tolo Highway, which has been shut with barricades below. Control this bridge and you control the road. On a lookout structure flies a flag: 'Free Hong Kong. Revolution now'. On the siding is more graffiti: 'We never surrender'. (The Polytechnic in Hum Hong is doing the same. The overpass they control runs over the cross-harbour tunnel entrance, which is also blockaded. They intermittently torch the toll booths. This morning, behind the umbrellas put up to hinder photographers, piles of stone and bricks and dozens of Molotov cocktails were ready to launch if the police tried to clear the road below.)

Nearby, someone has strung up a banner with US Republican Senate leader Mitch McConnell on it. 'Sooner or later, the rest of the world will have to do what the protesters are doing—confront Beijing,' reads the quote. Is this representative of the activists' political loyalties? Hardly. But it is representative of a certain anything goes attitude prevalent among protesters. And because the students are up against a formidable enemy in Beijing, their desperation for allies can lead them in peculiar and contradictory directions. It also feels representative of the seeming absence of any serious political debates. The attitude appears to be: let everyone think freely, as long as they agree with the five demands. Beyond this, it is all about tactics and organisation. In the heat of the moment, that's understandable. But this radicalisation has been going for months, longer perhaps, and there is still little to suggest—at least to an outside observer—that clear ideological poles are emerging. Just an intense hatred of the cops and determination not to give in to Beijing.

The situation gets tense fast when word comes in that police are nearby. How close? 'A few kilometres over there—three police cars.' The students have spotters everywhere. Everyone at the bridge puts on a breathing apparatus. Young women grab metal bars. Back at University station, someone is megaphoning for all frontliners to get to the barricades. Another group of young women and men, skinny and between five and five-and-a-half feet tall, walk by with baseball bats.

Standing alone is a man in his late forties. Does anyone know his son? Has anyone seen him? He's worried. He ought to be. The international students have packed their bags and are all leaving. The remaining staff are leaving too. Soon, it will just be these kids and whoever can be mustered in solidarity. Soon, the police are going to take back the Tolo Highway. What else are they going to take?

**Names have been altered.*

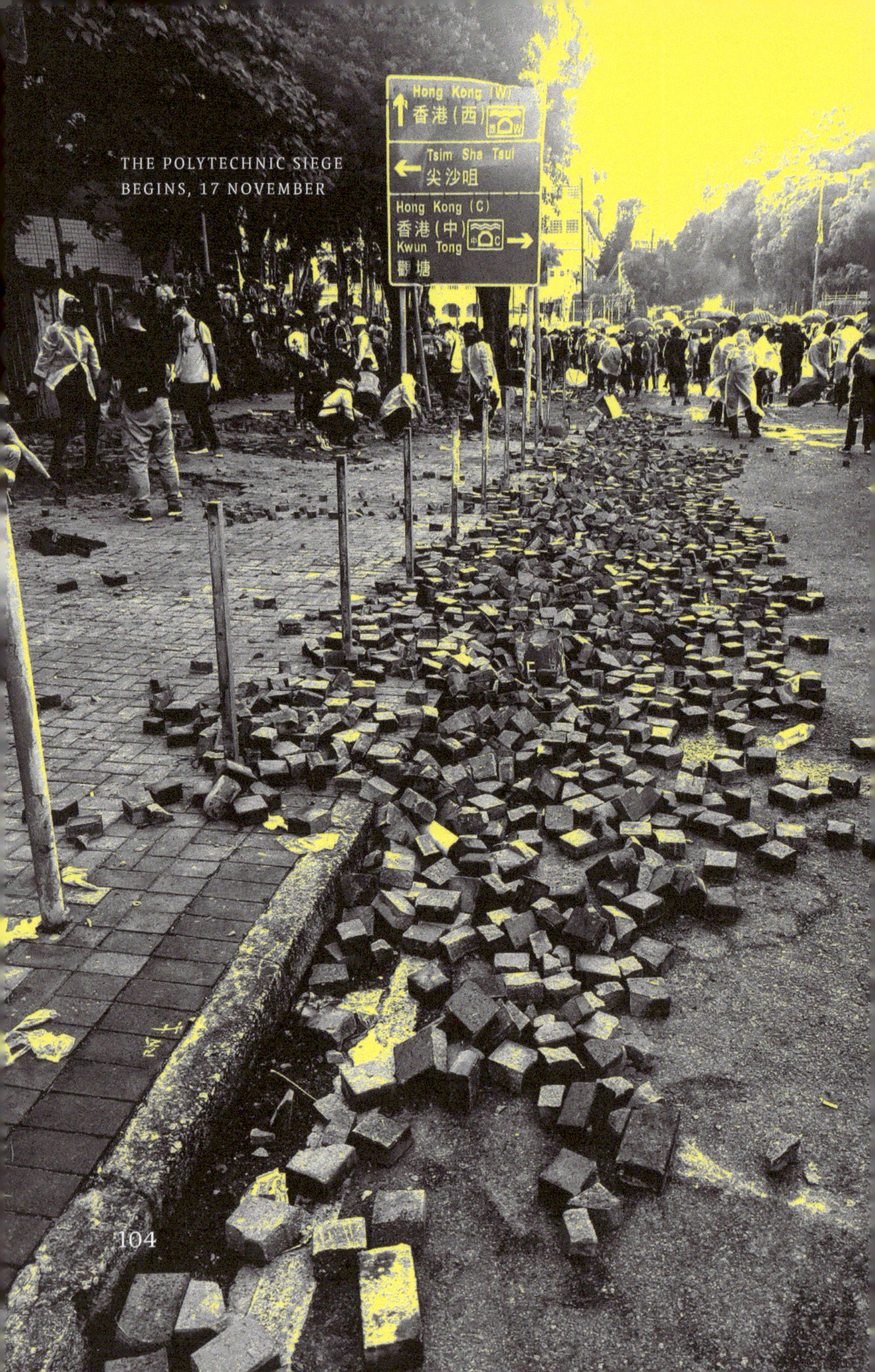

THE POLYTECHNIC SIEGE
BEGINS, 17 NOVEMBER

FRIDAY NIGHT LIGHTS

FRIDAY | There have been explosions at the number two bridge at CUHK and the metro is shutting down at 10pm. The eastern line is partially open, but the last train from the Polytechnic University at Hung Hom is going only as far as Fo Tan, the stop before University station, which has been destroyed by the students. At Fo Tan, a taxi driver waves his hands in the air and shakes his head. He's not going anywhere near the campus. A couple of young people say it's only a thirty-minute walk but don't worry—they will send a message out to get a car. Their friend is here within five minutes and will get me as close as he can.

Wo is a recent graduate and explains the situation on the way. This morning, the students opened a lane each way on the Tolo Highway as a gesture to locals and to reiterate that the blame for all the chaos lies with the government. Tolo has been blockaded for several days because it is an important arterial linking the New Territories and Kowloon. Many workers use it to commute, though, and the students don't want to start pissing them off. Whoever negotiated the opening allegedly gave a twenty-four-hour ultimatum for the government to guarantee that the impending council elections will go ahead. 'I don't know why they did this—no-one cares about these elections and they have never been part of our demands,' Wo says. When the general student population found out, they instead gave a twenty-four-hour ultimatum for the fulfilment of the five demands. After nightfall, they shut down Tolo again.

Whatever's happened with the explosions, the campus is being evacuated by the activists. The vice-chancellor sent out a letter today as well, threatening to call the police in to clear the campus if the activists don't leave. Tai Po Road, which leads to the university, is a log jam. 'All these cars have responded to the call to get people out,' Wo says. 'They are the parents.' They're not real parents, although some may be. Parent is the name given to those in the movement, like Wo, who volunteer to get people in and out of places quickly. Often, it's getting people home safely after demonstrations when the transit system has been shut down or in the early hours of the morning so they don't get taken by cops or beaten by thugs.

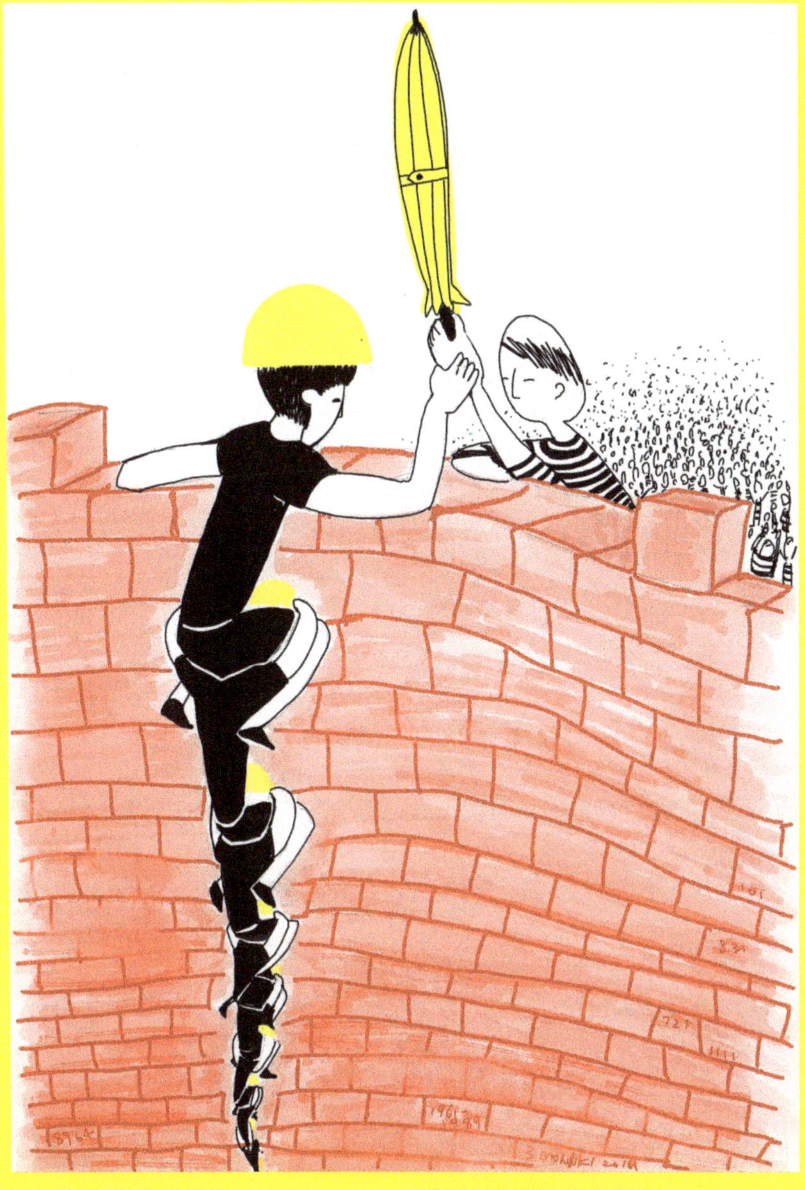

'FROM 1989 TO 2019'

THREE HANDS MONKEY
@THREEHANDSMONK1

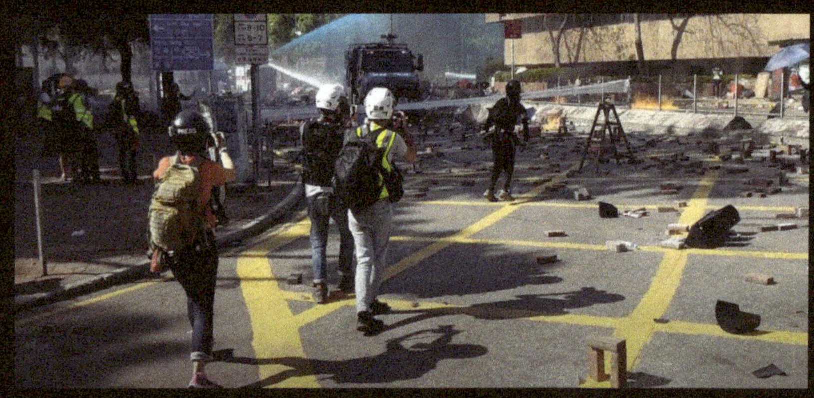

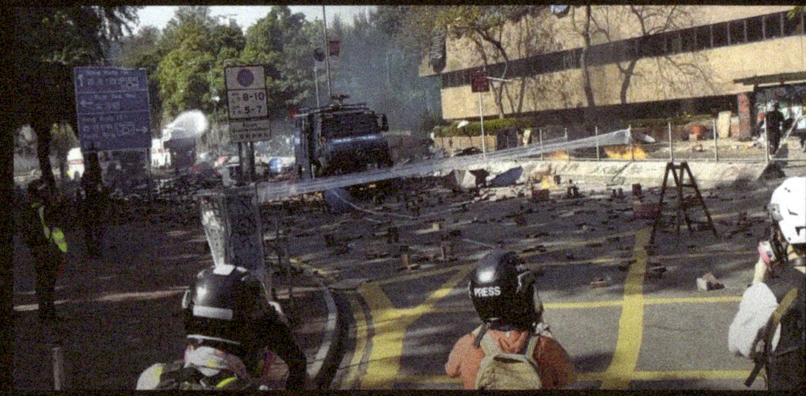

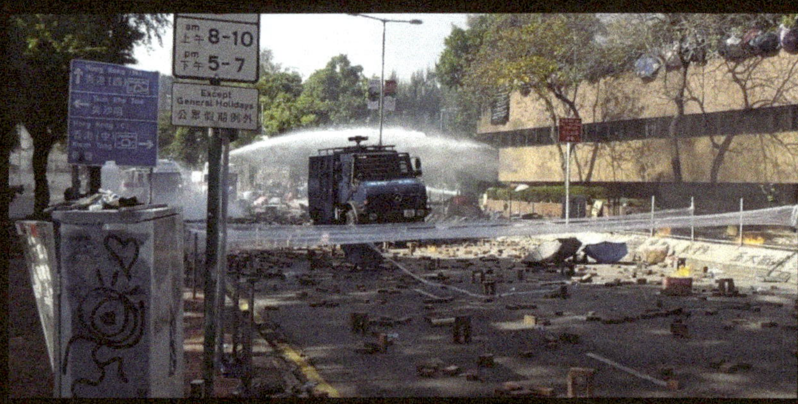

CLASHES OUTSIDE THE POLYTECHNIC

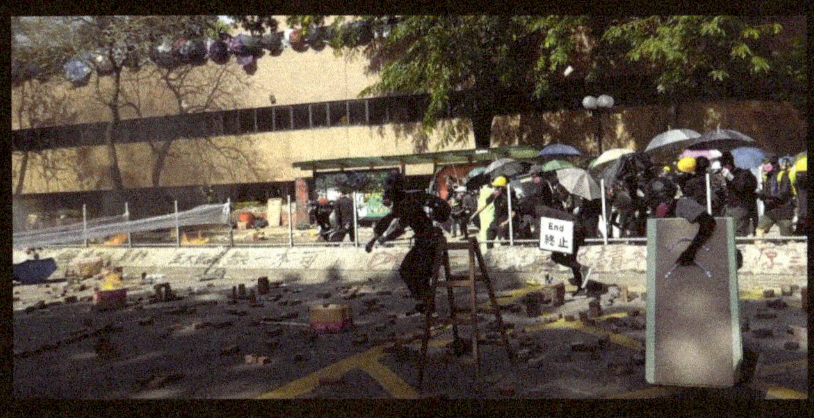
End
終止

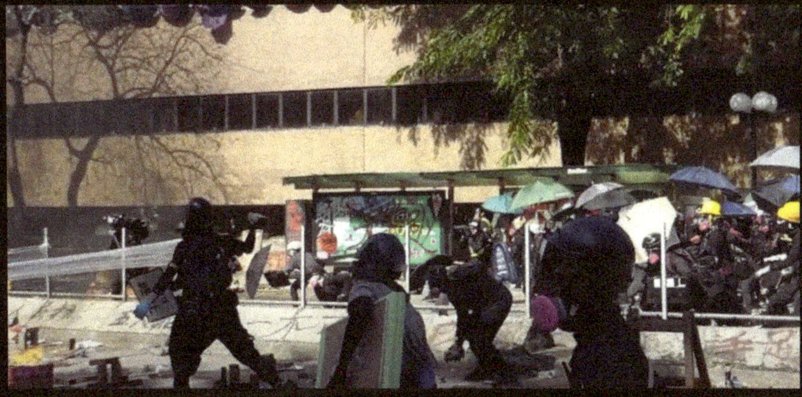

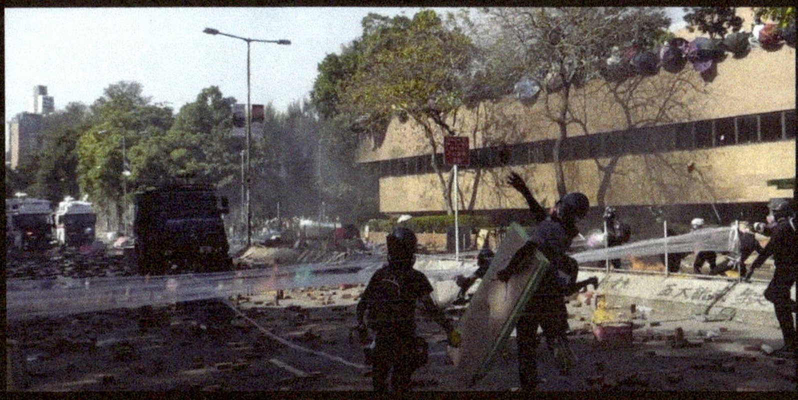

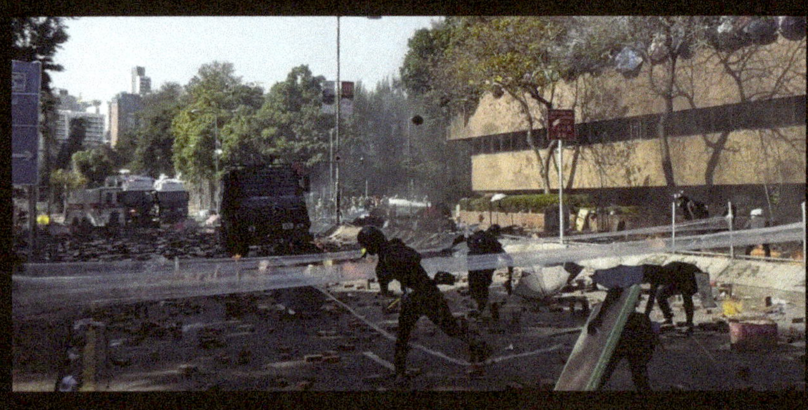

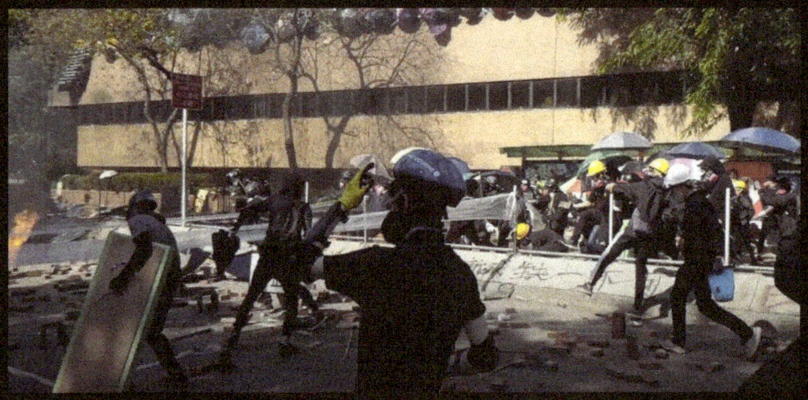

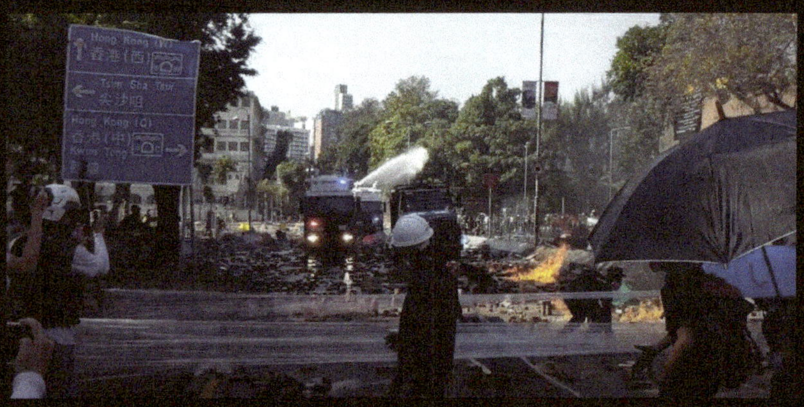
Hong Kong (W)
香港(西)
Tsim Sha Tsui
尖沙咀
Hong Kong (C)
香港(中)

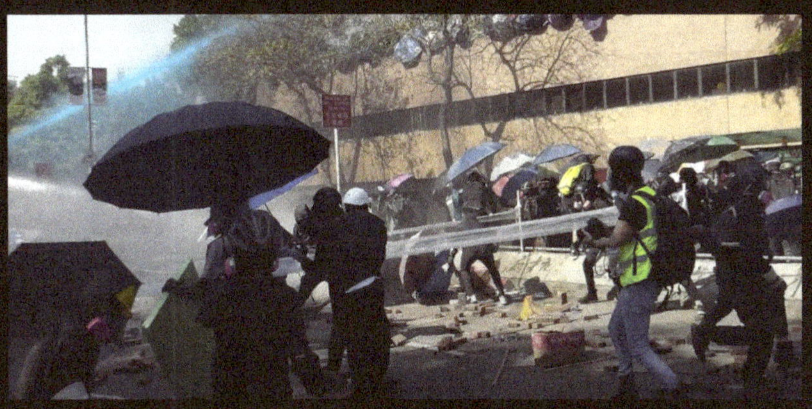

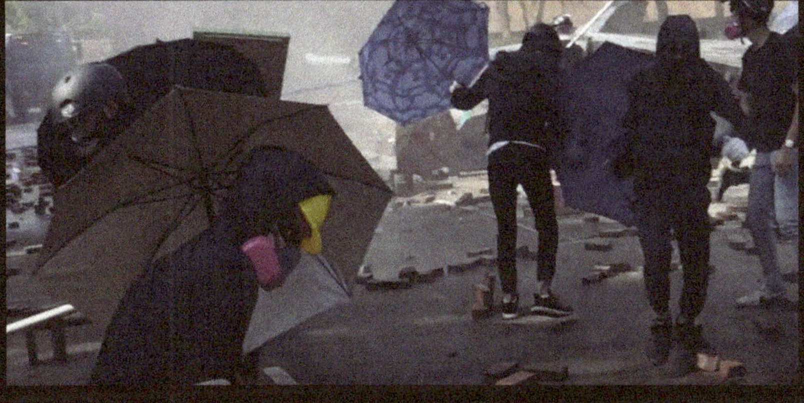

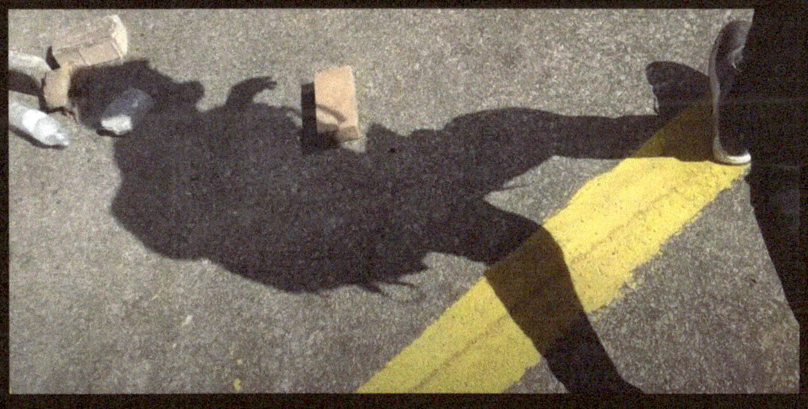

Nothing is moving, so I have to walk the last part of the way. The barricade at Lai Ping Road is being dismantled rapidly to get the cars in. There's a large commercial removal truck. The most useful parts of the barricade are loaded in, along with other material being brought from up the road. At the campus entrance, a student stands with several boxes of Molotov cocktails. 'I'm not sure why. There was a van explosion at number two bridge,' he says. Was it the police? Was anyone hurt? 'No, but we had no defence. There were not enough people to rebuild. Without the bridge, there is no point staying and fighting. We will lose. Most people have gone now, before the police come.' Are they giving up? 'No. We are taking as much as we can to other universities to reinforce them.' That explains the pace at which people are moving.

For the fourth night in a row there are protests in town. I wave down the first scooter to come past. 'Can you take me to Mong Kok?' Such is the support for the movement that nothing else needs to be said. He pulls out a helmet and we're off at a cracking pace. The streets are again occupied, bricks again litter the place and the barricades are up at Nathan and Mong Kok roads. There are no police, but they were here earlier. In the middle of the intersection, frontliners make more Molotovs. Someone stuffs it up and the road is on fire. The culprit pretends to have done it on purpose and rubs his hands above the flames as though he is just trying to warm up

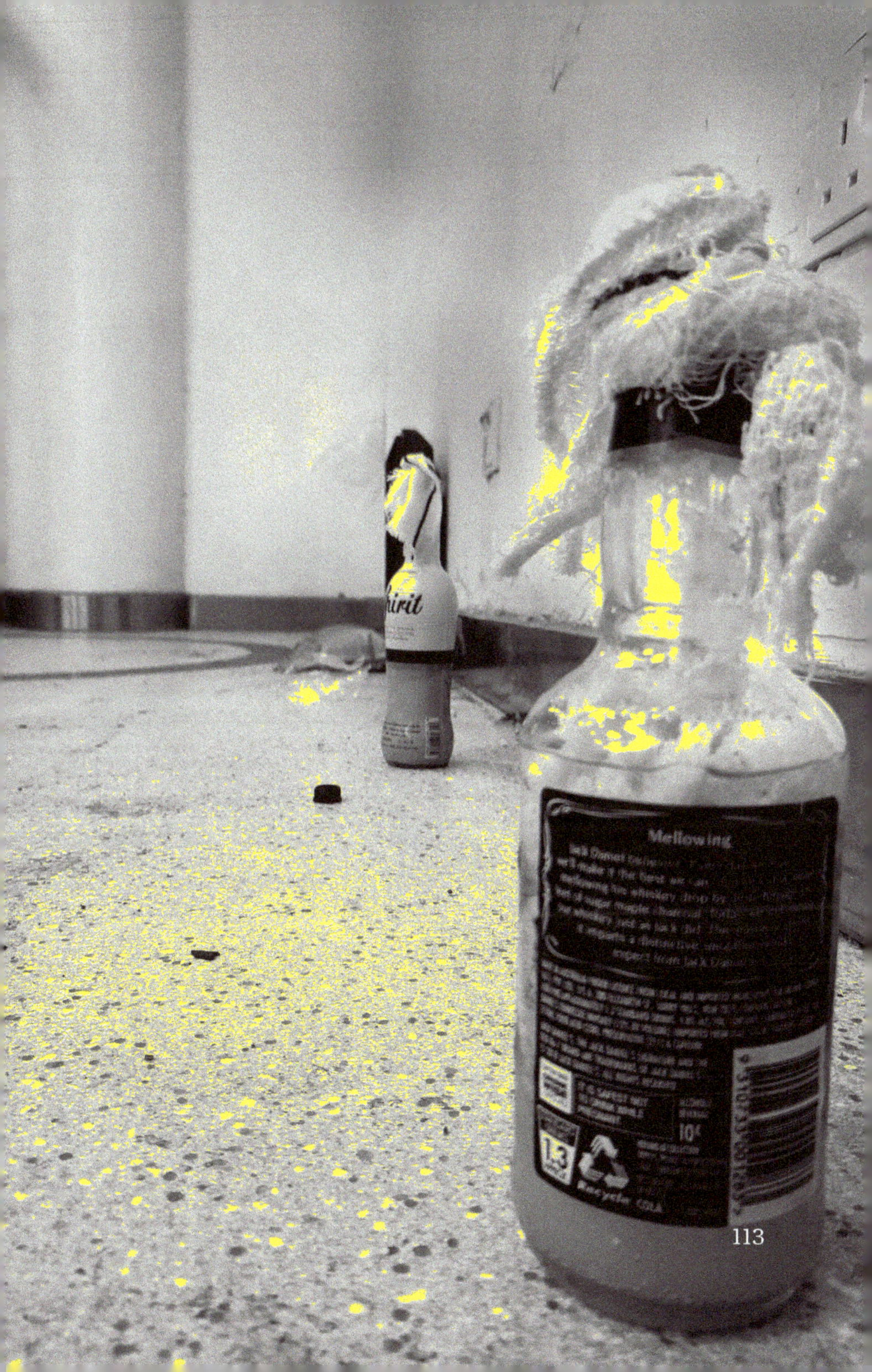
Mellowing

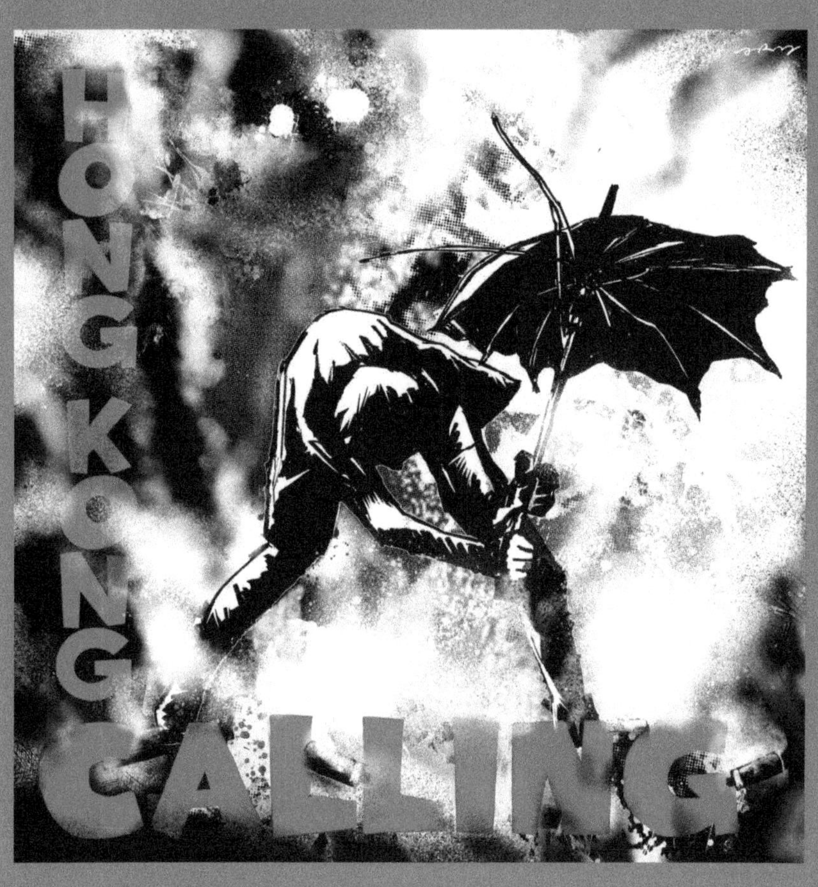

A RAY (20190
@A RAY

on this balmy night. Everyone finds this very funny.

The numbers and intensity are well down from Tuesday. And barricades are more rudimentary; firefighters walk in unchallenged to put out small blazes. When, after midnight, the police come firing tear gas and advancing south along Nathan, only thirty or forty of them are needed to push everyone back. The frontliners get the umbrellas up and launch a volley of Molotovs. But they are probably outnumbered even by the international press corps, whose ranks have swelled significantly over the last two days. Tonight, there is no strung-out advance-and-retreat battle. The cops just steadily move forward, firing tear gas every now and again and barking instructions. Then they leave as quickly as they arrived.

Over the last few days, everything seemed to be heading for a decisive confrontation. For two days, the cross-harbour tunnel has been blocked by the Polytechnic students and no attempt has been made to reopen it. The government appears to be in a bind. The students have overwhelming support, and hostility to the police has only grown since they lashed out at CUHK and Mong Kok on Tuesday night. Beijing continues to demand a crackdown. But the Hong Kong government so far has been unwilling to smash the students, perhaps fearing that such a move would provoke a citywide confrontation that they cannot control. It is significant that the only pro-cop counter-mobilisations calling for the restoration of order

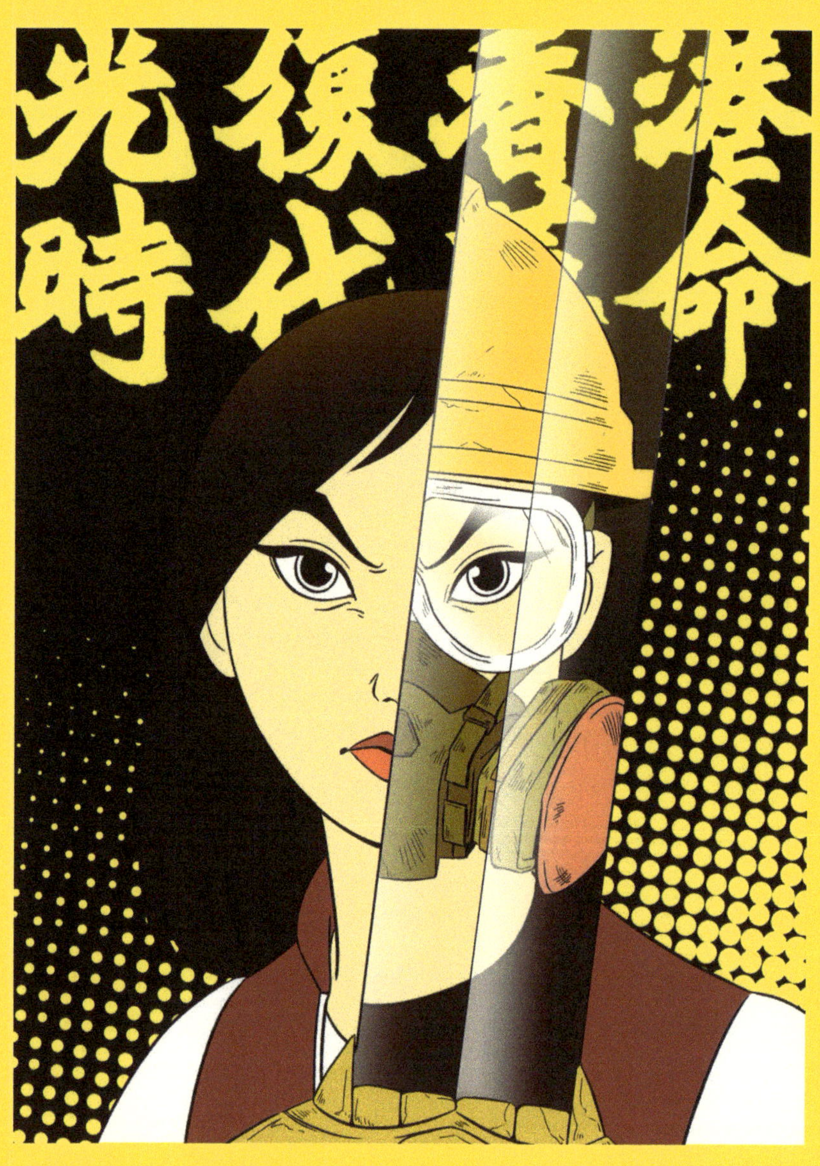

NEK
ECSTATICASUSUAL.TUMBLR

attract several hundred at most.

I haven't made it to Central district on Hong Kong Island yet, where demonstrations happen every day at lunchtime. Sue Sparks, a socialist formerly based in Hong Kong and who is following events here, noted on Thursday: 'We see plenty of workers joining protests, including office workers in financial services, lawyers, accountants, IT workers, retail workers (Hong Kong no longer has any manufacturing) ... As individuals they take days off, often with the sympathy of the bosses.' Reports suggest that these protests continue to grow; the government is threatening public servants with suspension if they get too involved.

On a side street, the intersection of Shantung and Shanghai streets, a small group smashes traffic lights. One protester is unperturbed about the loss of CUHK tonight. Isn't this the central campus to hold? 'I'm not worried. We have so much support and other campuses,' he says. 'Maybe the [CUHK] students are tired. But the population is not. I feel things have shifted in the last days. Two elderly Mandarin-speaking [mainlander] women yesterday saw me in this mask. They said stay safe. That to me is very unusual. It says we are getting even more support. And there was an elderly man with a [walking] frame. I started to clear the bricks for him to get a path, but he said no don't do that they'll catch you and beat you.'

The group of traffic light smashers now turns its attention to a branch of China CITIC Bank International. Before long, the place is ablaze and bystanders are cheering and chanting 'Fuck China!' The cops are moving in again, but it's 2am and things are petering out. With the CUHK activists and some of their materials redeploying to the Polytechnic and other occupations, the ball is in the government's court.

[NOTE: On Saturday afternoon, police attacked the occupied Polytechnic University. After several hours, they retreated. On Sunday, they attacked again, eventually surrounding the campus on all sides and laying siege. Most of the fighting was over by the early hours of Monday—until the city mobilised to defend the students stuck inside the campus.]

THE POLYTECHNIC AND AFTER

TUESDAY 19 NOVEMBER | There's a construction boom in Hong Kong, but no-one is getting paid to build the barricades everywhere around town. The youth rebellion is not only the biggest in China since the 1989 protests in Tiananmen Square, it is one of the most explosive student radicalisations of modern times. The depth of their rage, and willingness to risk everything in a fight that most think they can't win, is almost beyond words. 'Unrelenting' is the closest approximation.

Activists believe that mainland police are rotating through the riot squad to quell the protests. They say that behind the scenes, the police and the mafia are carrying out extrajudicial killings and raping young women activists. Cops have started to use live rounds and have promised to unleash greater levels of violence to bring the situation under control.

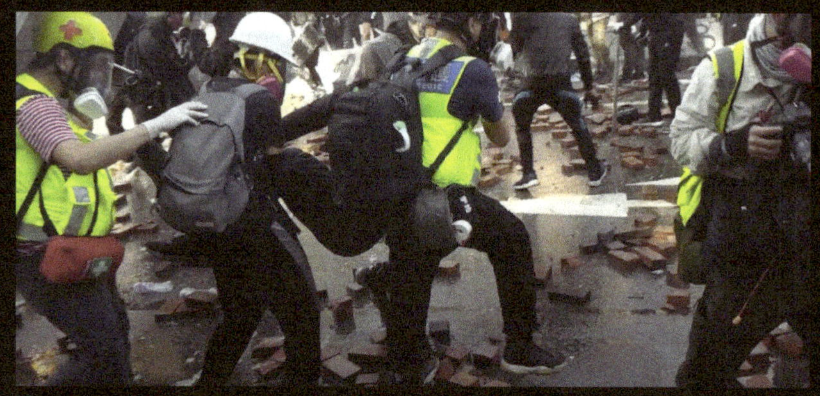

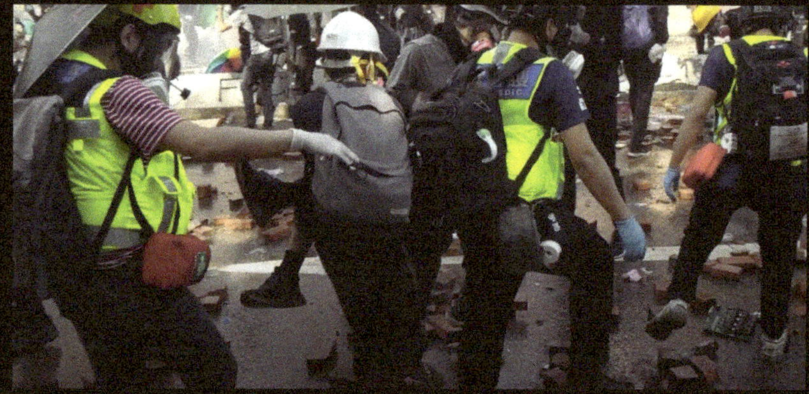

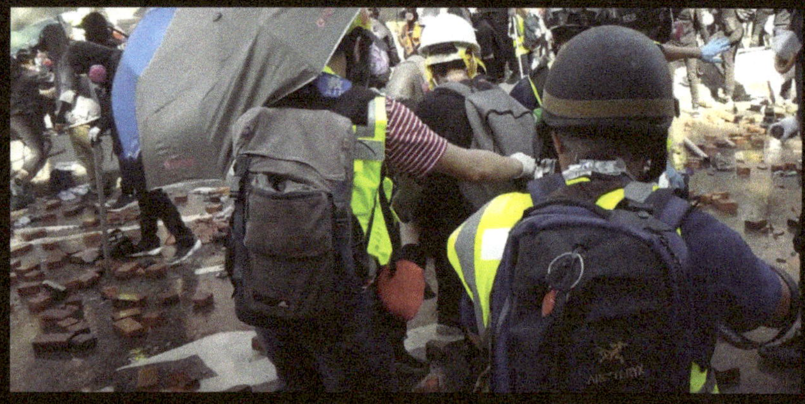

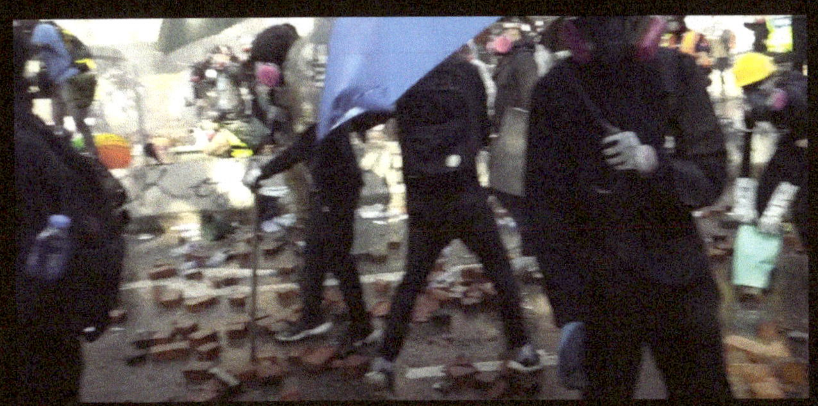

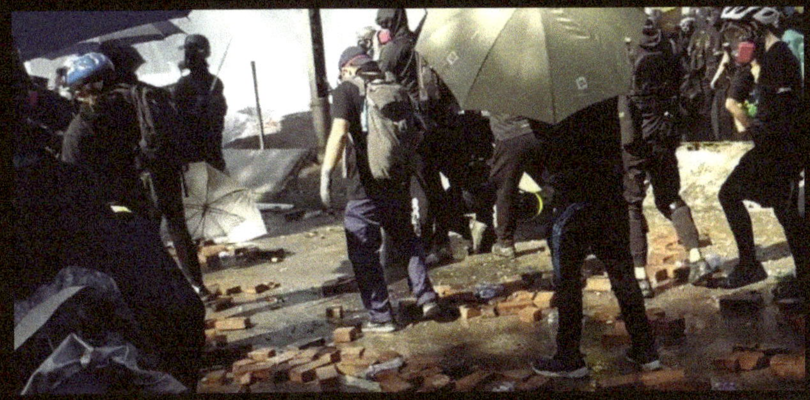

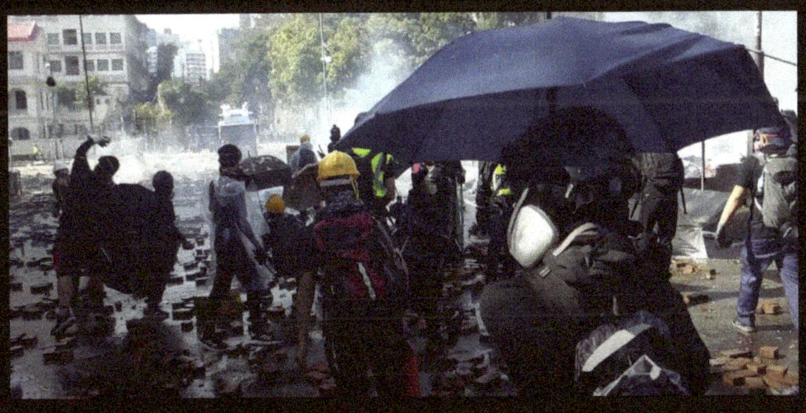

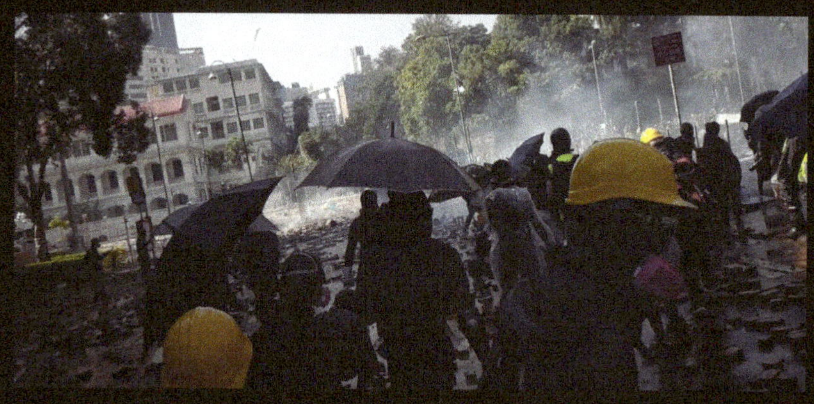

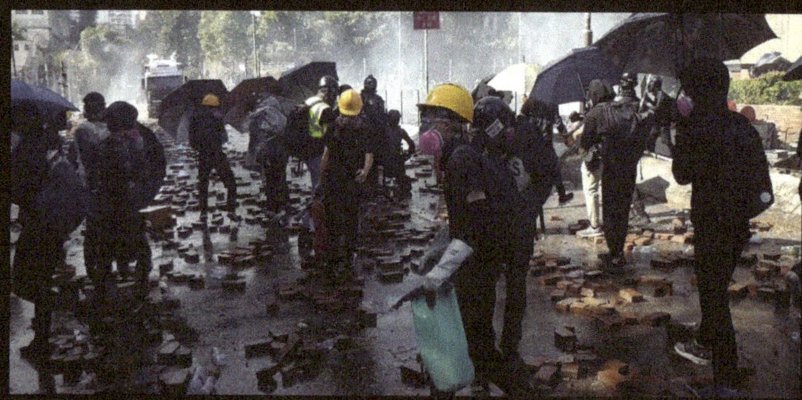

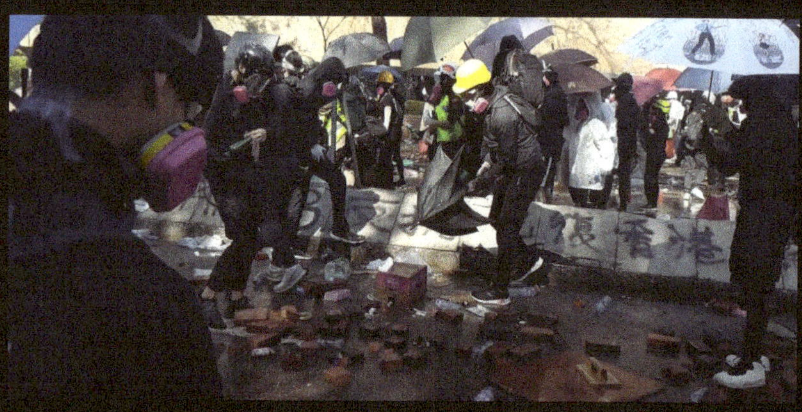
香港

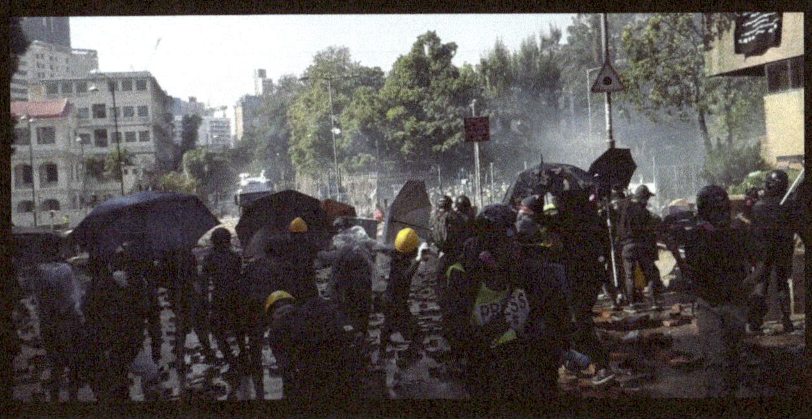
PRESS

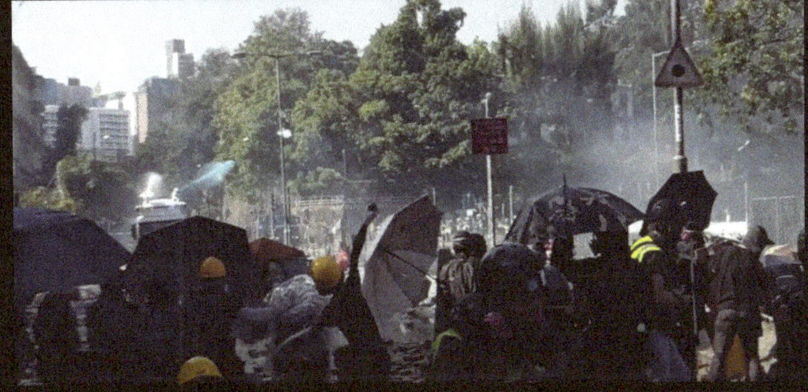

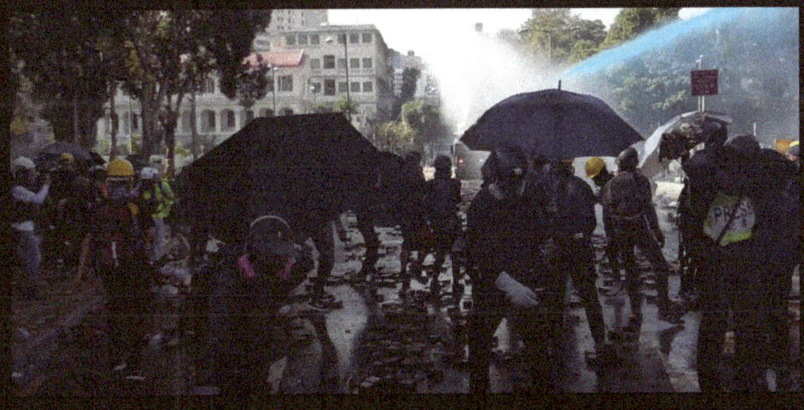
PRESS

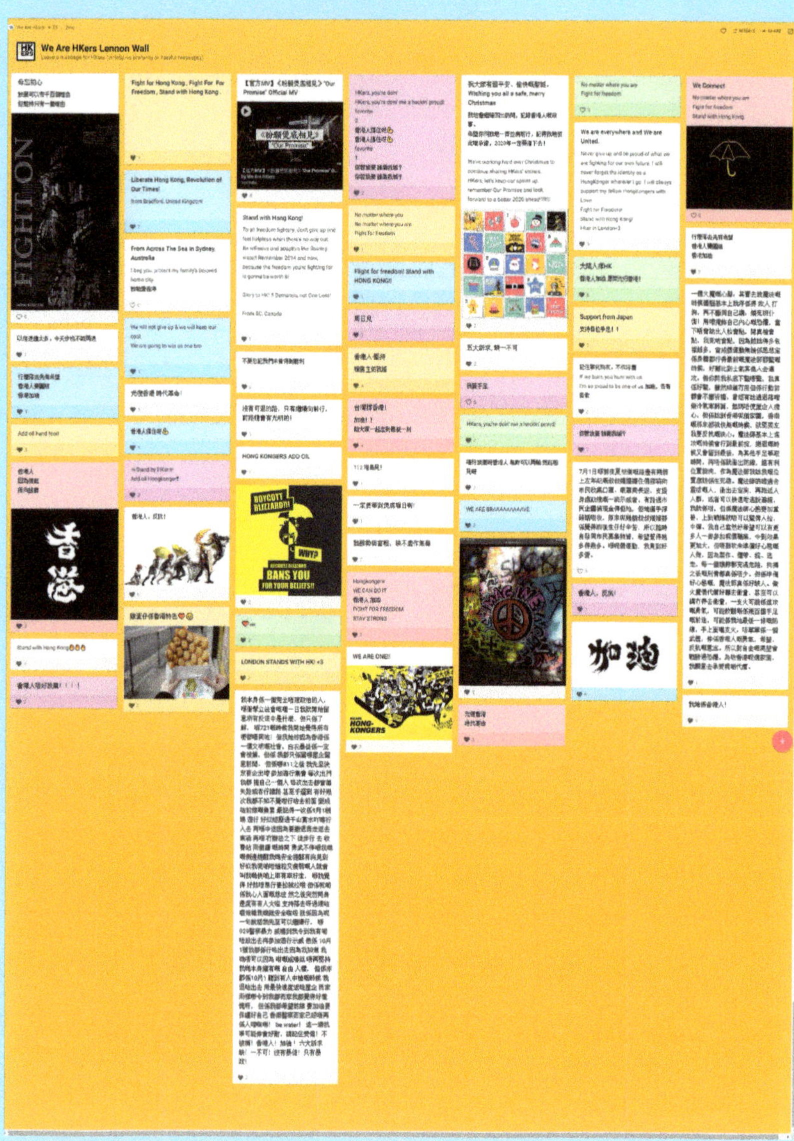

DIGITAL LENNON WALL
WE ARE HKERS

And news of the People's Liberation Army emerging from barracks to clear Baptist University students' blockade of Waterloo Road—a not-too-subtle warning to cease and desist the disruption—was widely viewed.

Yet on Monday, after a weekend of the most intense fighting so far between activists and police, pitched battles continued to rage in Hung Hom around the Polytechnic University, which has been under an intense police siege. In neighbouring suburbs Yau Ma Tei, Jordan and Tsim Sha Tsui, where roads everywhere were blocked, it was the same story. In some places, it wasn't the back-and-forth of last week, when protesters and police fought largely at a distance—but street brawls at the margins as cops made arrests and activists de-arrests. Central district on Hong Kong Island has also exploded in protest. Incoming police chief Chris Tang Pingkeung, due to be sworn in today, is quoted in the *South China Morning Post* saying that the cops have effectively lost control.

The last week at the Polytechnic is illustrative of the lengths the young people here will go to make the point that is scrawled in graffiti around the city: 'If we burn, you burn with us.' For days, hundreds of young women and men raced frantically to barricade every entrance and exit. In the canteen, they stockpiled noodles, biscuits, muesli bars and bottles of water. Along with their supporters, they took over the retail

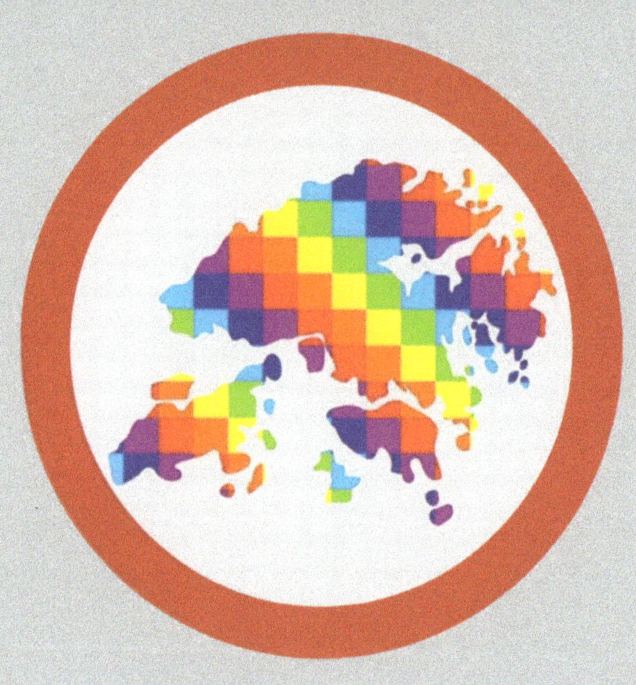

PheSti/HKER/MTR/0056

shops and turned them into twenty-four-hour communal kitchens. They set up medical stations with boxes and boxes of supplies. They collected for distribution hundreds of gas masks, goggles, fresh clothes, towels and soap. They armed themselves with bins full of broken paving bricks and garden stones, baseball bats, hammers and metal bars pilfered from railings along the roadsides. And they built an arsenal of Molotov cocktails, gas bombs, flour bombs and dye bombs. By Saturday afternoon, there were hundreds of petrol bombs to feed the frontlines—and for the next thirty-six hours, a group of about thirty young people worked tirelessly to keep production going as the war raged around them.

'The rule is dead, and our life is alight,' Tin, a recent graduate from another university, said as he rested outside PolyU's smashed up administration building. 'The world has been reversed. You are supposed to follow the rules and that makes things work smoothly. But now the rules are the problem; we have an obligation to protest.' Tin is a member of what Au Loong Yu calls 'Generation Catastrophe', otherwise known as the '97 generation—those born several years each side of the return of Hong Kong to Chinese sovereignty. 'This generation is very unlucky,' Au says. 'At first, the older generation couldn't understand—why are they so without hope? Why do they talk about revolution? It's because they sense the catastrophe. Like Greta Thunberg and the climate, but much more intense in some ways. This generation has continuous bad news.'

Generation Catastrophe is, like all generations living under capitalism, economically and socially alienated. There is extreme wealth polarisation and many jobs are menial and low paid. But the political issues are decisive in this rebellion. I've asked every young person I have spoken to about the impact of inequality, house prices and job prospects, but I've found them to be myopically focused on the political demands, particularly universal suffrage and an investigation into police violence. And while some are arguing to add a sixth demand—for the sacking of the entire police force—there are no signs of the demands being broadened to include social grievances.

The rebellion is not animated by the same issues that have inspired young people in the US and Britain—poor health care, high student debt, high unemployment and so on—to rally behind Jeremy Corbyn and Bernie Sanders, for example. Nor is it like the Arab Spring, which, while democratic in aspiration, was underpinned by class inequality and economic immiseration. Here there are problems, but unemployment is low, the health service is good and, while there is unease about the price of apartments, public housing abounds.

The issue is impending totalitarianism. In the West, we have anxieties about the rise of figures such as Donald Trump and the mainstreaming of the far right over the last five years. This pales in comparison to the situation in

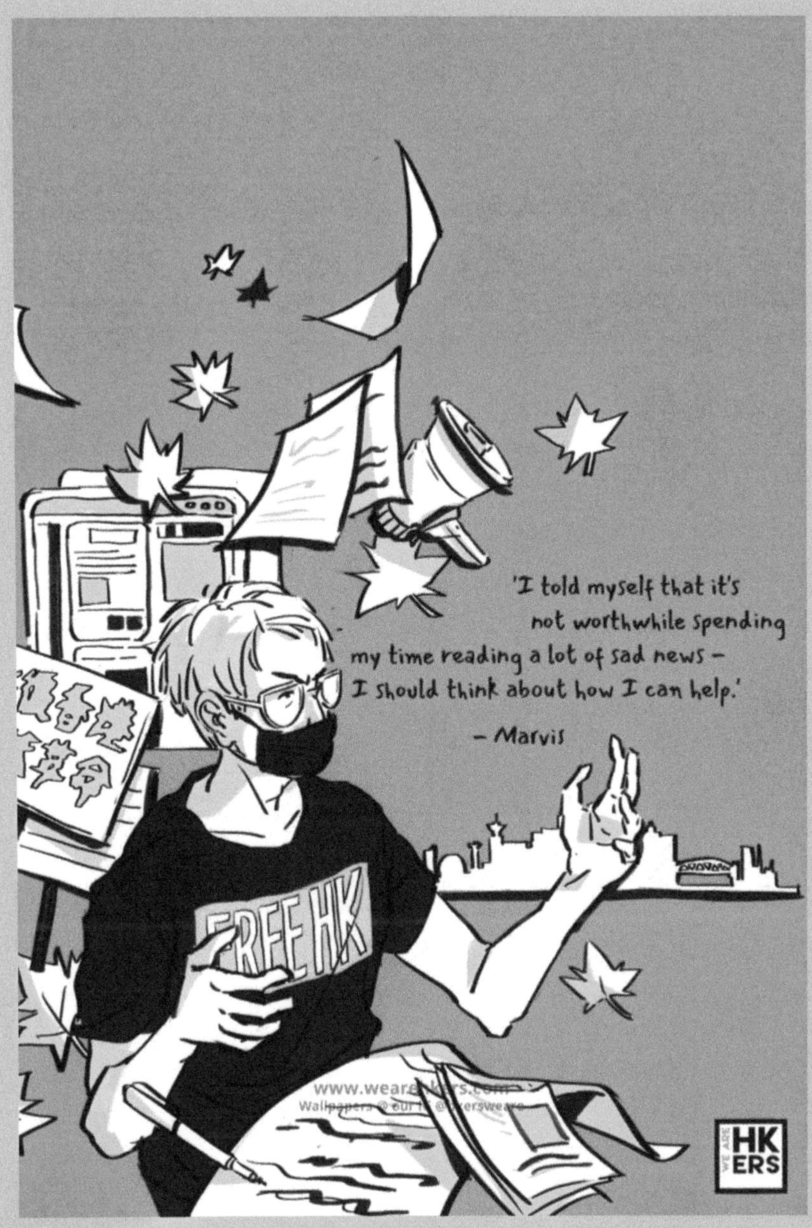
'I told myself that it's
not worthwhile spending
my time reading a lot of sad news –
I should think about how I can help.'
– Marvis
FREE HK
WE ARE HKERS

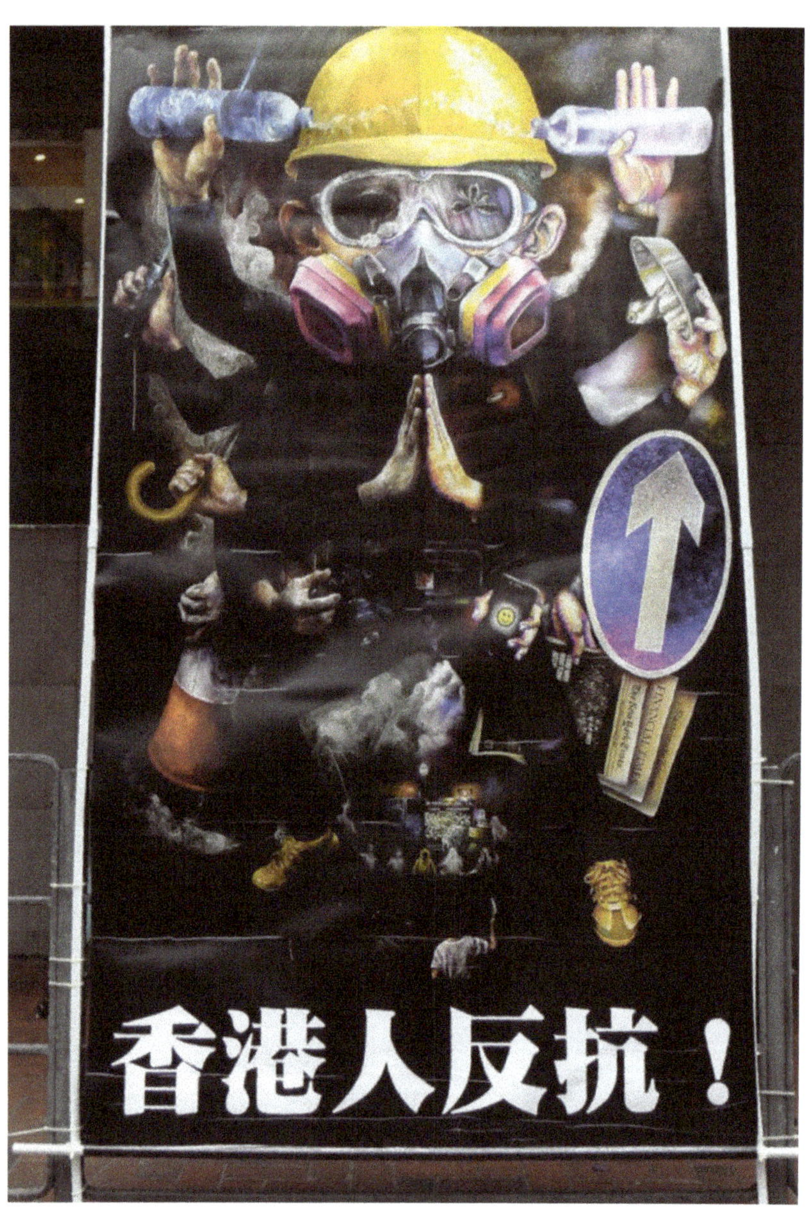

LUMLILUMLONG
@ LUMLILUMLONG

Hong Kong. By law, the city will be subsumed under China's authoritarian dictatorship by 2047—the end of the fifty-year transition period when 'one country, two systems' ceases to operate. But the Chinese Communist Party is fast-tracking the transition—integrating Hong Kong as quickly as possible through its control of nominations for the executive branch of government, through its influence over the composition of the legislature and through its effective control of the police and the city bureaucracy through the appointment of Beijing loyalists. This is what the young people are raging against.

Local factors also help to explain the apolitical nature of the movement, which is not quite the same as the sort of 'anti-political' moods in the West resulting from the long-term decomposition of centrist parties and the decline of the union movement. The mainstream democratic forces in Hong Kong, the pan-democrats, have been discredited in recent years. But the main issue is that Hong Kong is transitioning from a bourgeois colonial society to a form of state capitalism widely regarded as communism. Under the circumstances, it is next to impossible for the left to grow—after all, 'communism' is what everyone is afraid of. But the absence of a recognisable left should not inform Western attitudes towards the rebellion. All its demands are ones the left should support. The movement may be messy, but it could not be otherwise given the history and the circumstances.

There is a widespread belief that Beijing will prevail, which gives the movement a distinct mood. Unlike the Western student rebellion of the 1960s and 1970s, which built the last solid left-wing generation and deployed slogans of hope figuring a new world—'All power to the imagination!', 'Be realistic, demand the impossible!', for example—the spirit here feels vengeful, tied not to visions of a new society of equality and liberation, but reflecting the almost hopeless task of clinging to something imperfect before inevitably falling under the heel of something much worse. There is more bitterness and reflexive defiance than hope in the content of 'If we burn, you burn with us' and 'Liberty or death'.

This extraordinary rage, manifest in the destruction of symbols of Chinese capitalism in the more working-class districts, is precisely what has rallied behind them a huge section of the population, which continues to offer support. One small example happened on Sunday: before police surrounded the Polytechnic on all sides to prevent anyone leaving, an armoured vehicle approaching the protesters was hit by a Molotov. On a corner at the rear, a group of a dozen older locals walking past started cheering; one of them joined the young people digging up paving bricks, which were being smashed with hammers to use as projectiles.

There is, of course, talk about US influence. High-ranking Beijing officials have accused the protesters of trying to

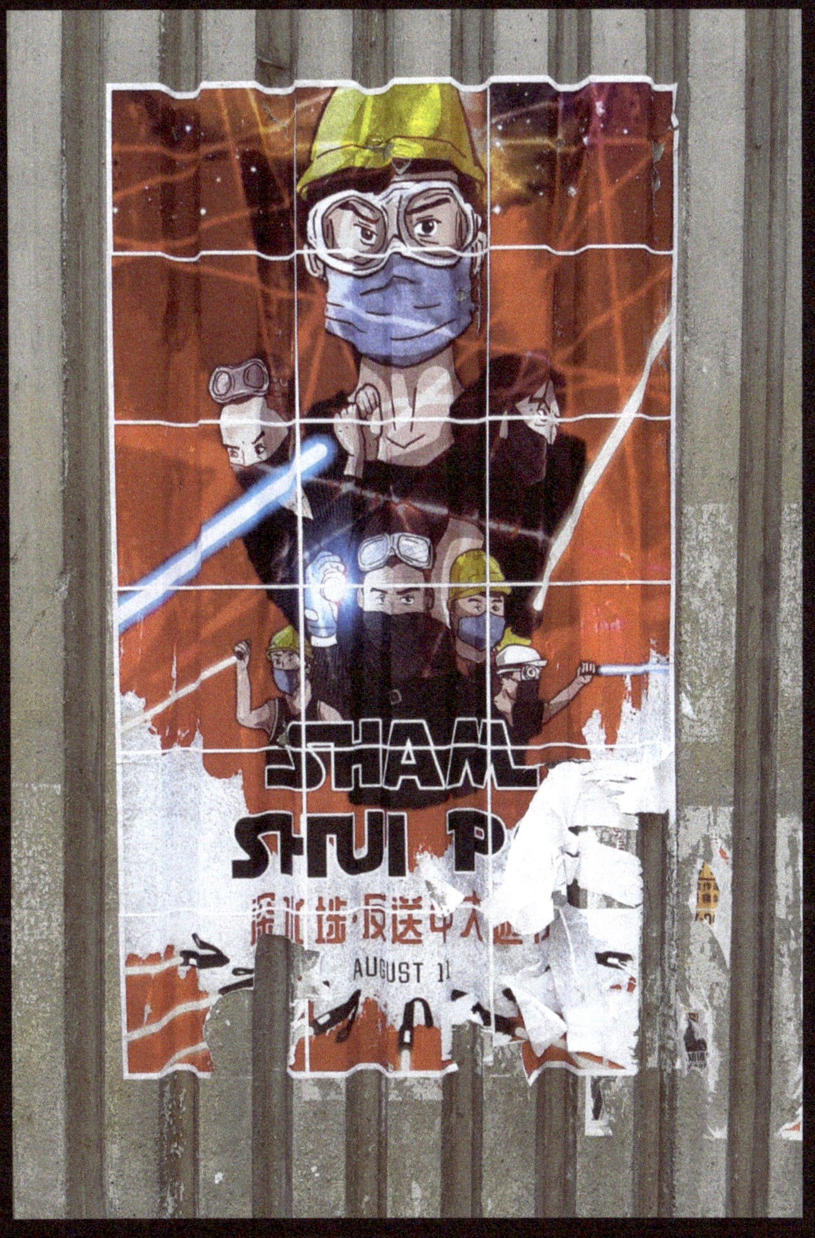

USP

foment another 'colour revolution'—a movement purportedly for democracy but in reality just an intrigue to install a government favourable to Washington. Certainly, the students are groping around for allies, and many don't see any that are powerful enough, except perhaps the US. But the idea that the US can be a saviour is primarily a product of desperation, not a considered political analysis. And it certainly doesn't mean the US state is in a position to influence events. Any honest witness would be quickly disabused of such a notion if they saw first-hand what is going on: a widespread grassroots rebellion clearly reliant on the resources it can muster locally.

As gas and dyed water from the cannon rained on activists outside on Sunday night, medics worked overtime inside the campus tending to the parade of injured being carried up the entrance stairs. In one of the tutorial rooms turned into makeshift medical centres, a text from the library was abandoned temporarily: *Ethics*. It may not be Marxism, but the activists here are putting theory into practice. Even if the students recognised that an important potential ally is the mainland working class, they have incredibly limited means of reaching it. Perhaps workers across the border, in the Pearl River Delta industrial zones, would be inspired to act in solidarity if they witnessed the rebellion. But more likely, and perhaps Hong Kong's ultimate hope, is that those workers rise in their own interests and test the cohesion of the Chinese state.

The East Timorese, for example, were able to free themselves from Indonesian domination only because a revolution in Java loosened the military's grip on the archipelago. The problem for the young rebels here is that the Chinese state is vastly more powerful and cohesive than was the Indonesian state in 1999. The students understand its power, but they are not going to die waiting for ripe conditions: they willed a one-day general strike and delivered a week of mayhem. That in itself was an enormous achievement. And, as the streets yesterday attested, they are not done yet.

Late on Sunday, when police through loudspeakers warned that everyone would be gassed, sprayed with water cannon and charged as criminals if they did not disperse, the Polytechnic occupiers respond by blaring the opening notes of Beethoven's 'Für Elise' over the top of them. Not only do they brawl, they do so with panache. Generation Catastrophe is showing the world how to resist.

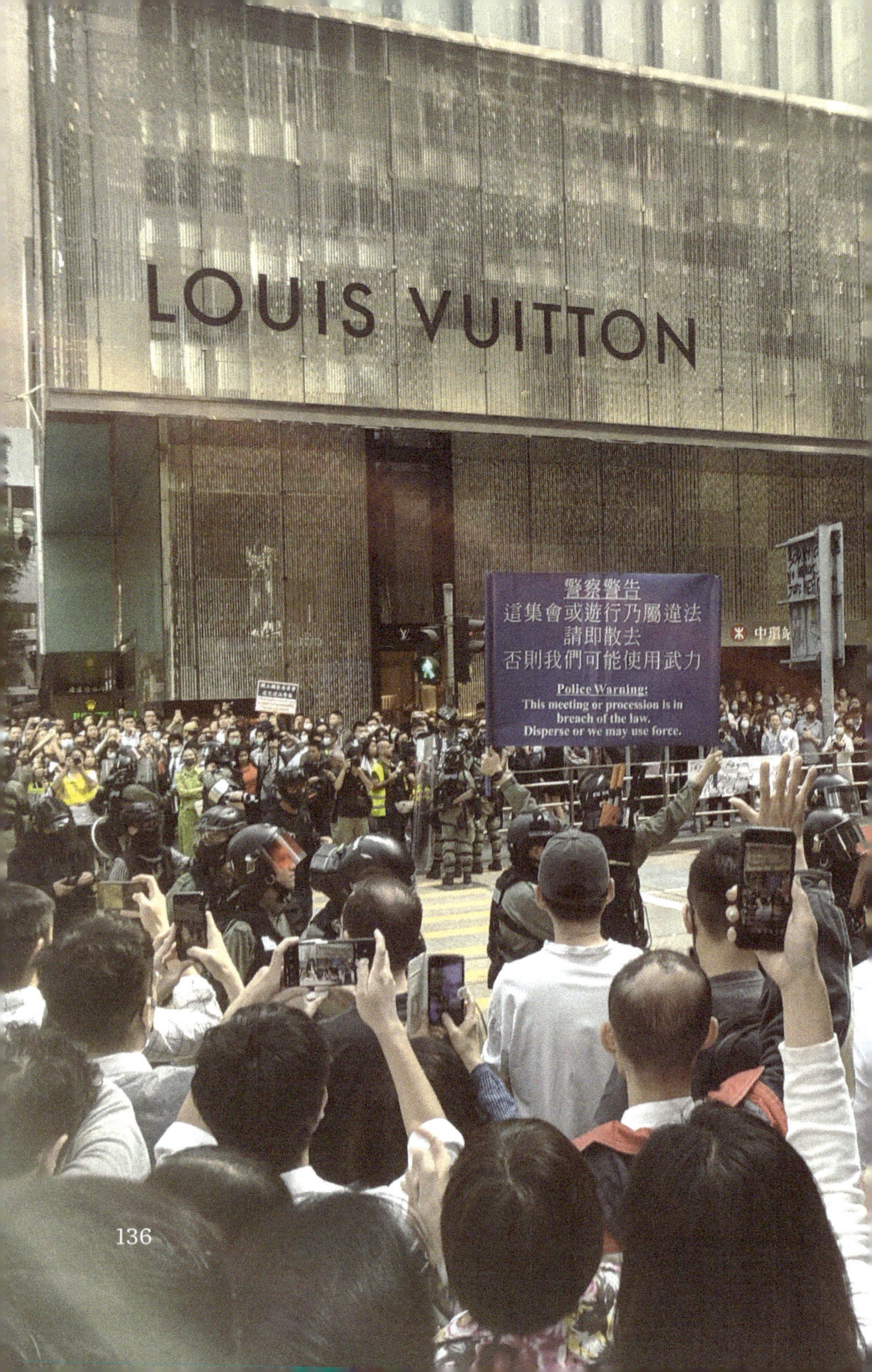

LOUIS VUITTON
警察警告
這集會或遊行乃屬違法
請即散去
否則我們可能使用武力
Police Warning:
This meeting or procession is in
breach of the law.
Disperse or we may use force.

'A CIVIL WAR SITUATION'

WEDNESDAY | It's lunchtime at the intersection of Des Voeux Road and Pedder Street. Several hundred protesters are chanting and jeering at police. They each raise a hand with all fingers spread as signifiers of the movement's five demands. One chant berates the cops as triads. Then there is the call of 'Rapists! Murderers!' Another is for the immediate disbanding of the force. Perhaps the most ultra-militant chant is the one wishing death on officers' family members. One wearing a red helmet raises a small canvas banner, which reads: 'Police Warning: This meeting is in breach of the law. Disperse or we may use force.' In response, a cacophony of boos and cheers.

Two things stand out here. First, when the riot police move in (they were waiting in eight vans for the assembly to begin), the protesters immediately clear the road and shift to the pavement, where they are legally allowed to congregate; there is no street fighting like at Mong Kok and other places over the past week. Second, the assembled are impeccably dressed and without weapons—this is Central district, Hong Kong's banking centre and one of global capitalism's most important financial hubs. Picture employees from Sydney's Martin Place, New York's Wall Street or the City of London screaming 'I hope your mother dies!' at on-duty police and you will have an accurate representation of what is going on here.

'I feel like it's like a civil war situation,' Howard says in between joining the chants and translating them from Cantonese into English. Wearing a grey tailored suit with brown pointed leather shoes, he works for one of the big firms here and has been coming to these demonstrations, which occur every lunchtime, for the last week and a half. 'The disruption is for economic effect. This is one of the few things we can legally do,' he says. 'We might be a bit depressed after what happened at PolyU [the siege of the student-occupied Polytechnic has resulted in more than one thousand arrests]—but we have so much support. There are seven million of us, so this will not stop us. If you support the police, I think you are brainwashed.'

The demonstration today is down in numbers from the heights of last week, when they had enough people to block the roads, but the militancy remains. As two of the unneeded police vans drive off, all corners of the intersection erupt in

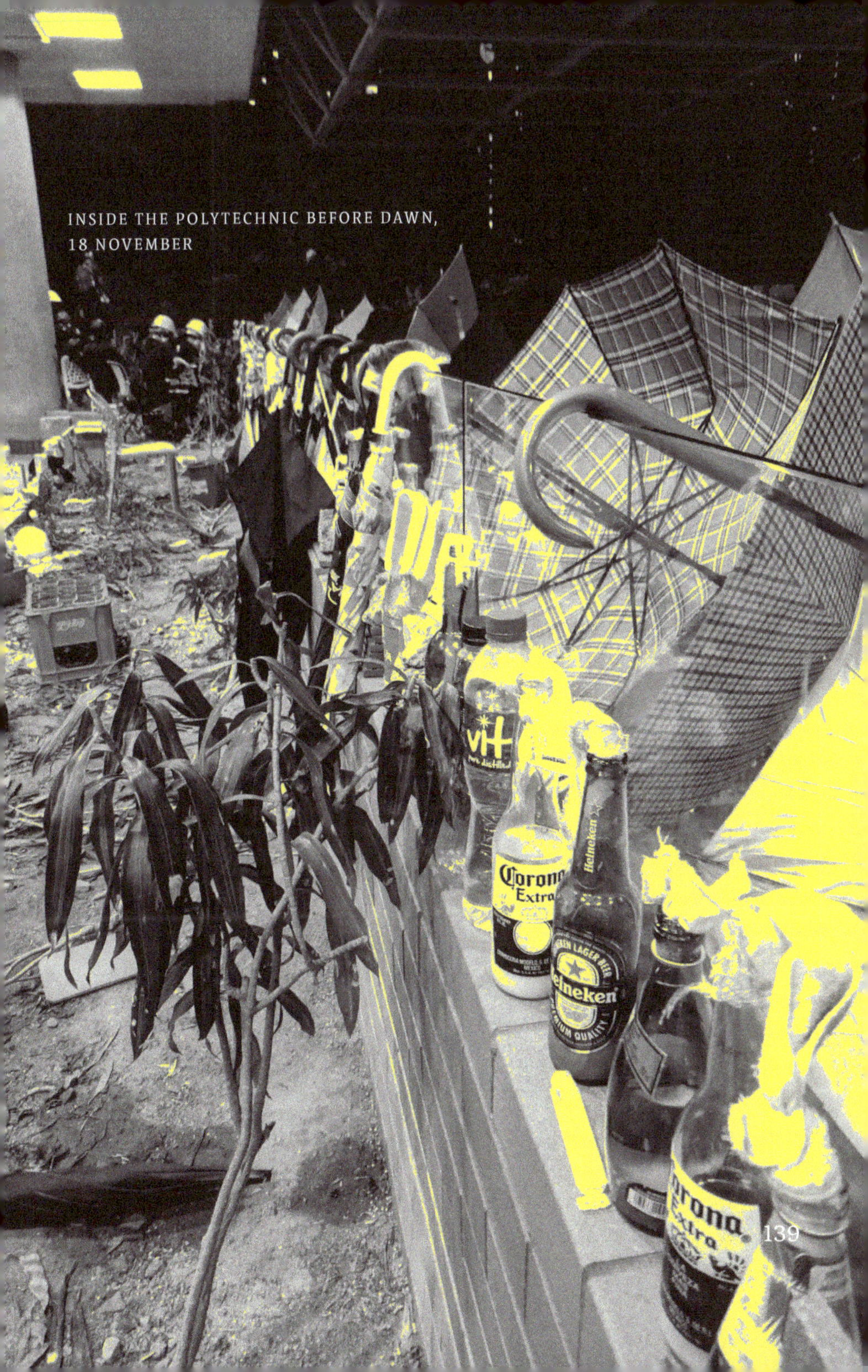

INSIDE THE POLYTECHNIC BEFORE DAWN, 18 NOVEMBER

jeering. 'We're not blocking the road! You are! We're legal—you're illegal!' How is it that even the financial district has become a hotbed of anti-cop rage? 'It has been building for some time, five months. But I think Monday was a turning point,' Howard says. Monday last week, an officer shot a young protester in the abdomen at point blank range. Video footage of the incident went viral. Three people now have reportedly been shot by live rounds, a young woman says that she was gang raped by cops in a station, and everyone says that these publicly known incidents are only the tip of the iceberg. Because the police investigate themselves and no-one is being disciplined, other victims will not come forward. 'That's why we chant, triads! They are gangsters who can do what they want with no control.'

Howard isn't the first person here to have used the term 'civil war'. At the Polytechnic, Tin said the same thing. He wasn't referring to the students' actions. The police, he said, are taking people out behind the scenes. How true this is I don't know. But it is a widely held belief. 'The students say it is true,' Howard says. 'I believe them. The police are liars.' It's not just the students who say it. And it's not just their supporters who believe it. *Financial Times* journalists Sue-Lin Wong and Nicolle Liu yesterday quoted a young officer admitting, 'No-one follows the rules and guidelines anymore. When my colleagues break the law, they never admit it and our supervisors provide cover for them.' Today, the BBC has run a story quoting Simon Cheng, a former trade and investment officer at the UK consulate, saying he was taken by mainland police and tortured for two weeks in August:

'I saw a bunch of Hong Kong people getting arrested and interrogated. I heard someone speak in Cantonese saying: "Raise your hands up—you raised the flags in the protest didn't you?" ... The secret police clearly stated that batches after batches of Hong Kong protesters had been caught, delivered and detained in mainland China.'

These sorts of stories, and the police handling of the situation, have turned a society of decorum into a rage. 'The relations between people and the police used to be quite good,' an older labour movement activist says. 'Before June, there was a sense that there was accountability.' A Chinese University of Hong Kong survey last month found that about fifty percent of the population doesn't trust the police at all. Before the protest movement, the figure was seven percent. It would be interesting to see the figures now. Footage of officers kicking the heads of already subdued protesters lying on the ground have gone viral since the Polytechnic siege. So too footage of young high school students being arrested in their uniforms on the way to school.

Police claim that they have been restrained. But it is astounding, given the situation, that more people have not

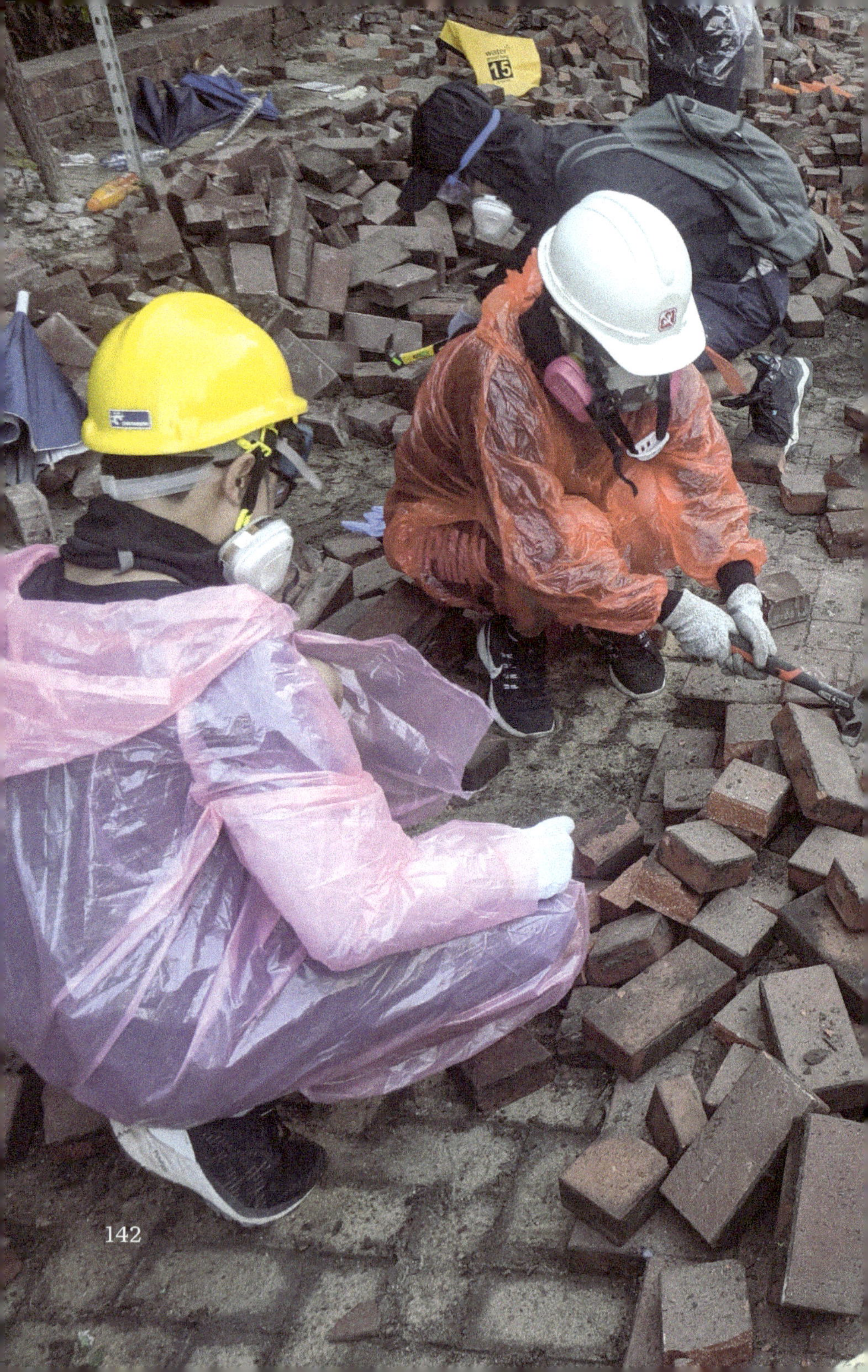
water
15

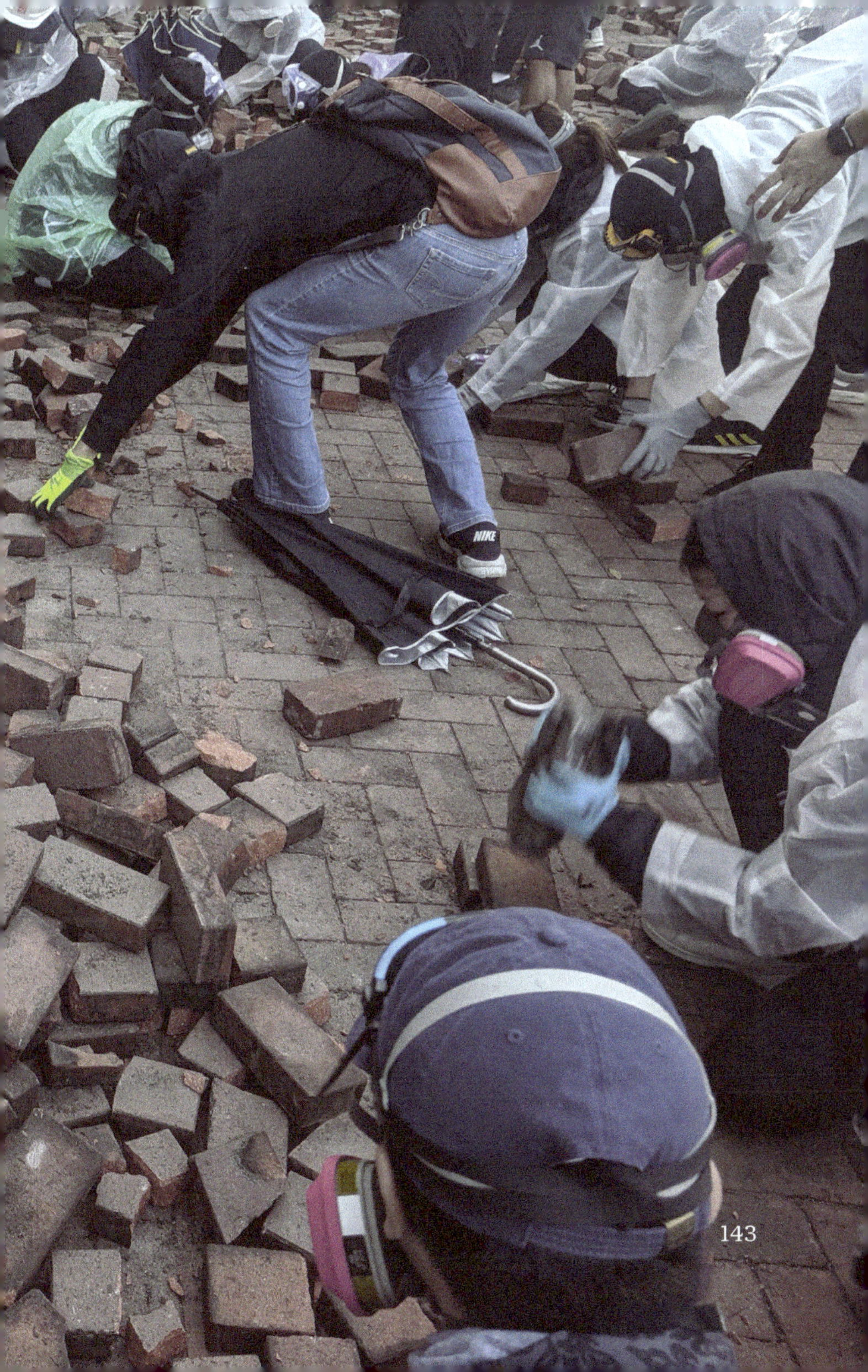
NIKE

been killed during the recent clashes, in which officers have fired countless rounds of potentially lethal rubber bullets. The have also concentrated on chemical warfare: gassing the hell out of the place to suffocate everyone into submission. At Mong Kok last Tuesday and at the Polytechnic on Sunday, even frontliners with high-end gas masks sometimes succumbed. People were being dragged away semi-conscious by medics. Some were throwing up as first aiders drenched them in water to wash the residue from their eyes and skin.

The blanketing of protest sites with tear gas has been so intense that the Cleaning Workers Union today held a press conference/protest calling on the government to stop the police deploying it. The cleaners are overcome by the residue, which is stirred up when they sweep the streets. One worker says that she is constantly coughing at work now. It's not safe and the government doesn't care, she says. 'They think our lives are cheap.' Danny To, an organiser with the union, says after the conference:

'They [the workers] don't have enough protection. We want the government to supply proper masks and goggles and rubber gloves. In the areas heavily affected with tear gas, they should have professional teams with full equipment. The government said they don't know very well the chemical substance of the tear gas. It is ridiculous—they are using it everywhere. If they don't know, they don't know the threat to

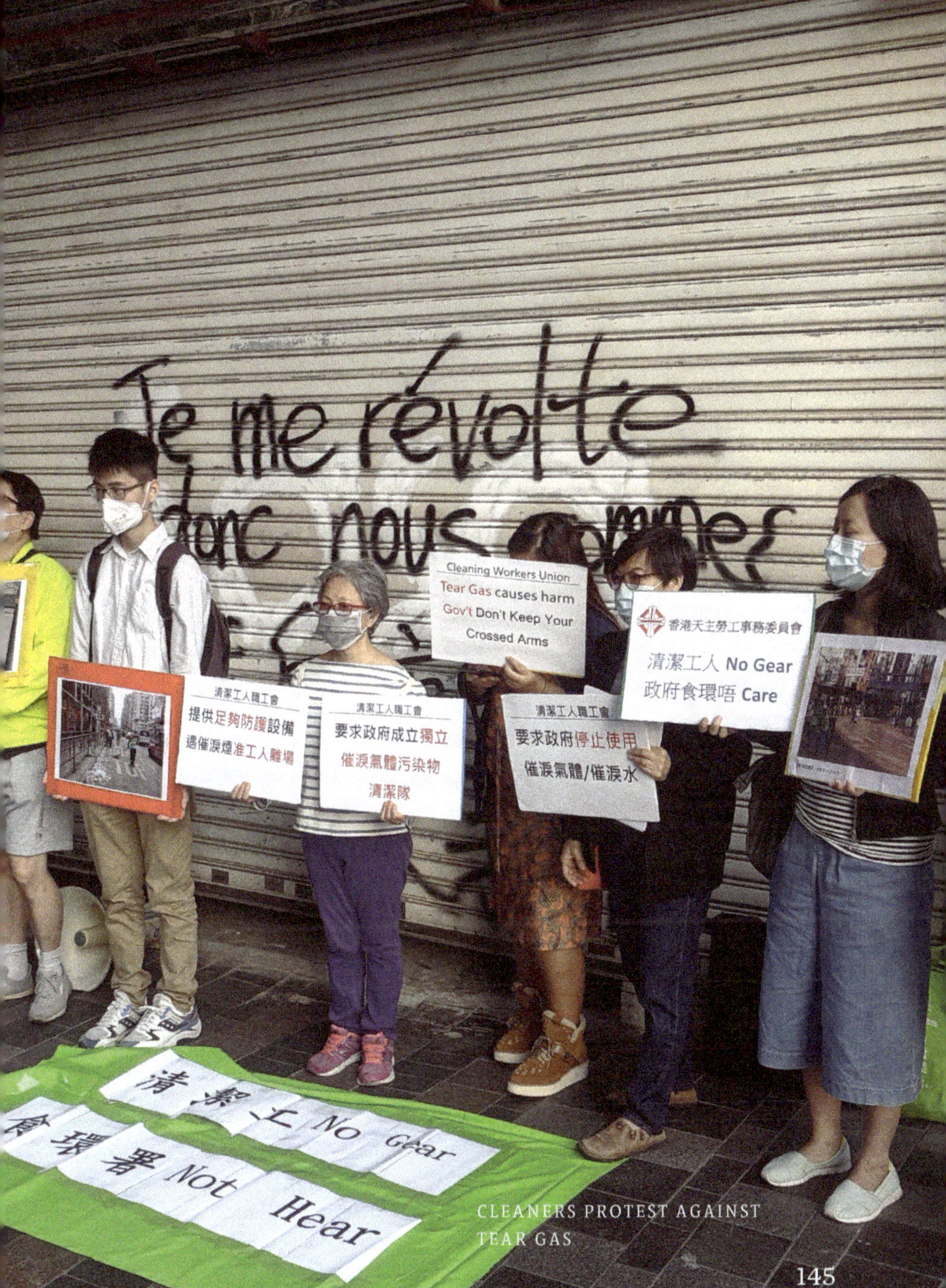

CLEANERS PROTEST AGAINST
TEAR GAS

public health. They should stop using it.'

Debates are raging in activist forums. Some frontliners are upset that many people at the protests don't wear gas masks. When the police volleys come, everyone runs, leaving the advanced guard exposed. Others say that the frontliners' Molotovs aren't effective—or they just don't have arms to throw them far enough. One lesson reportedly being drawn (how widely I cannot say) from the Polytechnic siege is that activists cannot hope to counter the full force of the police. Some are saying that too many have been arrested for little gain. They must return to where they were two weeks ago: with Bruce Lee's 'be water' approach of smaller actions from which they rapidly scatter before the police have a chance to respond.

Only the activists will know what is really going on and what is to come. It's unclear how many of the Polytechnic arrestees were central to the movement. A lot of people seem to have gone to ground after the police rounded up so many of their comrades. If things return to the frenzy of last week, however, it might get messy. Some of the cops—already partially off the leash, according to that *Financial Times* article—seem to be baying for blood. As I left the siege of PolyU while the sun was coming up on Monday morning, a pack of riot police was going feral. The officers weren't performing; it was pure rage if ever I've seen it, even if their yells were

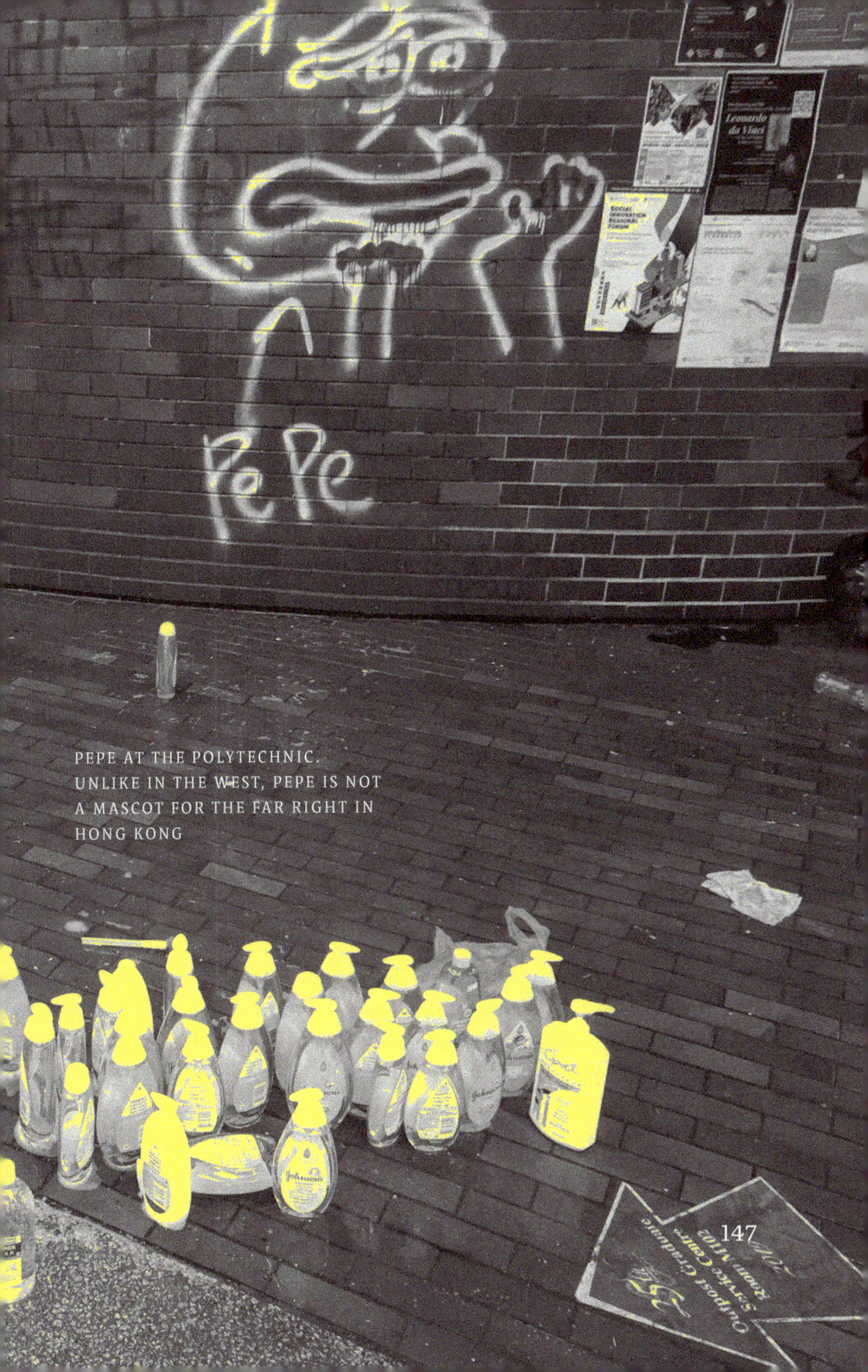

PEPE AT THE POLYTECHNIC. UNLIKE IN THE WEST, PEPE IS NOT A MASCOT FOR THE FAR RIGHT IN HONG KONG

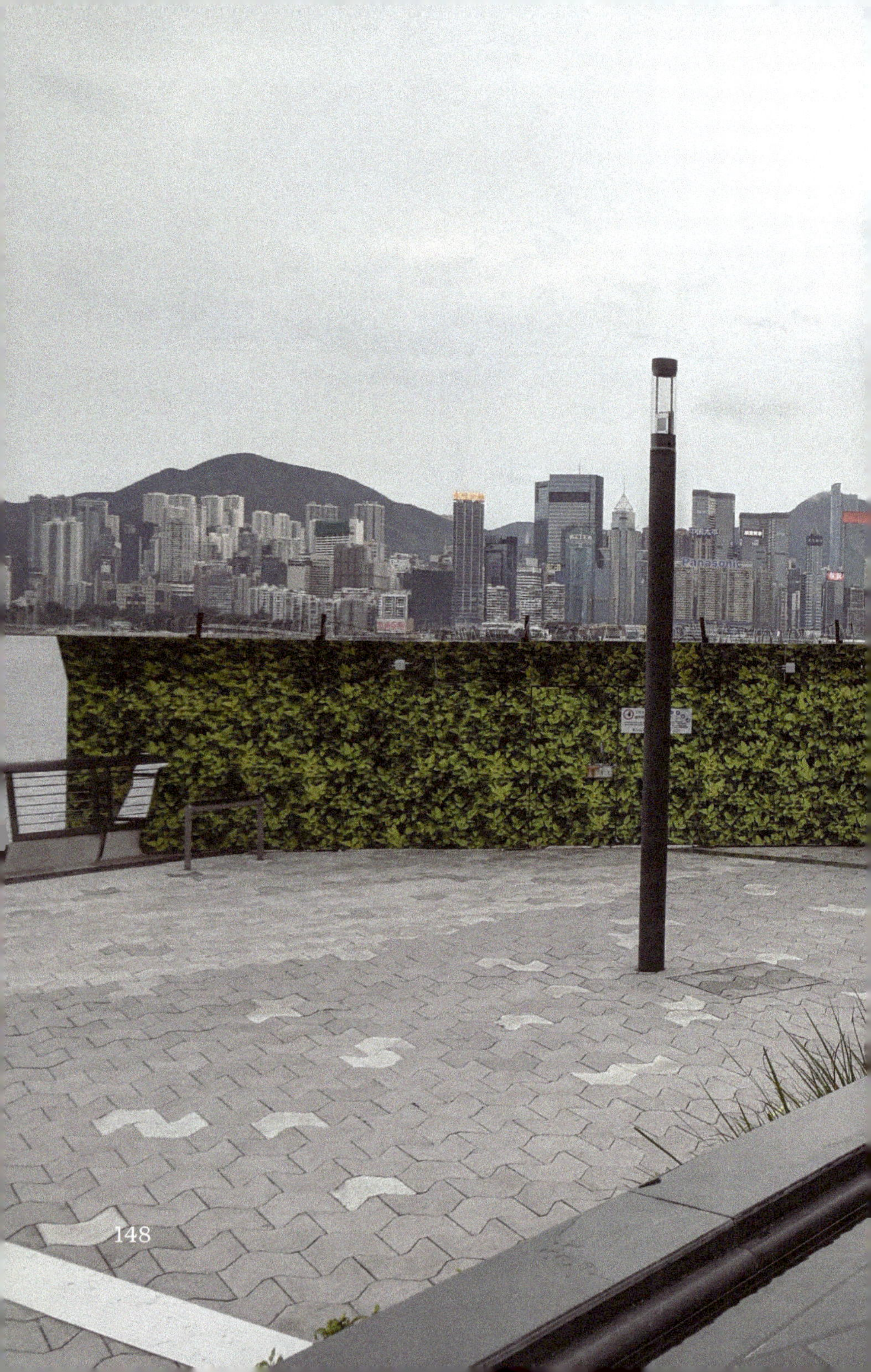
Panasonic

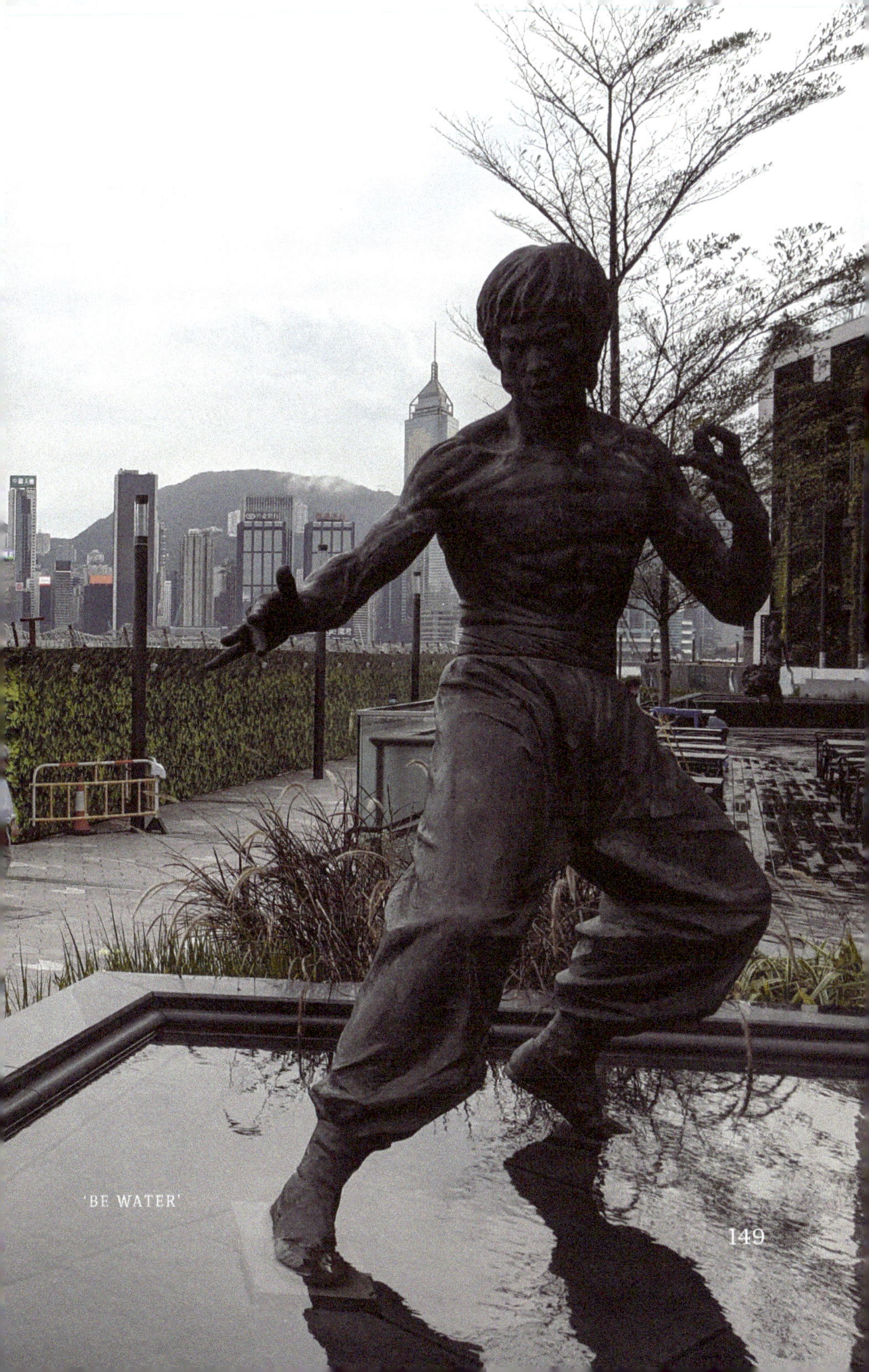

muffled by gas masks. By anecdotal accounts, it is the fury of a rank and file desperate to drown the rebellion in blood, if only their superiors would give the green light.

'Honestly, police have been very lenient,' former Superintendent Clement Lai Ka-chi told the *South China Morning Post* yesterday. 'They have a lot of options, in terms of tactics and weapons—way more than you can imagine. But they have only used the tip of the iceberg of what is available to them.' This seemed an ominous warning from someone still plugged into the officers' circles: you ain't seen nothing yet. Police have started carrying AR-15s and other semi-automatic weapons. Commanders are making clear gestures about what they may be prepared to do to bring the situation under control. Are they bluffing? Who knows? But a heavy responsibility must now weigh on the activists. Will they respond to the fall of the Polytechnic and the mass arrests? If so, how will they stay safe?

THE ELECTORAL WAVE

MONDAY 25 NOVEMBER--Pro-democracy candidates across Hong Kong stormed to victory in Sunday's district council elections as politics here continues to be turned on its head. For the first time since the territory's handover, the pro-Beijing forces lost control. The pro-democracy camp has taken at least three-quarters of the four hundred and fifty-two contested seats and won more than fifty-five percent of the votes; the Democratic Alliance for the Betterment and Progress of Hong Kong (DAB), the main pro-Beijing party, has been reduced from one hundred and nineteen seats to fewer than two dozen.

The result has shattered the government's claim that a silent majority backs its crackdown on the protest movement that has raged for six months. It has demonstrated that the

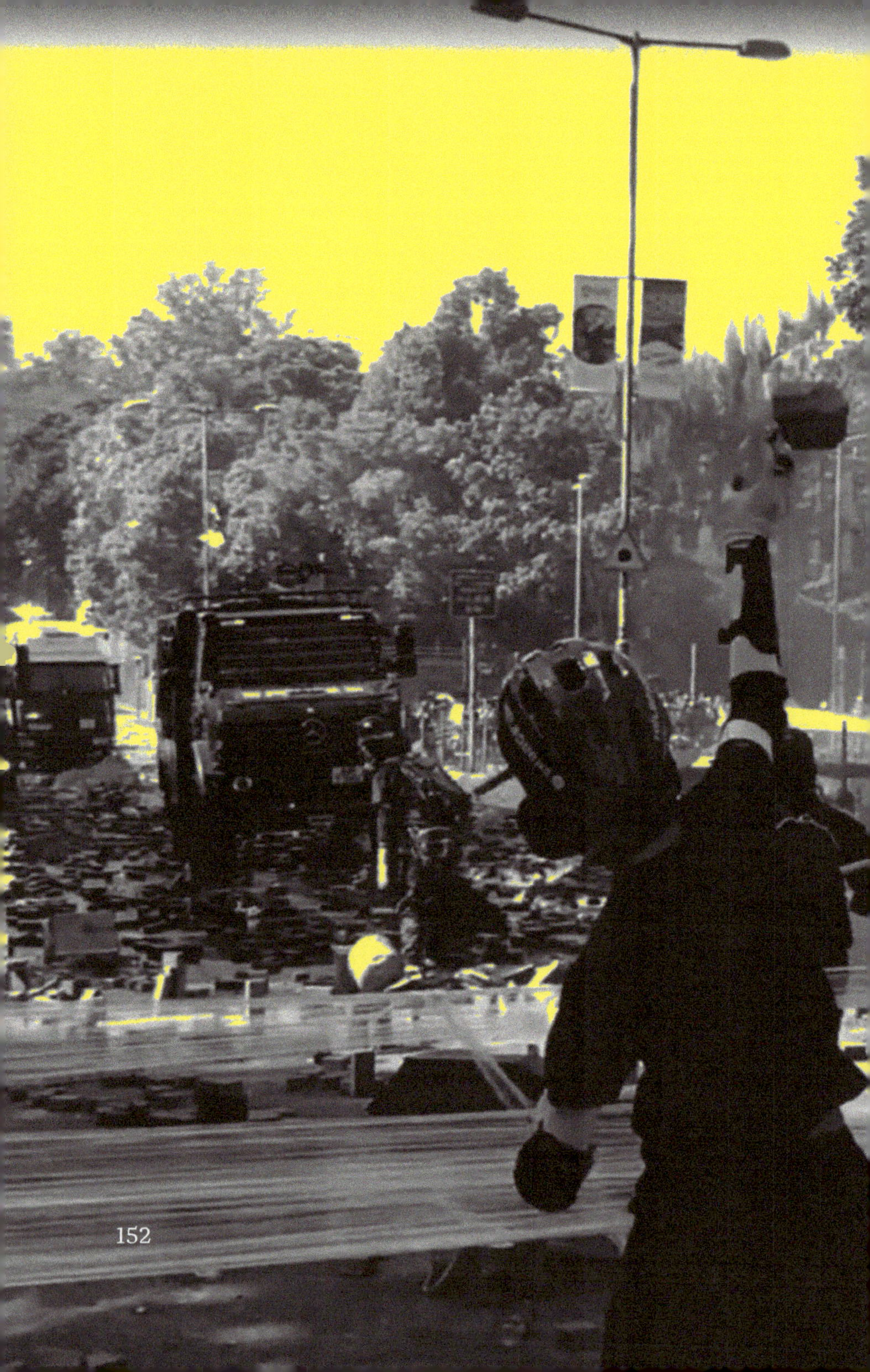

intense street fighting, disruption and direct actions of the radicalising students and youth, far from scaring the horses as some observers believed, galvanised a huge section of the population. A week ago, the city was engulfed by protests and huge confrontations between masked demonstrators and riot police. In recent days, however, calm descended. Frontline activists stopped lobbing Molotovs and went to ground as the population prepared to cast their ballots. The electoral mobilisation was unprecedented: the turnout was a record seventy-one percent—twenty points higher than in 2015. District council elections are the only properly democratic polls in the city and were widely viewed as a referendum on the pro-democracy movement, which could not have hoped for a more decisive vindication. No-one now can credibly question the democratic legitimacy of the rebellion.

It is significant that the DAB, which has had a majority lock on the district councils for twenty years and is known for its financing and mobilising operations—and for its bribery—was overwhelmed by the surge in young voters. However, despite the drubbing, there is scant evidence that the DAB machine faltered or that its support fractured. While losing one hundred seats, the Alliance increased its vote from just over three hundred thousand in the last council elections to almost five hundred thousand this year, indicating that far from all momentum being with the pro-democracy movement, there is

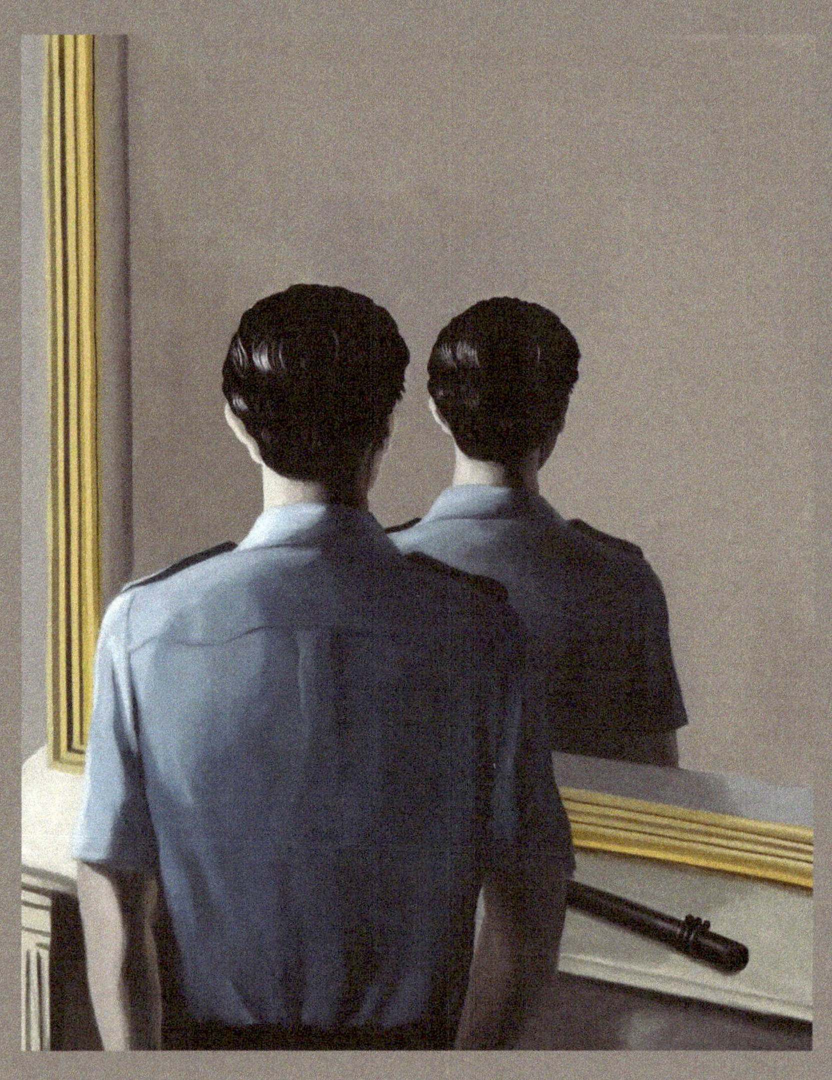

INSPIRED BY RENE MAGRITTE'S 'NOT TO BE REPRODUCED'
JUSTIN WONG

a polarisation. And DAB received the single largest share of the votes of any party or alliance—seventeen percent. In total, the pro-Beijing camp received forty-one percent of the vote, which is pretty much in line with the 2016 Legislative Council election. (In the LegCo, as it's called, only half of the seats are allocated by popular vote, which has allowed the pro-Beijing bloc to maintain a majority.)

Nevertheless, this is a symbolic and moral victory for the democratic forces. Chief Executive Carrie Lam, to wide public ridicule, today said that the outcome was a vote to 'restore order'. But the DAB has announced an internal review. With a dozen of its heavyweights having lost their seats, it will have to regroup and restructure. And the mainland press reportedly has been muted in its response, with the Communist Party hoping for the situation now to settle after weeks of major disruptions and confrontations.

With the pro-Beijing camp in disarray, it seems a perfect time for the opposition to go on the offensive and call mass mobilisations in support of the five demands, one of which is universal suffrage for all government positions. Despite widespread euphoria, among some there is a sense of foreboding. 'Still we feel not safe,' a local trade unionist said on Monday. 'I'm not sure what the government response will be to the election. This is a little victory. But people have made so many sacrifices. People have been killed. So many arrested. We have paid a lot for this. We have to push the government. That's why we want a strike. We need to show the government we are not backing down. And we need to shut down the city so that the students don't have to fight like this and risk their lives.'

In August, airline workers, transport workers, engineers, construction workers and more joined what has been described as Hong Kong's biggest strike in fifty years. But since then, workers have joined demonstrations only as individuals, rather than an organised bloc; there is little yet to indicate that labour unions will mobilise for strike action. And the main union federation, the Federation of Trade Unions, is pro-Beijing. It holds mobilisations in support of the government, although they reportedly are small, attracting a couple of thousand at most, with union officials overrepresented.

The desultory situation in the labour movement has not been lost on some of the radicals in the student movement. The day before the poll, outside the mammoth Tin Yiu estate in Tin Shui Wai near the Chinese border, 'John'—an activist from the Education University—related some of the current debates. 'We still believe that we must shut the city down. People are talking about the labour unions. Frontline protesters are upset. [They are saying about the last two weeks of intense clashes:] "We all took a risk, why didn't you support us by going on strike."' John refused to vote, although he

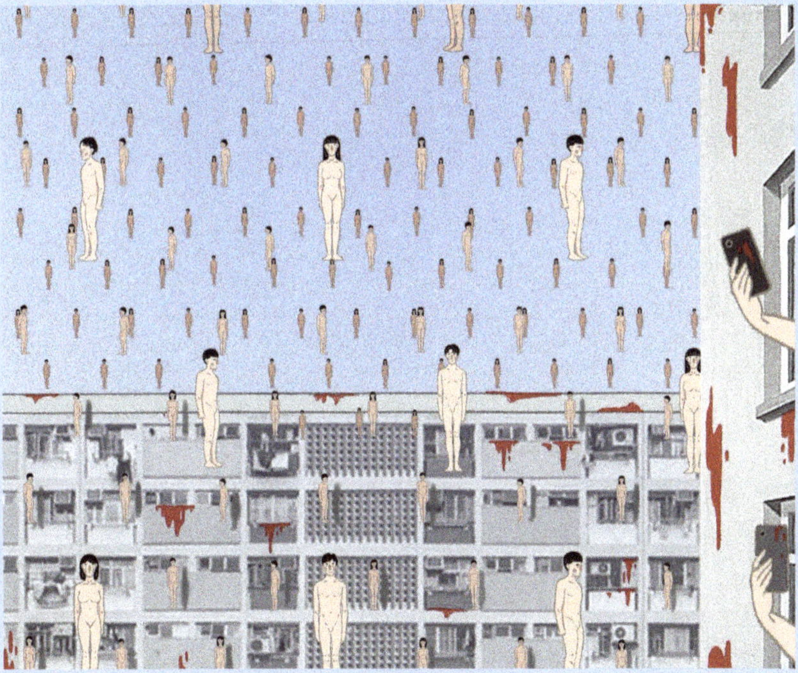

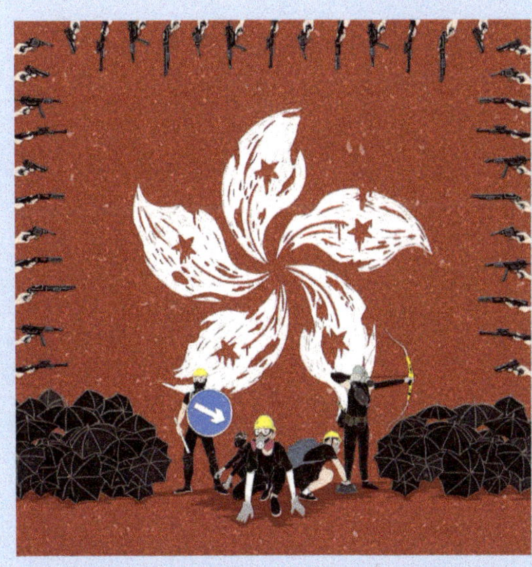

PON'SEED

ARTWORK ABOVE
INSPIRED BY
RENE MAGRITTE'S
'GOLCONDA'

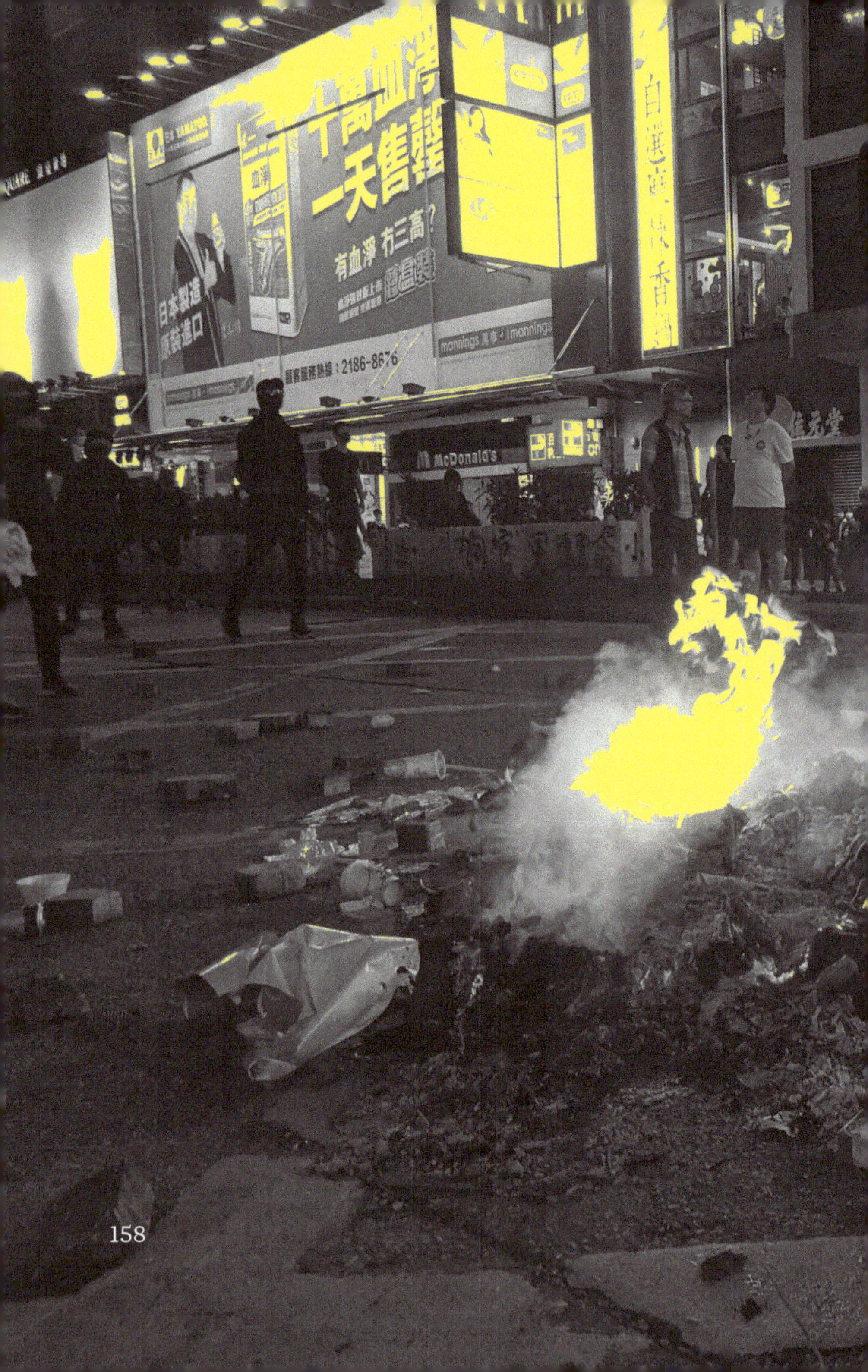
十萬血淨
一天售罄
有血淨 冇三高?
日本製造
原裝進口
2186-8676
mannings
McDonald's

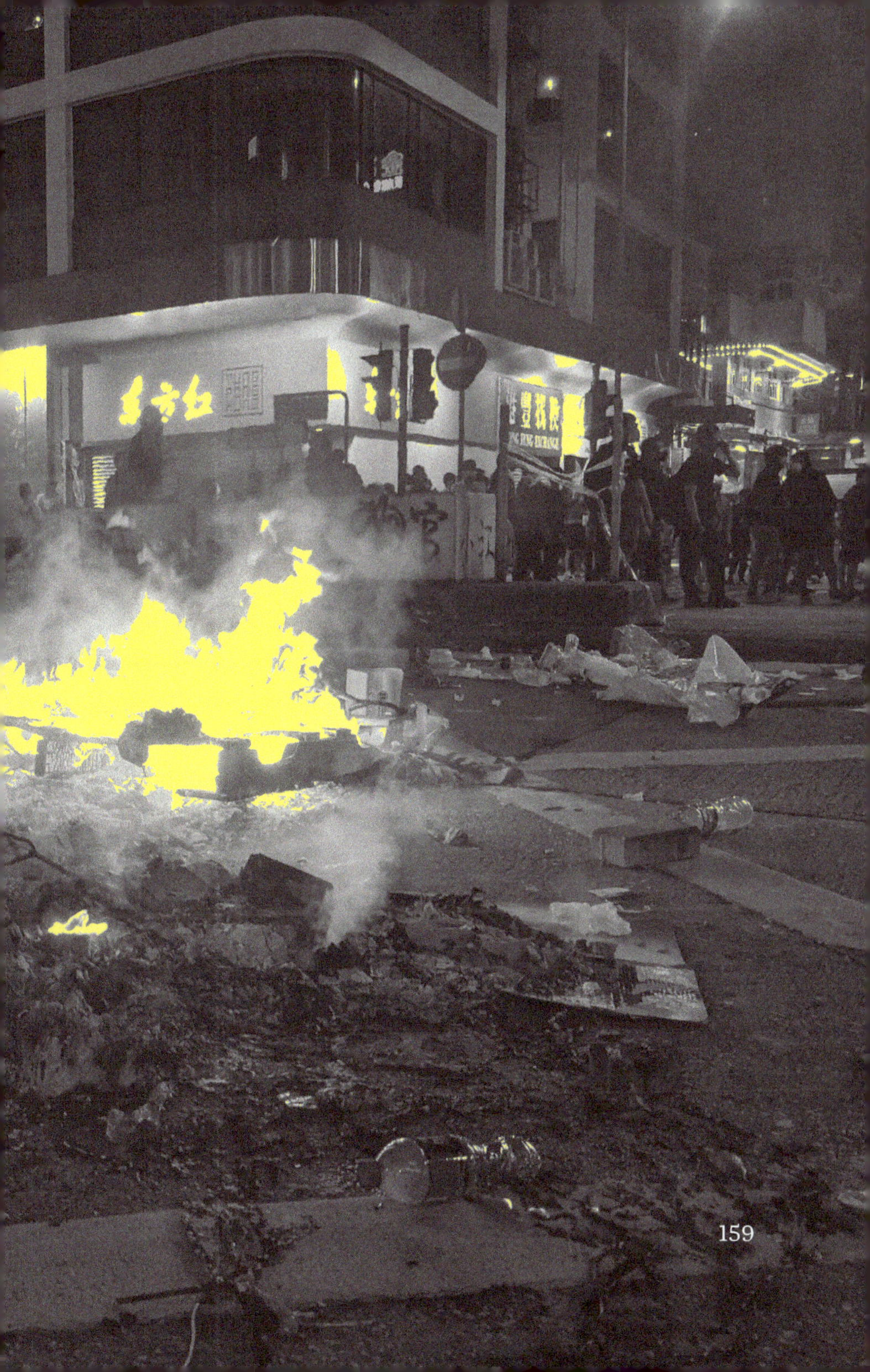

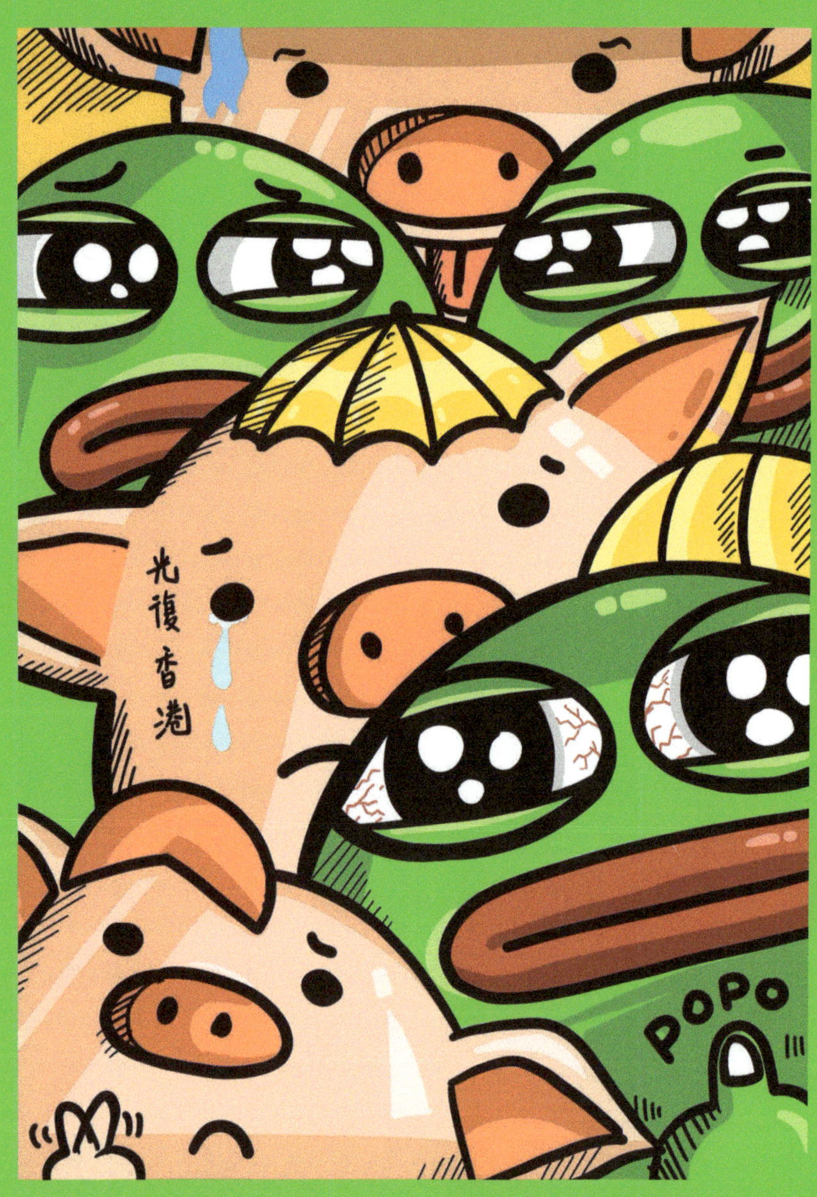

CHILD LI
@CHILDDDDLI

acknowledged that his is a minority position. 'I don't believe in these elections,' he said. 'First reason is I don't trust the government. Second reason is the problem is coming from the system—the whole political system is not fair. If we vote, we endorse this system.'

There will be some constitutional ramifications from the democrats sweeping the districts—they will slightly shift the balance in the electoral college and nominations committees for the LegCo and the chief executive, for example. But despite the moral victory for the movement and the egg on the face of Carrie Lam, the results are not a blow to the real structures of power in Hong Kong, which increasingly are rooted in Beijing.

While there is unity around the five demands, how exactly to win them, and whether they are even winnable, is a source of great confusion. The radicals are aware that they cannot sustain the massive confrontations with the police without enduring significant casualties and mass arrests for little gain. If they were joined in their militant actions by tens of thousands of other citizens, they would provoke a crisis of immense proportions, dramatically shifting the political terrain in the city. Yet while they have generated much sympathy, there have been few signs of their direct actions drawing in significant layers of others except as supporters. Many were waiting for the election results before deciding on a new course of action, but there is no consensus on what to do in

EVEN THE DARKEST NIGHT WILL END

TOGETHER WE FIGHT

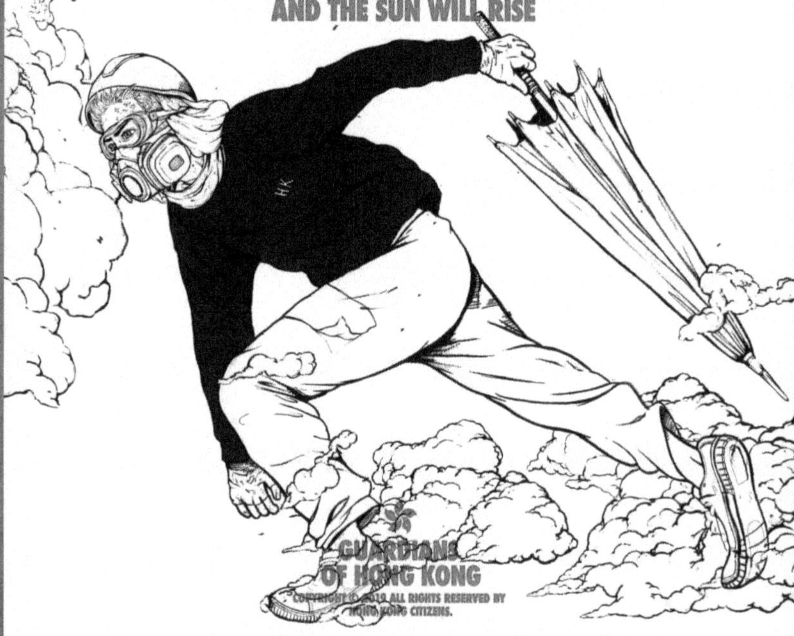

the face of the increasingly violent police force.

One suggestion is for a united opposition political bloc, based on the five demands of the movement, with the same discipline as the pro-Beijing forces. But a united opposition focused on the elections doesn't seem realistic. While the district elections were a success, district councillors wield no budgetary or legislative power. The LegCo and the chief executive are the key institutions, but not only are they not elected by universal suffrage, when oppositionists do make it in, they can be disqualified, as half a dozen legislative councillors were in recent years for allegedly being at odds with the 'one country, two systems' doctrine enshrined in the Basic Law. Nowhere does the phrase 'you can't change the system from within the system' seem truer than with the governing structures of Hong Kong.

Furthermore, the pro-democracy forces sit on two axes ranging from naïve constitutionalists to militant direct actionists and from far-right xenophobic 'localists' to the small far left. Given the balance of forces and the apolitical nature of the student rebellion, it is not at all clear that a cohesive opposition—if it were even possible—would be anything other than a vehicle for bourgeois liberals or nationalists to hegemonise the movement while using a few activists as their radical face.

Time will tell how the situation develops. Some things at

least are certain. The electoral victory has highlighted the depth and breadth of the pro-democracy movement and has underlined its moral authority in the city. The pro-Beijing camp has been rocked and the government thoroughly embarrassed. But the fundamental contradiction remains between the people's desperation for democracy and the Chinese Communist Party's will to incorporate the city into its totalitarian regime. This is the heart of every serious political dispute in Hong Kong. If the resolve of the movement has been tested and found unwavering, so too has the attitude of Beijing. This is not going to be settled any time soon.

EVEN THE DARKEST NIGHT WILL END

TOGETHER WE FIGHT

AND THE SUN WILL RISE

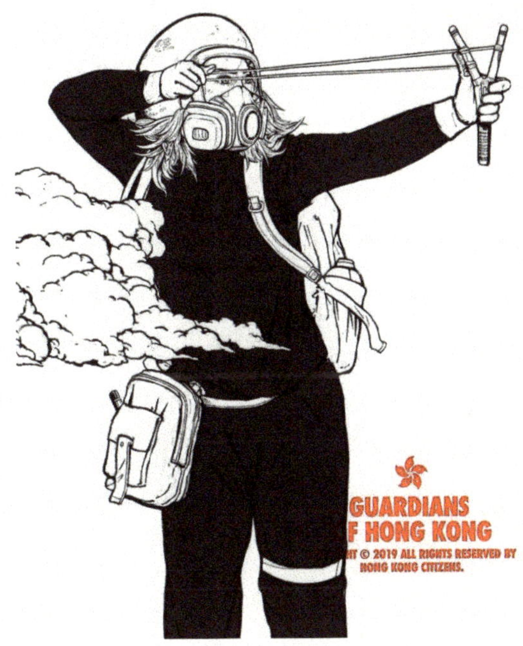

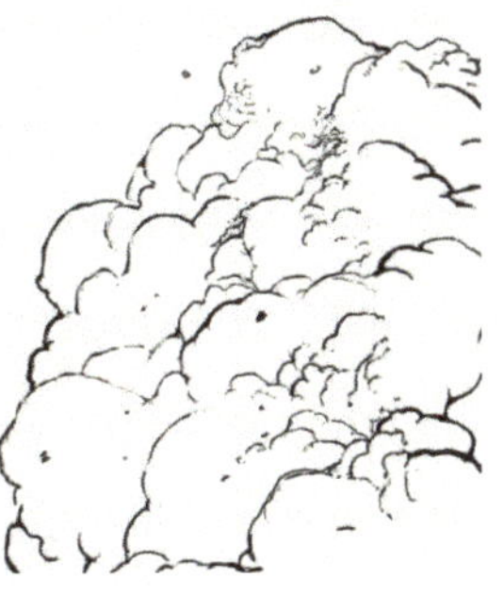

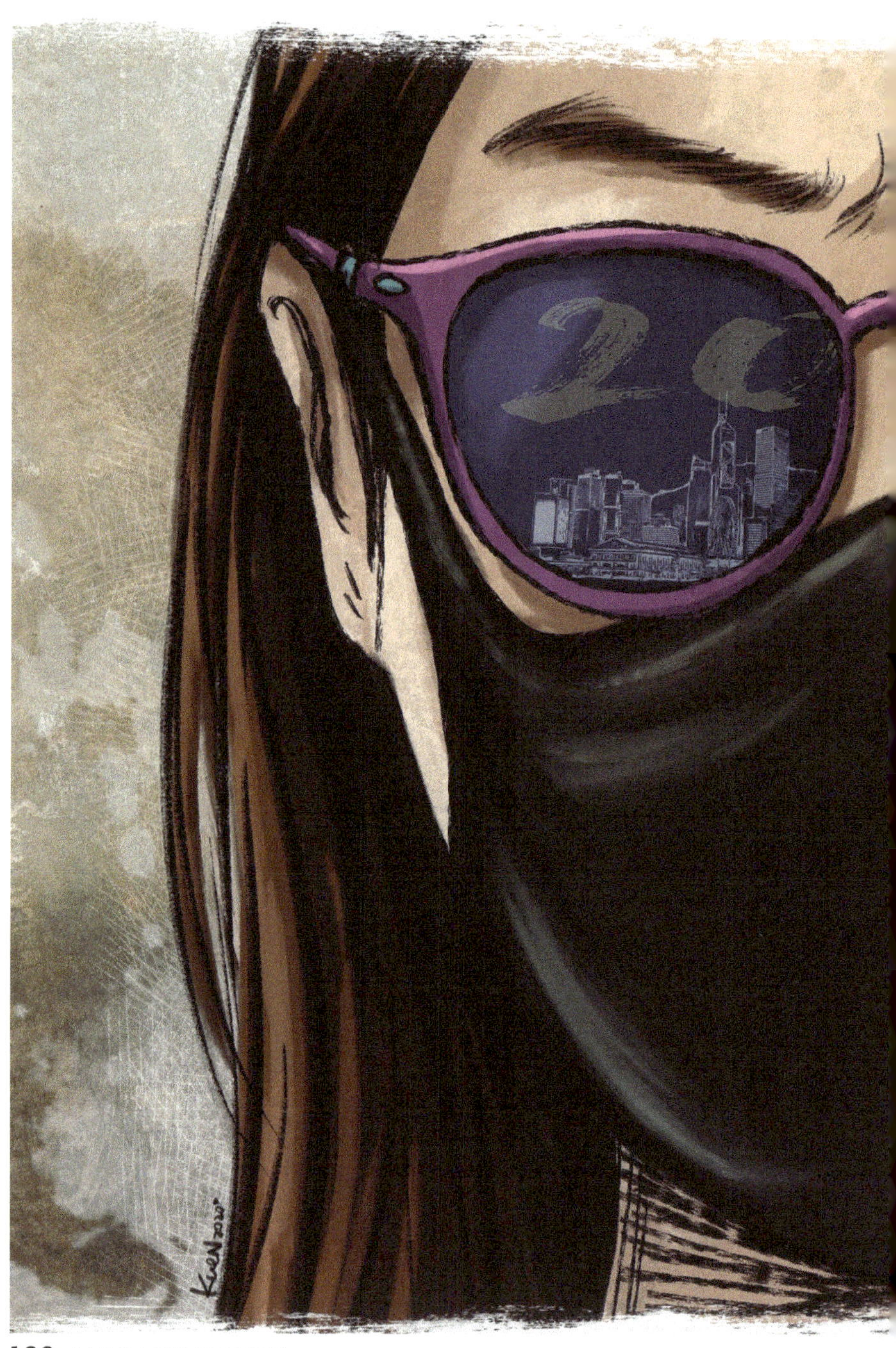

 LAU KA-KUEN (2020)

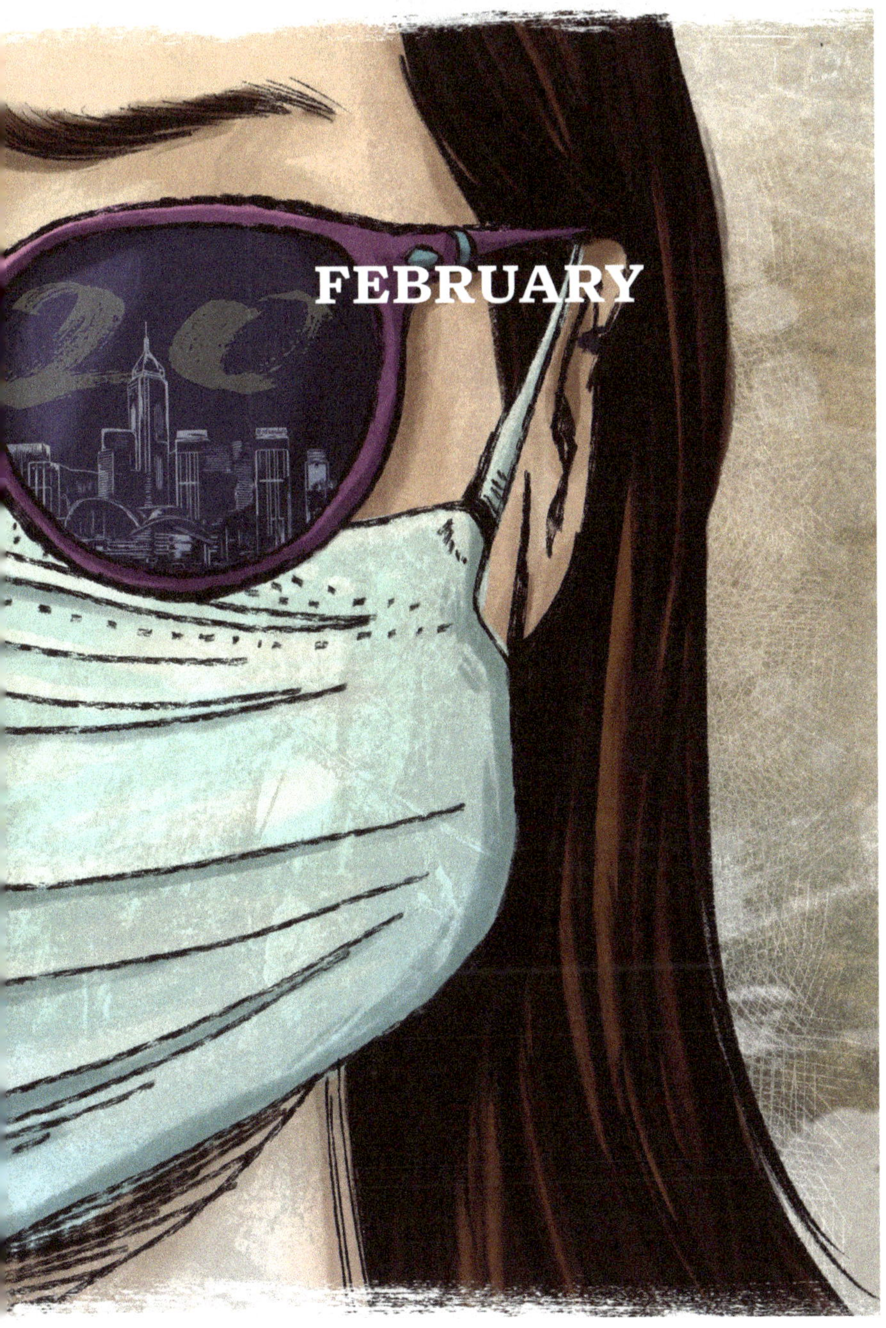

FEBRUARY

FEBRUARY

DREAD

THURSDAY 13 FEBRUARY | Viewed from the shore at Lau Fau Shan village fish market in the New Territories, Shenzhen is an imposing behemoth of high rises and skyscrapers. Guangdong's second largest metropolis was China's first global city, designated a special economic zone and opened to foreign capital in 1980. From a semi-rural county, it grew to be the Silicon Valley of the People's Republic in just a few decades. More than eight million of its estimated thirteen million population are migrant labourers. This week, they are returning to work after the extended Lunar new year holiday, but the city remains in a partial lockdown due to the coronavirus outbreak, after Guangdong became the second most infected province in China.

One thousand kilometres north, the largest quarantine in

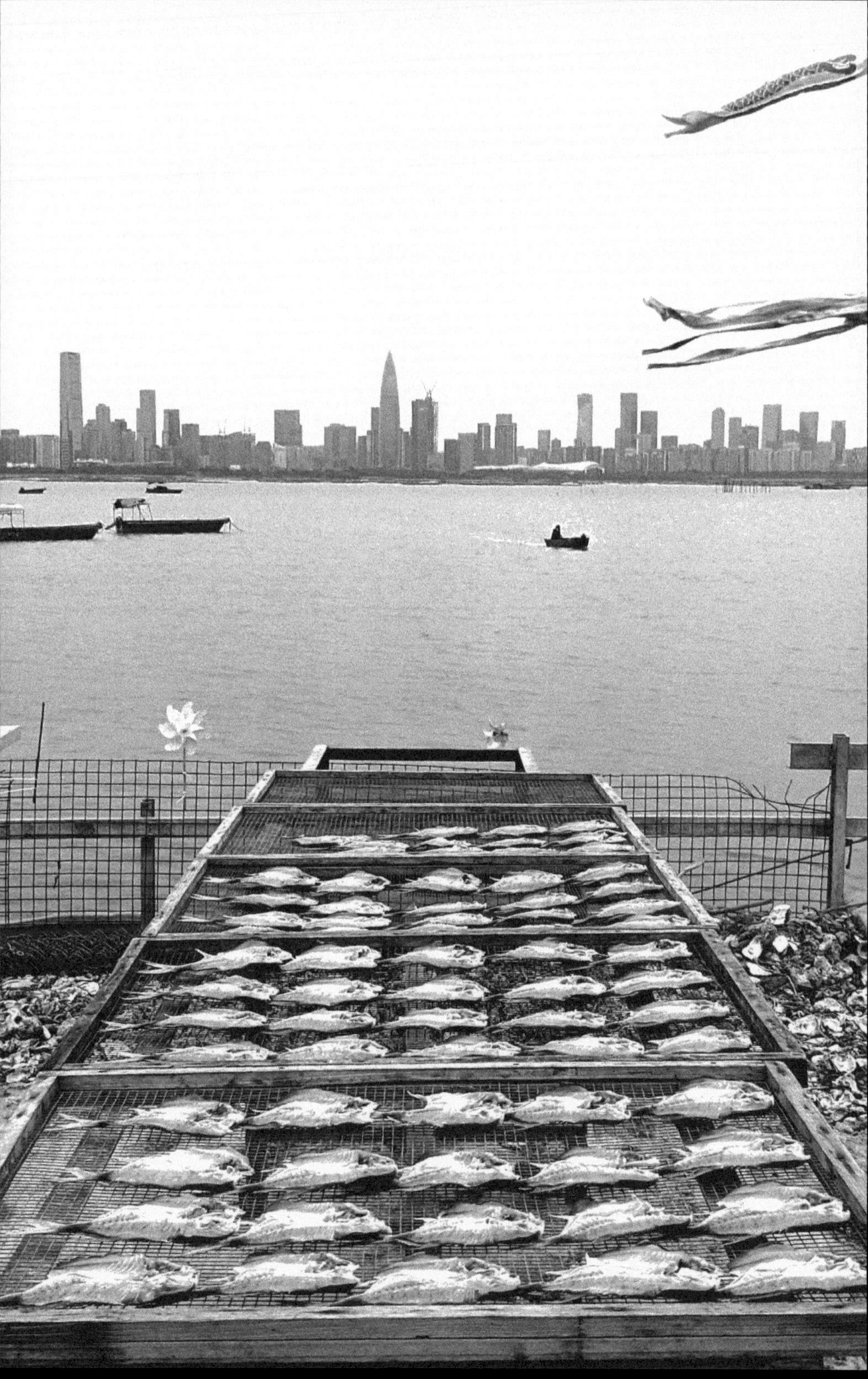

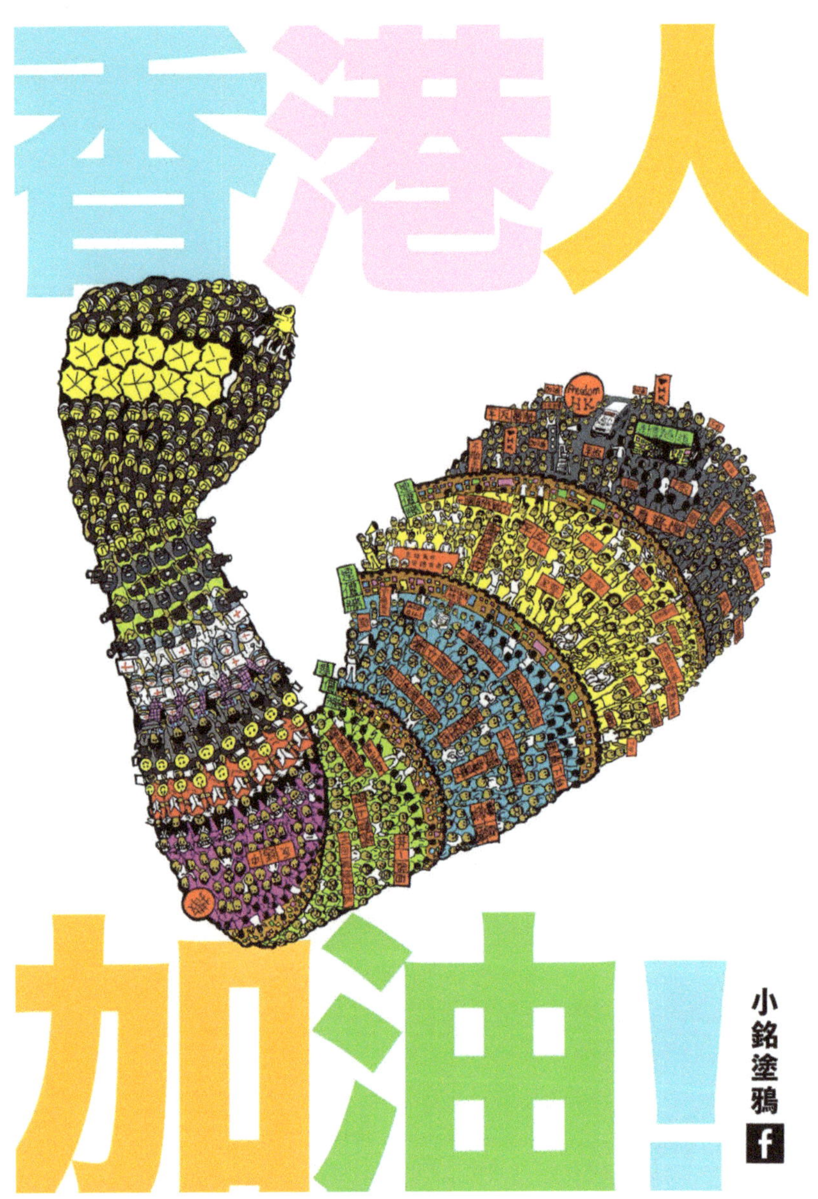
香港人
Freedom HK
加油！
小銘塗鴉

human history is ongoing: a total lockdown of maybe sixty million people in Hubei province and its capital, Wuhan, the centre of the epidemic. Partial lockdowns continue in Guangzhou and China's key industrial zone, the Pearl River Delta (which includes Shenzhen), and the four big coastal cities of Zhejiang province in the Yangtze Delta, another important industrial zone exploiting millions of migrant workers. So too Beijing and Shanghai. At least two cities, Tianjin and Xian, have imposed entry restrictions for people from affected areas. In all, more than eighty cities in twenty provinces are reported to be affected.

'It's every province. Every province has shutdowns,' Lu (not his real name) says over the phone from Handan, a city of about ten million in Hebei province (not to be confused with Hubei). 'Here all buses have been stopped. The schools are shut until March. All businesses are shut except supermarkets and the vegetable markets—although I haven't been outside for five days so maybe it is changing with people going back to work. Everyone is upset about the cover-up. Even pro-government people. But mainly the anger is with the local government [in Wuhan], not Beijing.'

More than one thousand people are dead in Hubei. The Communist Party initially failed to respond to warnings from medics in Wuhan. City officials are accused of orchestrating a cover-up, ignoring or suppressing information about the outbreak and harassing and detaining doctors who sounded the alarm. Before the shutdown in late January, several million people potentially exposed to the coronavirus had already left (Lunar new year celebrations are a time of great human movement in China). The pathogen hitched a ride with some of them. When the authorities flipped from censors to crowd controllers, the quarantine declaration came eight hours before its enforcement, prompting an estimated one million people to flee to other parts of China. Again, the virus travelled with some of them. The lockdowns soon proliferated.

'The situation is very tense. There have been no notifications when it is going to reopen again,' a resident says via email from a quarantined Hubei city. 'The closures came very suddenly, and there are no exceptions at all. But the problem is that the logistics support to go hand in hand with this closure has not been ready at all. There are now lots of SOS requests in Wuhan city coming from individual citizens. Here, all necessities are in short supply. Masks and hygienic wipes cannot be bought. People feel that the lockdown is necessary ... But we are all very angry at the government for lying about the virus ... They shouldn't just do propaganda in this type of situation. We want open information, transparency ... And we need professionals, mutual aid groups within the community so that individual citizens can have their needs met.'

The lockdown of Wuhan, Hubei and then other areas may

FREE
HONG
KONG

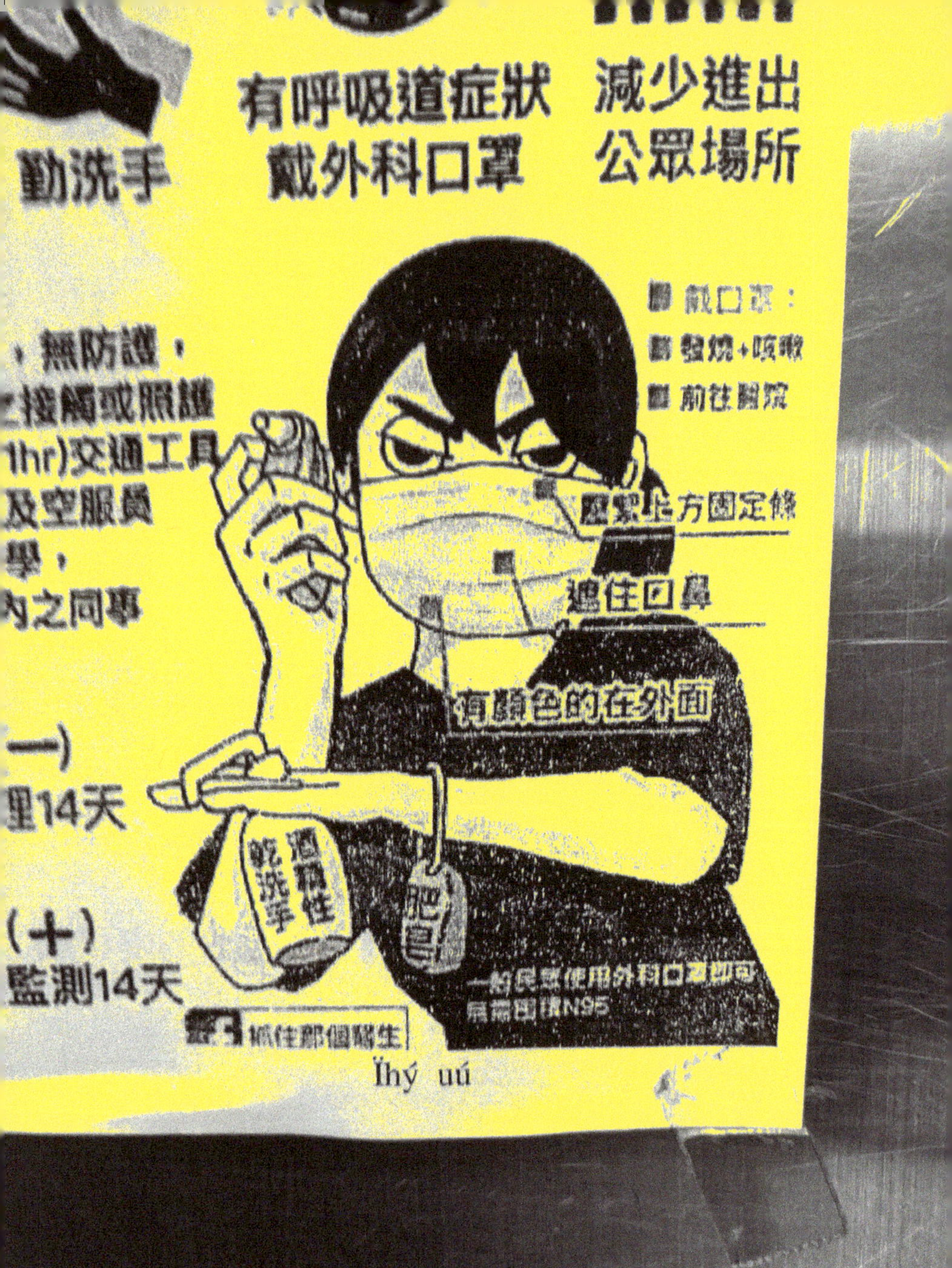

勤洗手
有呼吸道症狀
戴外科口罩
減少進出
公眾場所
發燒+咳嗽
前往醫院
壓緊上方固定條
遮住口鼻
有顏色的在外面
酒精性
乾洗手
肥皂
一般民眾使用外科口罩即可
監測14天

have been a panic or a belated display of decisive action from the Communist Party. Putting aside that it was botched from the start, and that greater death and suffering in Wuhan may well have been the result, it is not clear whether it has been effective in slowing the spread of the virus. But it unquestionably contributed to broader anxieties as the focus shifted to a perceived collective carrier: people from within the quarantine zones as agents of or proxies for the plague. As the death toll and the number of infections rose, the fear arrived.

'As the epidemic radiated out from Hubei's capital, Wuhan, in recent weeks, Chinese have turned against those who hail from the province,' *Washington Post* China correspondent Gerry Shih noted. 'Those from Hubei found in other parts of China are tracked down, accosted and locked at home by neighbors ... On social media, Chinese have condemned the five million so-called public enemies—Wuhan residents who fled the city in the days before and immediately after the government's lockdown order ... In the northern city of Shijiazhuang, neighborhood committees offered bounties of $280 to anyone who reported someone who had visited Wuhan ... In Jiangxi's provincial capital, Nanchang, hotels asked guests to answer surveys asking if they had travelled to Hubei. A receptionist at a major international chain assured a visitor that there were no guests from Hubei in the building. "We've rejected them all," he said.'

Panic is contagious. Travel bans and restrictions, and partial suspensions or full closures of borders were implemented by almost all of China's neighbouring states as it became clear that Beijing had lost control and that official information was unreliable: Afghanistan, Bhutan, Kazakhstan, Kyrgyzstan, Laos, Mongolia, Nepal, Pakistan, Russia, Tajikistan, Taiwan and Vietnam. Significantly, North Korea closed its borders the day Wuhan was locked down; Pyongyang shutting the gates on the country that guarantees its survival was an early indication of the potential seriousness of the outbreak. So too with Macau. The semi-autonomous territory shut its casinos for two weeks, a de facto border closure, while panicked authorities deported people from Hubei back to the mainland.

Dread is spreading through Hong Kong. The virus is here. Public congregations and family gatherings are discouraged. The libraries are closed. The schools are closed. The museums are closed. The universities are closed. Water is not flowing from public drinking fountains. Even the morning bird watching in Hong Kong Park has been cancelled. Public announcements at metro stations implore people to wear a mask, to wash their hands, not to touch their mouth or nose,

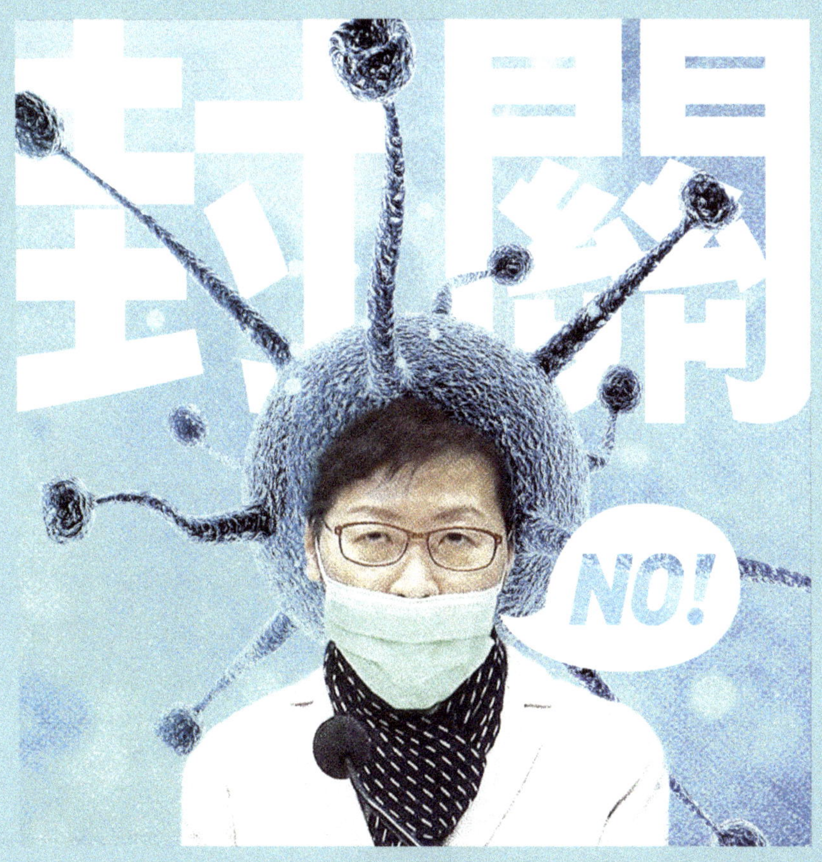

DEPICTION OF CHIEF EXECUTIVE
CARRIE LAM AS A VIRUS AND
CALLING FOR BORDER CLOSURES

HONG KONG DESIGN INDUSTRY
UNION (2020)

nor rub their eyes. Don't spit. Sneeze only into a tissue. Carry and use sanitiser regularly.

On the second floor of the Tang Lung Chau wet market in Causeway Bay, cleaners are nervous. Doctors without Borders is briefing about basic hygiene and how to stay safe. 'There's no-one here to help us—we have to help ourselves,' an elderly woman says once the presentation is finished. 'Be careful when working. Stay hygienic. We must stay optimistic.' When the NGO leaves, a volunteer with the cleaners' union makes a speech decrying government inaction. Another cleaner agrees. 'The government has not provided enough equipment,' he says through a translator. 'There may not be enough [masks and gloves] to get through next month.' When I pull out a stash of masks, hand sanitiser and alcohol wipes picked up in Australia, there are audible gasps. 'This is like gold here!' the union volunteer says.

Asia's world city, as Hong Kong likes to call itself, is in chaos. On Nathan Road in Tsim Sha Tsui, a queue outside a cosmetics shop stretches thirty metres. The woman at the front says she's been here for three hours, waiting to get medical masks. Two weeks ago, when a trading company announced it had eleven thousand boxes of them, more than ten thousand people queued overnight. On Sunday morning in Causeway Bay, hundreds are waiting in line. Is this for masks? 'Only for Indonesians,' a woman says. They are domestic workers.

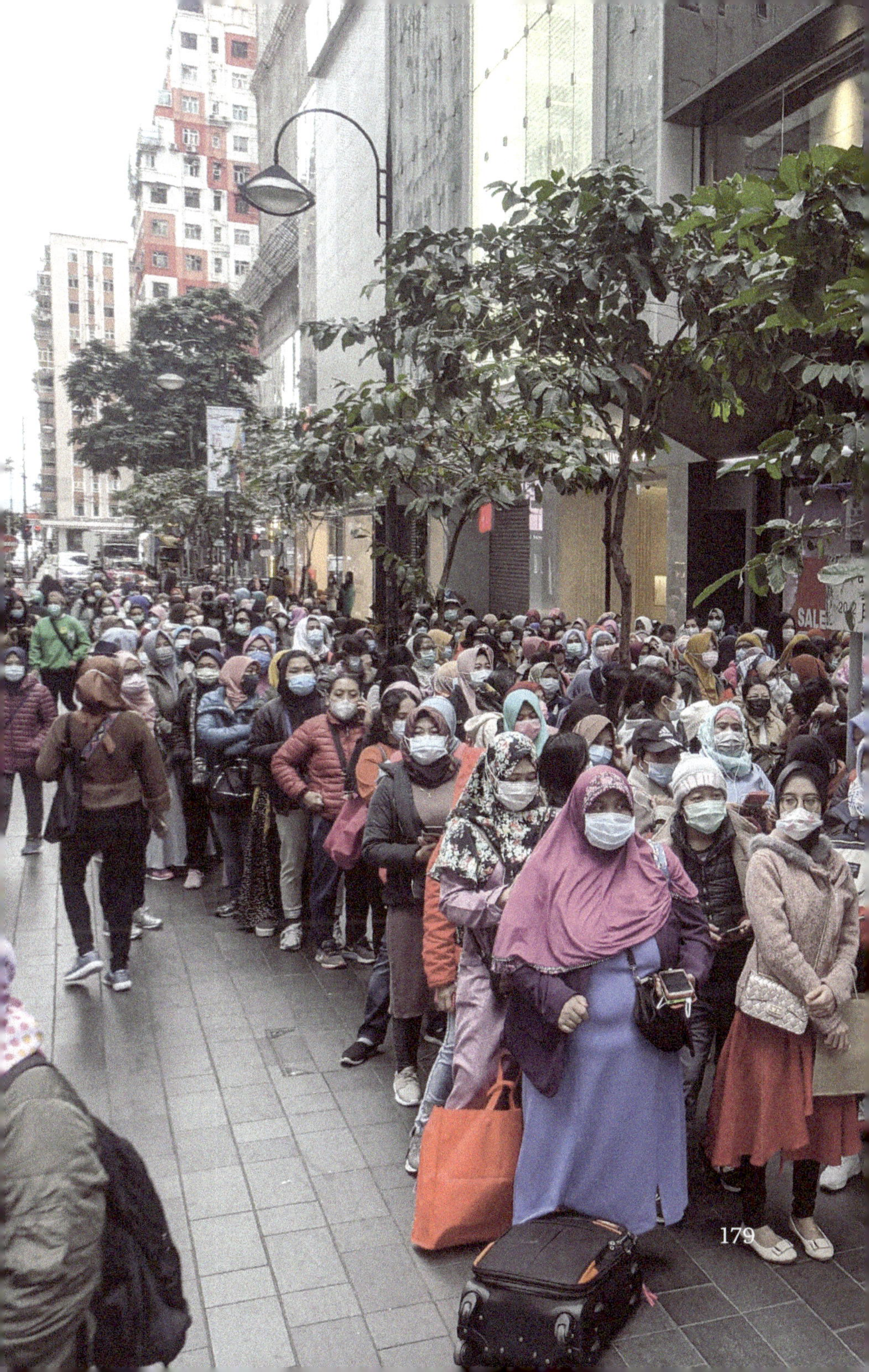
SALE

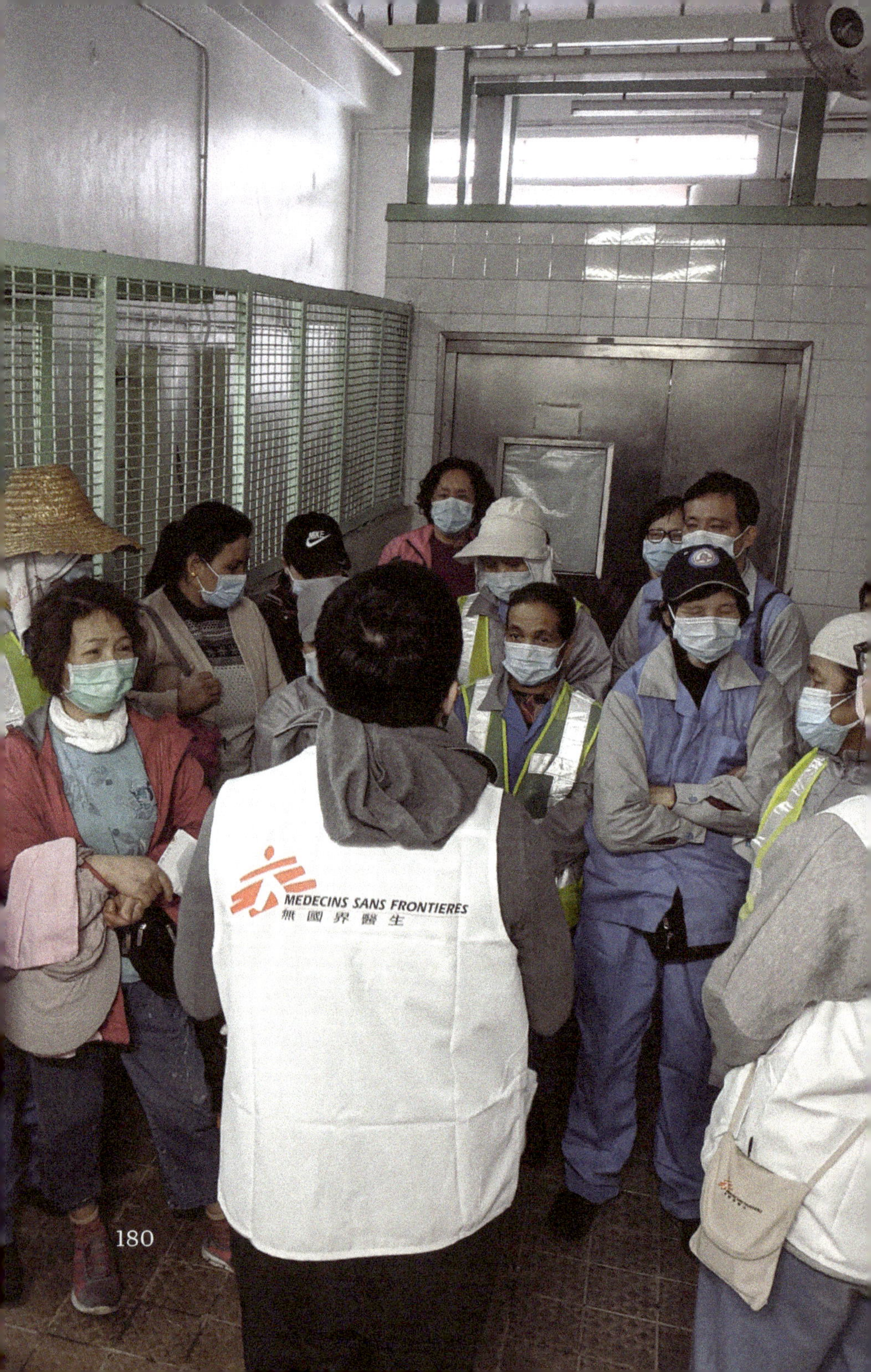
NIKE
MEDECINS SANS FRONTIERES
無國界醫生

Presumably their employers want them fit for duties. A young woman walks by with two bags full of boxes of tissues—panic buying. Many supermarkets have been cleared of rice and toilet paper after rumours of impending shortages spread much faster than the virus has thus far.

The government has fucked up big time. There's no other way of putting it. Almost two decades after severe acute respiratory syndrome (SARS, another coronavirus) killed almost three hundred people in the territory amid claims of cover-ups and inaction, Hong Kong appears thoroughly unprepared. The city's vaunted free market capitalism has failed. There aren't enough masks. There's no sanitiser. Four quarantine zones have hastily been declared, but they are either in or close to residential areas, and some of the locals are apoplectic. Why hadn't proper sites on government land been prepared earlier?

Last week, seven thousand medical workers from the newly formed Hospital Authority Employees Alliance went on strike to protest the government's response. They raised five demands: forbid all travellers from entering Hong Kong via China, ensure a sufficient supply of masks, provide isolation wards and stop all non-emergency services, provide support and facilitation for health care staff caring for patients under isolation, and publicly commit not to take disciplinary action against striking workers.

**Until the truth is revealed,
Hongkongers will never give up.**

Much has been made about the so-called xenophobia at the heart of the demand to close the border. But that is a misreading of the situation. Anti-mainlander sentiment certainly exists here—how could it not when the Communist Party is infiltrating every political and civil society institution in Hong Kong and the territory is being forcibly integrated into China? Yet while some groups are trying to use the panic to push an anti-mainlander agenda, the border demand is animated by panic—and a recognition that the already strained health system will collapse under the weight of a pandemic.

'The border closure has to be looked at in the context of SARS. 2003 is very close in people's memories,' a local activist says. 'China hid the outbreak until too late, and a lot of Hong Kongers died because of it. Closing the border is looked at from almost exclusively a public health perspective.' But what about the right wing of the movement for Hong Kong's self-determination: is it gaining support in such a reactive situation? 'The right wing of the movement is incredibly small, as most of the right wing in Hong Kong is the pro-government, pro-Beijing parties. That's where you find the anti-LGBT, anti-immigrant, anti-refugee candidates,' he says. 'That's not to say we don't have some nativists on our side, but they are a minority with not that much pull. They only look bigger than they are because both tankies [supporters of the Chinese Communist Party] and US far-right media latched onto them as something they could use for their political agendas and spread that imagery around constantly when it is totally non-representative of the movement here. The strike was supported, and unionising has been a huge part of the build towards finding more ways to put pressure on this government.'

A volunteer with the cleaners' union echoes this. 'Macau and Taiwan have done it, why not here? It's not against Chinese people—it's the virus,' she says. The issue is also intertwined with the collapse in the government's authority, which looms large. A Hong Kong Public Opinion Research Institute poll last month found that just nineteen percent of people trust the government. The territory's leader by law must be a China loyalist, and the current chief executive, Lam, is widely seen as a stooge. So when she labelled as 'discriminatory' the calls to shut the border, it riled people—Beijing's puppet telling everyone that their legitimate fears are just anti-Chinese racism.

Socialists generally, and rightly, are opposed to the national borders that divide workers from one another and create barriers to building a united movement of the oppressed against oppressors. But that arbitrary line that we despise is the only thing standing between Hong Kong and totalitarianism. Its disappearance, when it comes, will be the triumph of reaction over the already limited freedoms that

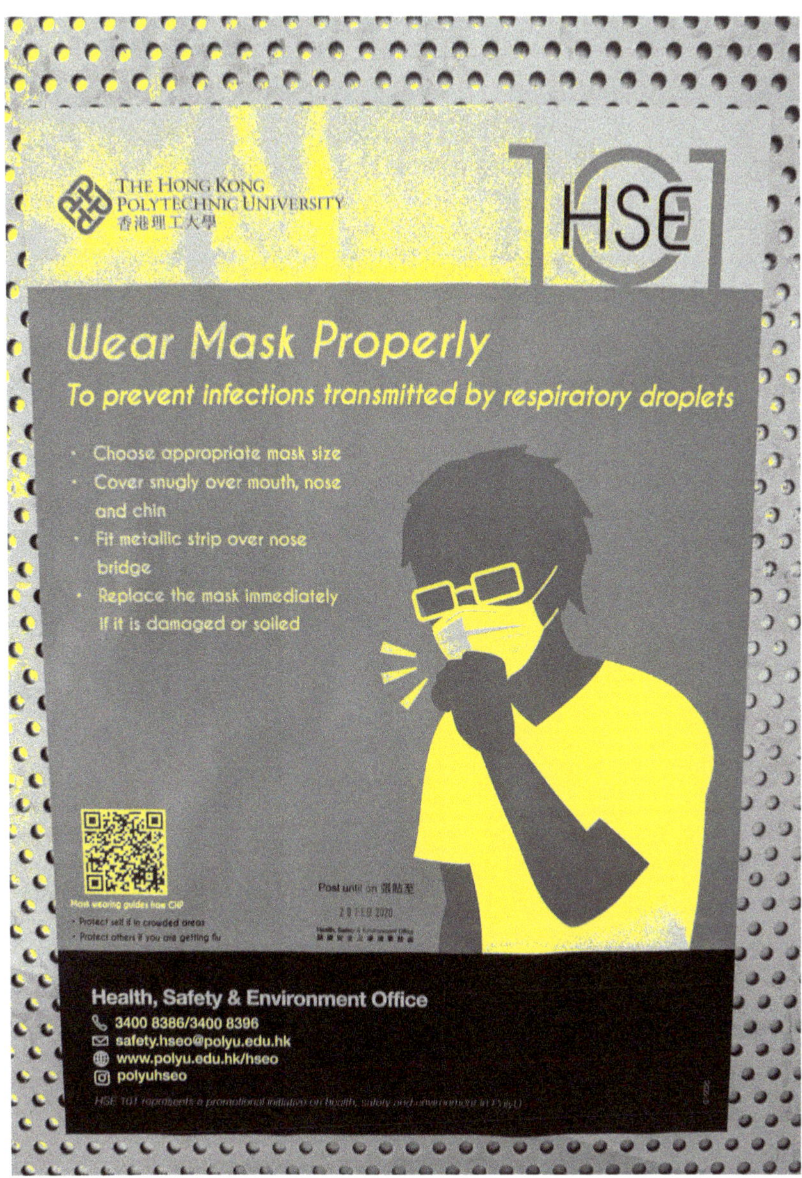
THE HONG KONG
POLYTECHNIC UNIVERSITY
香港理工大學
HSE 101
Wear Mask Properly
To prevent infections transmitted by respiratory droplets
Choose appropriate mask size
Cover snugly over mouth, nose and chin
Fit metallic strip over nose bridge
Replace the mask immediately if it is damaged or soiled
Protect self if in crowded areas
Protect others if you are getting flu
Health, Safety & Environment Office
3400 8386/3400 8396
safety.hseo@polyu.edu.hk
www.polyu.edu.hk/hseo
polyuhseo

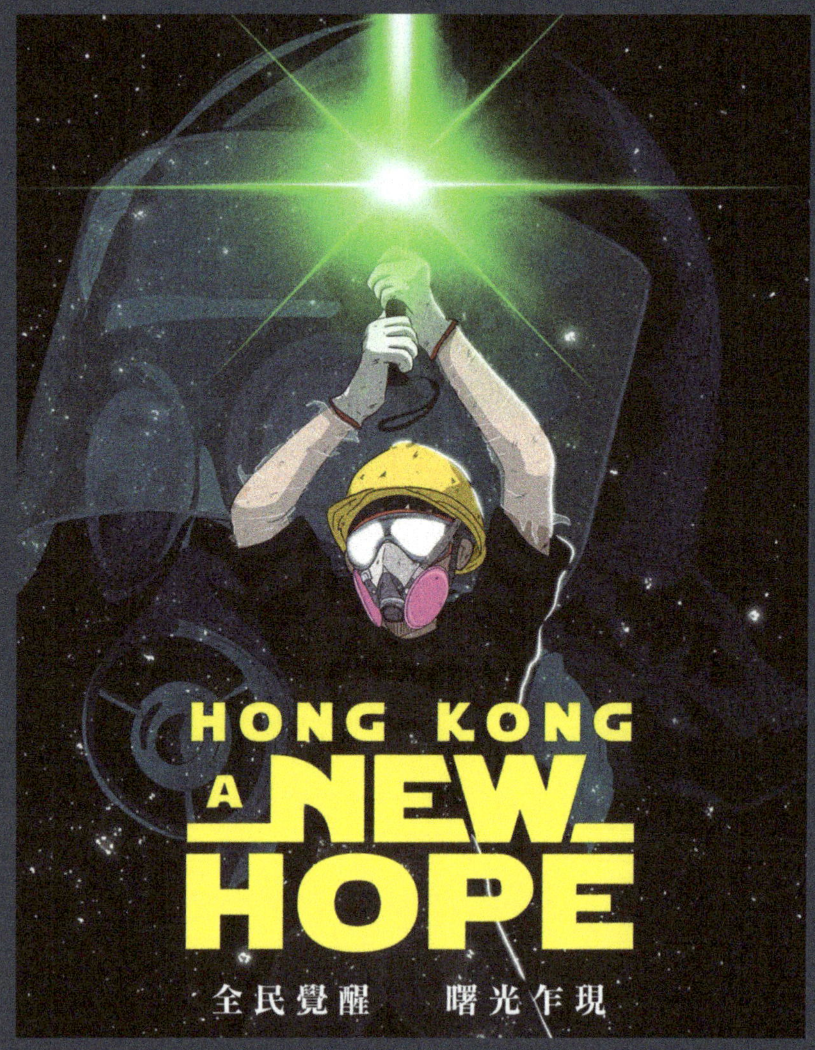
HONG KONG
A NEW HOPE
全民覺醒 曙光乍現

exist here. That fact should give people in the West pause for thought before branding all talk about border controls here inherently reactionary.

Time will tell whether these measures save lives, although there is quiet confidence on the part of Yuen that the situation is now manageable. But while Hong Kong holds its breath, across the border, the Chinese economy is stuttering and the Communist Party wants industrial production restarted. The markets demand movement—movement of goods and movement of labour. If the shutdowns were nothing but reactive, useless (or worse) political stunts, then switching to a focus on growing GDP, with all the attendant health risks that come with that enterprise in regular times, will at least be a good thing for lifting the restrictions on people's civil liberties. But what if cracking the whip on tens of millions of migrant workers in the middle of an epidemic results in a new wave of infections?

IS SPRINGTIME COMING?

THURSDAY 20 FEBRUARY | Barricades are up again at Hong Kong Polytechnic University. But unlike last November, during an intense occupation at the height of the city's extraordinary democratic rebellion, there's hardly a student in sight. The administration has taken control of PolyU, which is in an extended shutdown because of the coronavirus. At the main entrance on Cheong Wan Road, weighted one-and-a-half-metre-high yellow barriers run along the side of the building. The formerly paved footpaths, dug up by radicals for the bricks to be used as projectiles, are concreted and asphalted. Electronic gates like those at metro stations have been installed at the bottom of the stairs leading into the campus. Half a dozen security guards monitor everyone coming and going. When classes resume, anyone without a student or

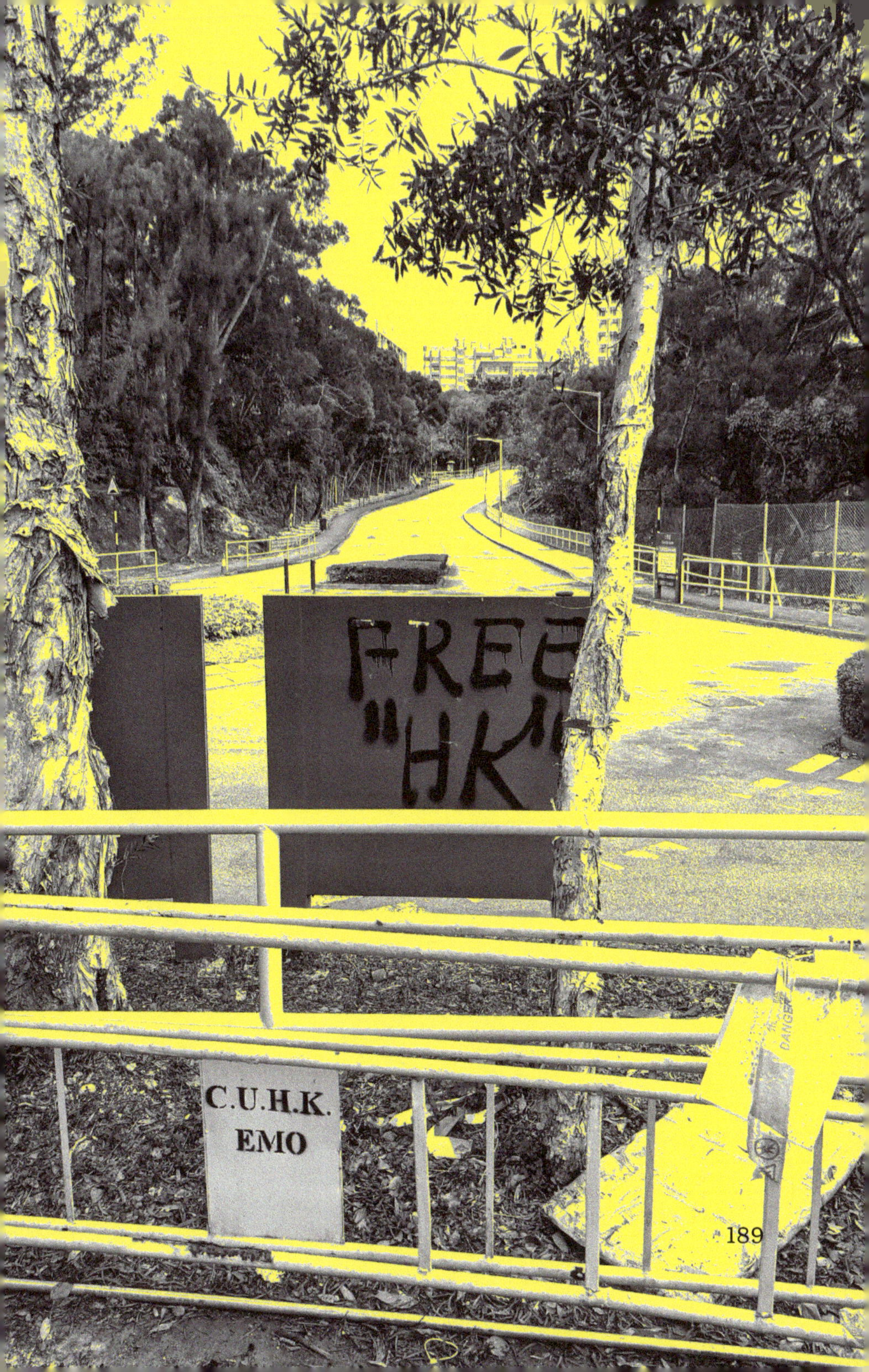
FREE
"HK"
C.U.H.K.
EMO
DANGER

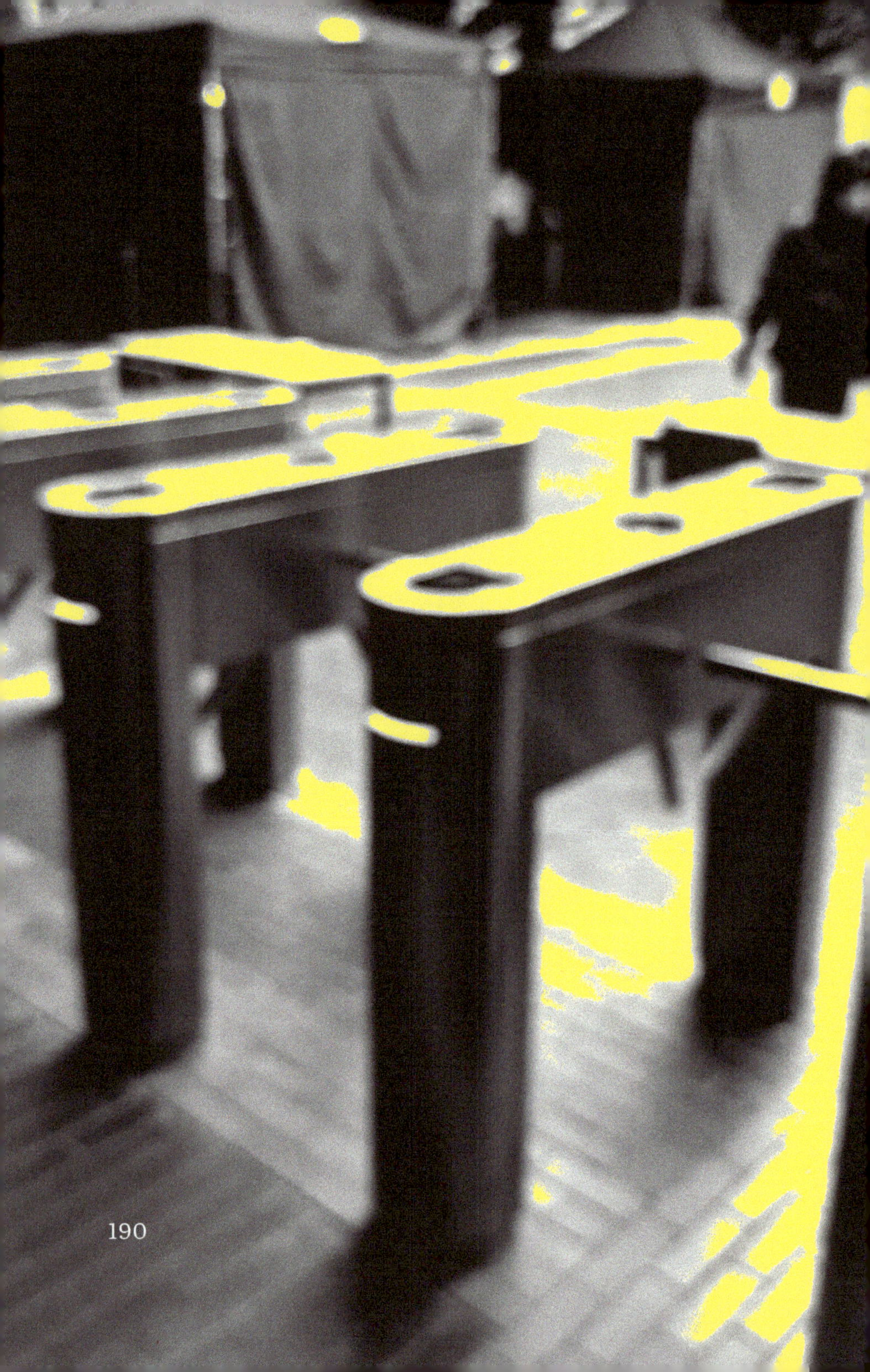

staff swipe card will have to register to gain entry.

Last year, when the police laid siege here, at the top of the entrance stairs to the left was a makeshift clinic run by students and their supporters. Medics carried in a steady stream of activists suffering from tear gas inhalation and rubber bullet wounds inflicted by the police. Today there's a new makeshift clinic, but it's set up by the administration to test temperatures and screen people for the dreaded virus. Last year, the government was attempting to ban face masks, which protesters used to protect their identities. Now, the university has posters instructing people to 'Wear Mask Properly' so no-one gets sneezed on. The cafeteria back then was a hive of communal activity. Free food, donated by supporters and cooked by volunteers, was distributed 24/7. It was a ramshackle mess of supplies, solidarity and people falling asleep on their feet. Today it's sanitised, which isn't so bad. But commerce has triumphed over the collective spirit; there is a new queue system leading to automated ordering stations for drinks—the ultimate in individualised efficiency, in which you need not interact with a soul to get what you pay for.

Graffitied bollards have been wrapped in grey canvas, the walls and ground washed of paint, and the garden beds, previously trampled and stacked with bricks and petrol bombs, hastily reconstructed. On notice boards and tied overhead between the supporting poles of a prominent walkway, bright

'Good Seed' advertisements offer several hundred thousand Hong Kong dollars to kickstart social projects. The administration initiative, backed by an array of NGOs and corporates, aims to 'INSPIRE, ENABLE and EMPOWER social innovation projects' and encourage returning students to 'Be Creative to Change the World!' It's a reminder that, while administrators and HR professionals from every continent talk a lot about diversity and cultural exchange, in the end they all speak the same language of respectable self-advancement under the guise of social responsibility. No doubt there will be the usual social climbers clambering to get some of the cash, along with a nice tick on their curriculum vitae. But thousands who participated in the street clashes and occupations last year will see through it.

There are reminders of the heroic occupation. Some campus entrances remain closed because of the damage caused when students torched barricades to hold off the cops. The student union noticeboards near the Registrar's Office are full of undisturbed agitational posters. In the meeting room on the second level of the union building, a garbage bag full of helmets sits on the table. Next to it is a bag of eye washes for flushing tear gas. A pile of banners is in the far corner near another bag, this one full of gas masks. And, of course, there's an umbrella here and there. Some of the offices are open and full of materials and supplies. Two vending machines, smashed and grabbed, have been neither refilled nor refitted. There's not a person around. It feels like a zombie apocalypse film—nothing has been touched for months, everything left as it was after a sudden catastrophe.

It's a similar story at the Chinese University of Hong Kong. Razor wire surrounds the MTR (Mass Transit Railway, Hong Kong's metro train system) station servicing the campus, which was almost completely destroyed by students in November and is now covered in tin and tarps, presumably awaiting refurbishment. A dozen security guards check the IDs of everyone arriving. Heading north toward the number two bridge, the embankment between the rail lines and Sea Side Drive is strewn with damaged umbrellas. The bridge passes over the Tolo Highway and was an important strategic site on campus when the students decided to halt the traffic underneath—their contribution to an immense effort to shut down the city to secure democratic rights. Today, there is a guard post in front, and the structure is barricaded. Only one entrance to the entire sprawling campus is open to traffic. Half a dozen buses, which had been commandeered by students during the occupation, have been fenced off and the graffiti on them sprayed over. But plenty is still visible elsewhere around the grounds. 'The history will NEVER forget', 'They give us corruption, we give them revolution', 'Live free or die trying', 'Free HK' and the *V for Vendetta* insignia.

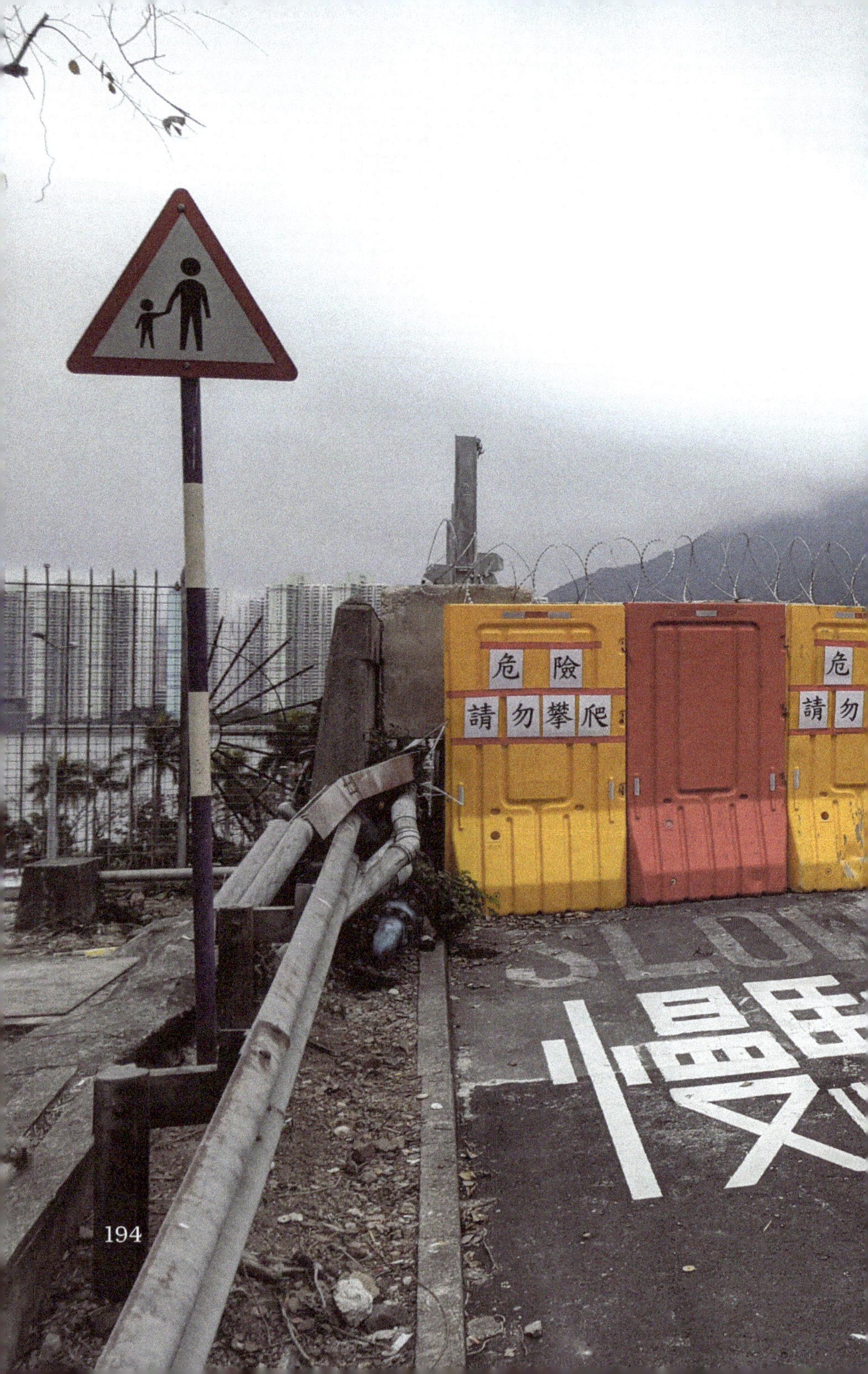
危險
請勿攀爬
危
請勿

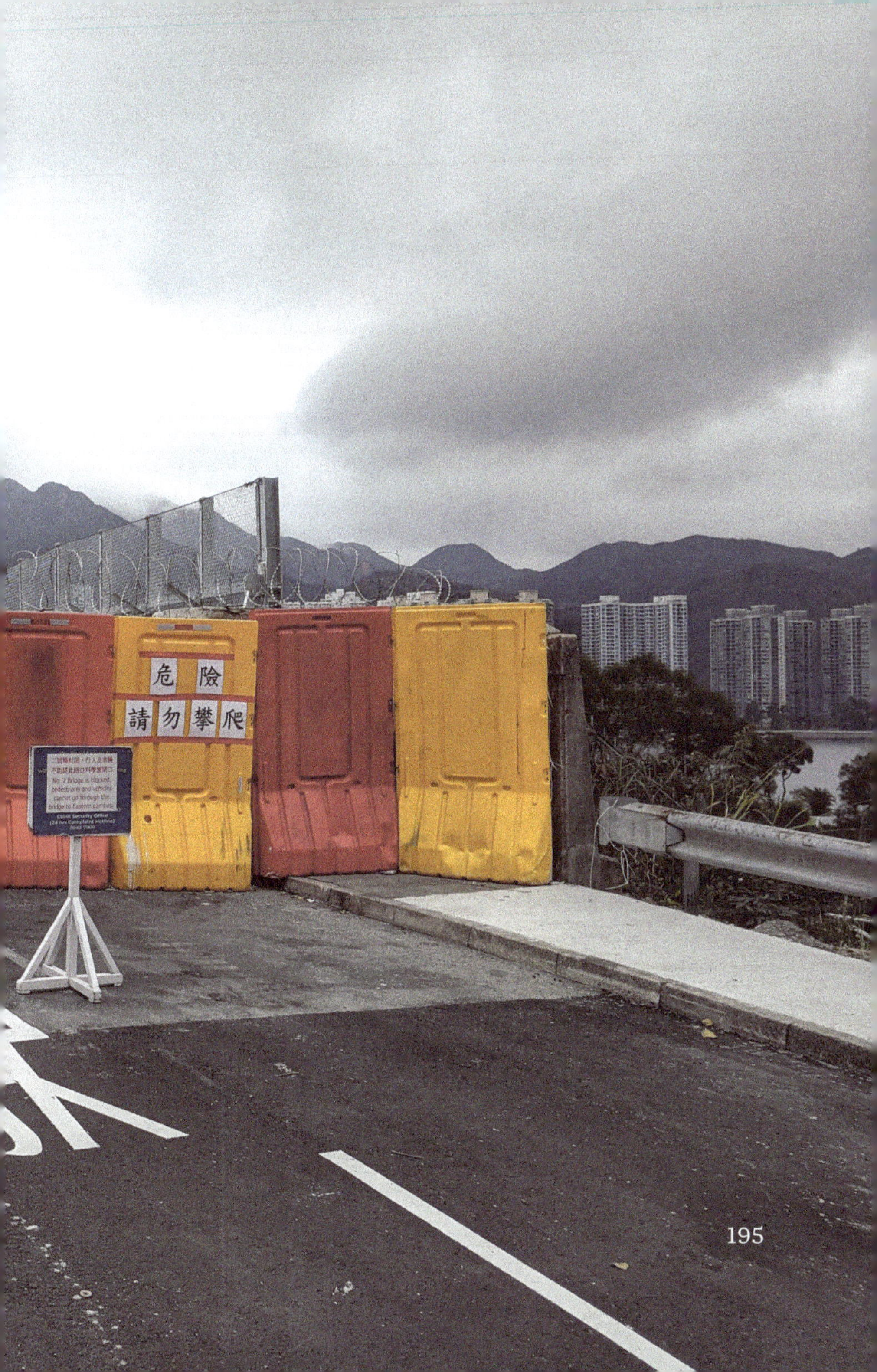
危 險
請 勿 攀 爬
No. 2 Bridge is blocked,
pedestrians and vehicles
cannot go through the
bridge to Eastern campus
CUHK Security Office
(24 hrs Complaint Hotline)

Au Loong Yu is keeping his distance in a small pagoda in a Tuen Mun park in the New Territories. Hong Kong is one of the most densely populated cities in the world, almost everyone living on top of one another in huge high rises. With an aggressive infection like this coronavirus, a single carrier undetected in public housing could quickly lead to an outbreak. He has a few extra medical face masks and gives one to a homeless person as we get up and walk. Between explaining the political and market failures that have left an old man to fill the sanitation gaps exposed by an incompetent and unprepared government, the veteran activist turns his thoughts to last year's revolt:

'The movement of 2019, the momentum, has been declining obviously. You can see a lot of symptoms. The Lennon Walls [where people stick post-it notes with messages of support for protests, general slogans of the movement and other pithy commentary]—there are fewer updates. And for a long time, several months now, there has not been people shouting slogans from their own apartment and getting the slogan echoed by people in other apartments. It used to happen every night at ten o'clock, but that has long passed. Maybe two months before the outbreak of the university

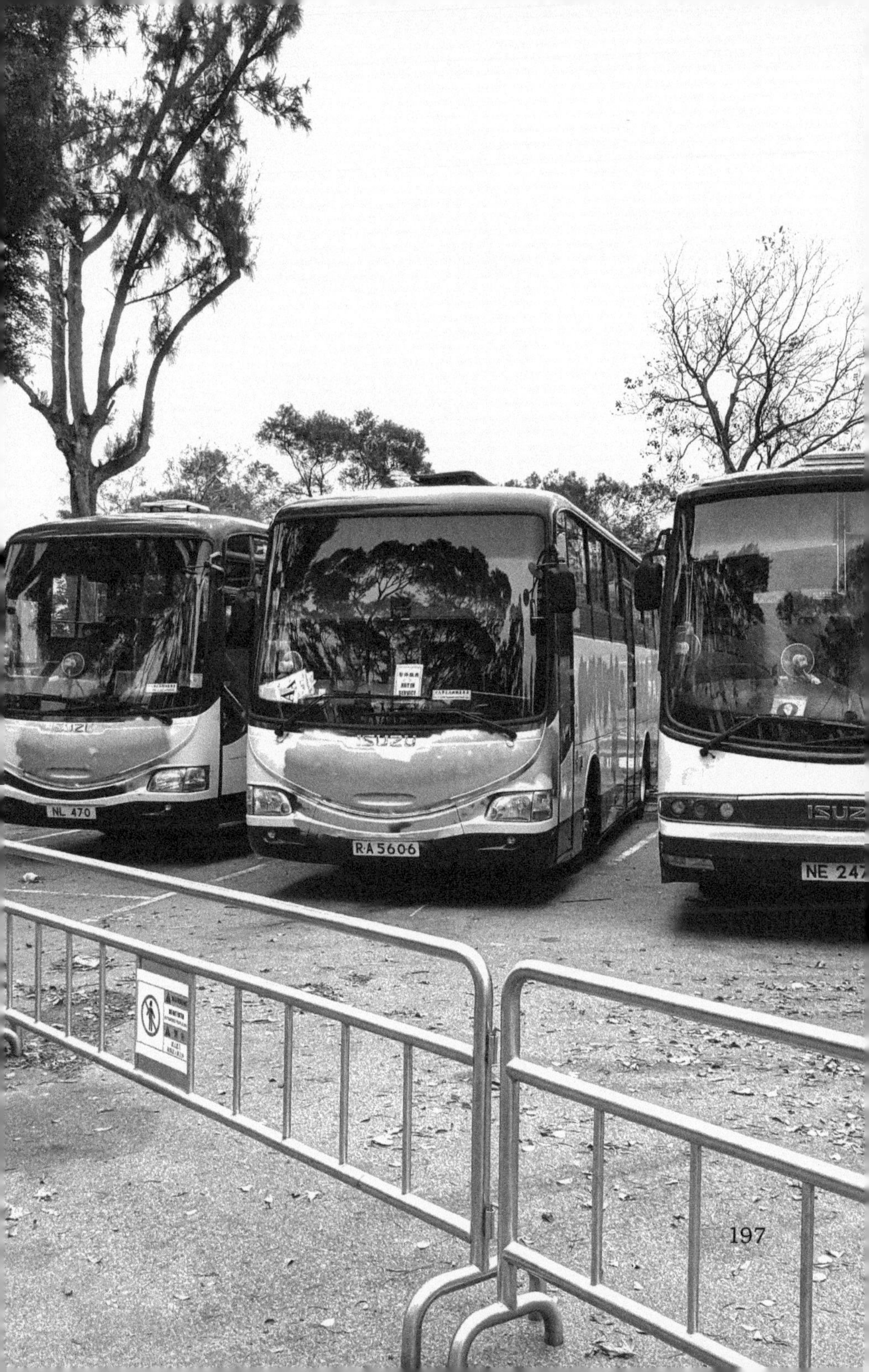
NL 470
ISUZU
RA 5606
ISUZ
NE 247

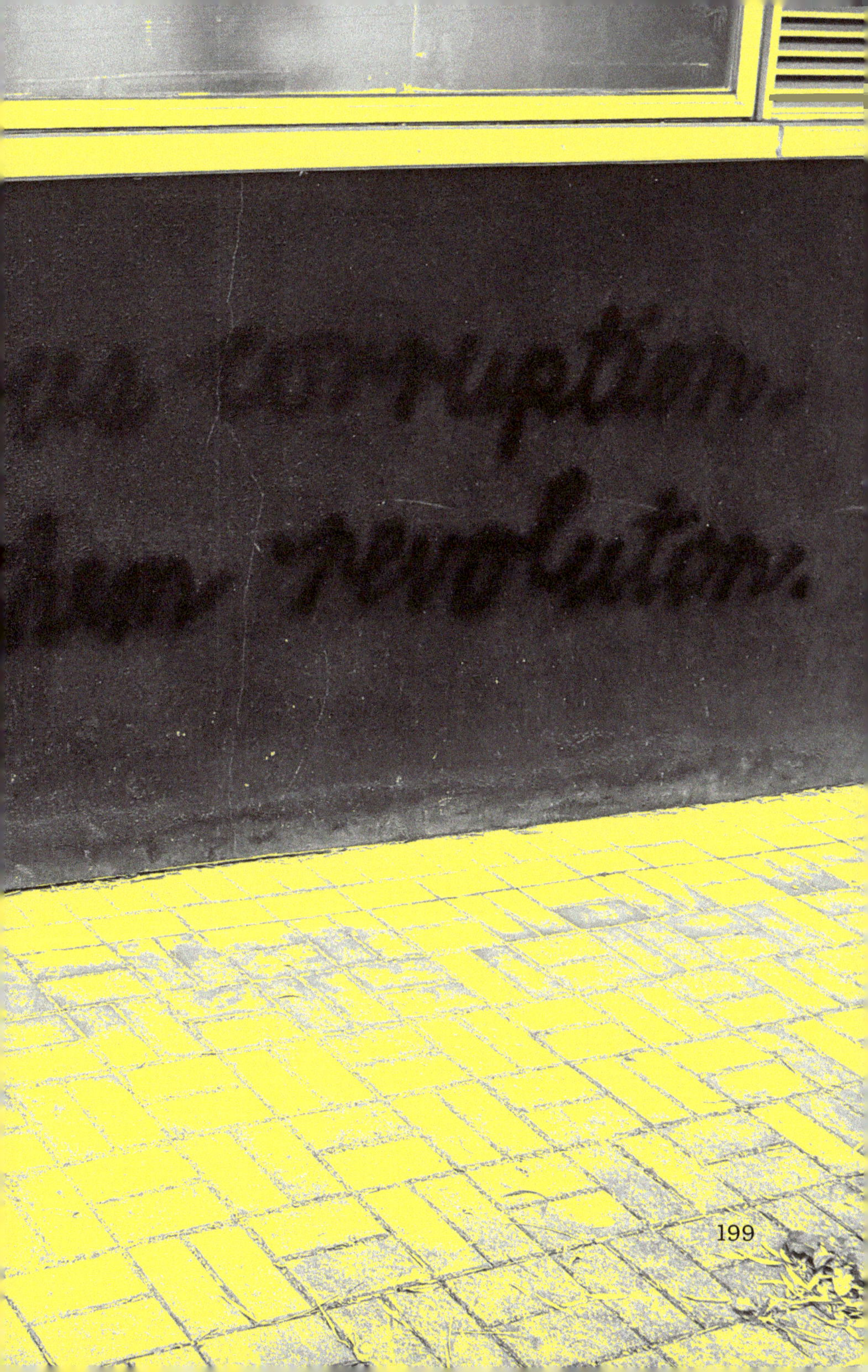
corruption.
revolution.

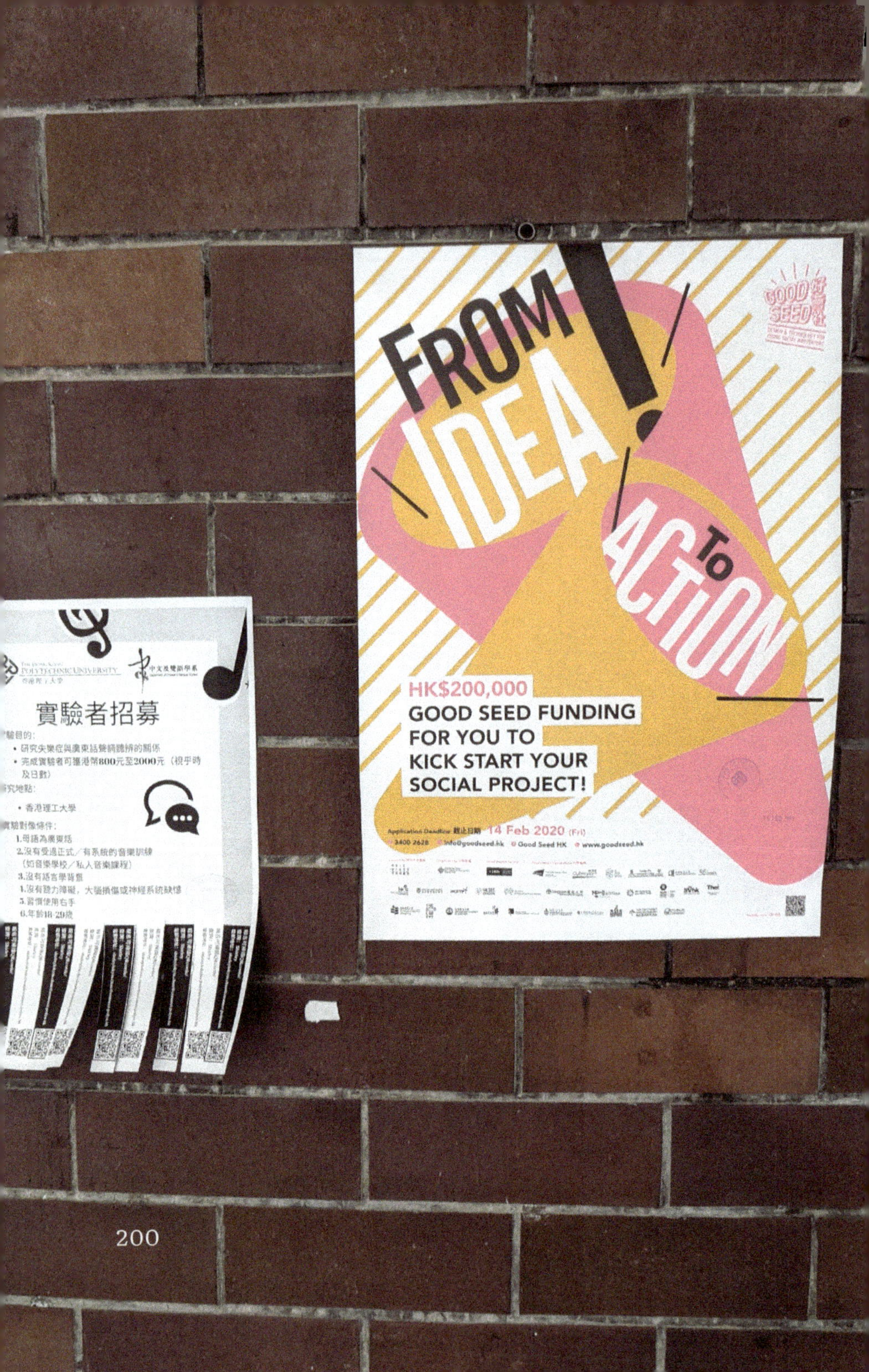
THE HONG KONG POLYTECHNIC UNIVERSITY
香港理工大學
中文及雙語學系
實驗者招募
研究失樂症與廣東話聲調聽辨的關係
完成實驗者可獲港幣800元至2000元（視乎時及日數）
香港理工大學
1.母語為廣東話
2.沒有受過正式／有系統的音樂訓練
（如音樂學校／私人音樂課程）
3.沒有語言學背景
4.沒有聽力障礙，大腦損傷或神經系統缺憾
5.習慣使用右手
6.年齡18-29歲
FROM
IDEA
!
To
ACTION
GOOD SEED
HK$200,000
GOOD SEED FUNDING
FOR YOU TO
KICK START YOUR
SOCIAL PROJECT!
Application Deadline 截止日期 14 Feb 2020 (Fri)
3400 2628
info@goodseed.hk
Good Seed HK
www.goodseed.hk

occupations, this type of activity had already died down. The students tried to save the movement. They came up with the brilliant plan of blocking roads, stopping transport and making people strike. But not being able to get to work—this is not the proper way to go on strike.'

There is broad agreement that when police relentlessly turned the screws, the movement could no longer continue in the same way. The state's firepower was too great. People grew tired and, while there wasn't mass demoralisation, the accumulation of defeats and the evacuation of the university occupations took a toll. More than seven thousand people have been arrested. One thousand have been charged; the nearly six thousand bailed are subject to curfews, reporting requirements and/or restrictions on their movement. 'There were so many arrests—these were often frontliners and more radical protesters, especially at PolyU,' says a young activist on Hong Kong Island. 'Since then, police have started shutting things down quickly. The big confrontations were organised on the spot during the events, not beforehand. With things shut down more quickly and more violently, people don't have time to organise themselves. And the regular protesters are more intimidated.' Another activist, a citizen journalist who goes by the name of Hong Kong Hermit to maintain anonymity, draws out the longer picture of shifting police tactics:

'There's been a constant sense of escalation over the last

few months. Currently, even the big peaceful marches get hassled before they begin. Then, once they start, they get attacked by undercover cops rushing in to tackle a couple of people. Riot cops pepper spray dozens, there's a little tickle of tear gas, the march is cancelled and everyone is hassled on the way home. And that's for the processions where there are babies and families present.

'In the beginning, the marches would go until five or seven in the evening, then the frontliners would take over and cause malarkey until midnight. Then, the teargassing started before sunset and frontliners would go on until the last train. Then, with the MTR moving from being neutral to being a military transport for the cops, and a staging ground from where they could launch attacks, the actions became smaller and more localised as we couldn't redeploy. The late-night actions were all around residential areas that the cops then started to invade and cause hassle in people's home estates. Shopping malls for daytime protests were the next step. Police routinely invaded those too, beating people senseless. Ultimately, people ran out of safe places to gather and protest even peacefully, as the cops have attacked everyone, everywhere, and with little reason or warning.'

The tremendous strength of the movement last year was its spontaneous character. But its weaknesses are starting to show in the face of the repression. The government lacks

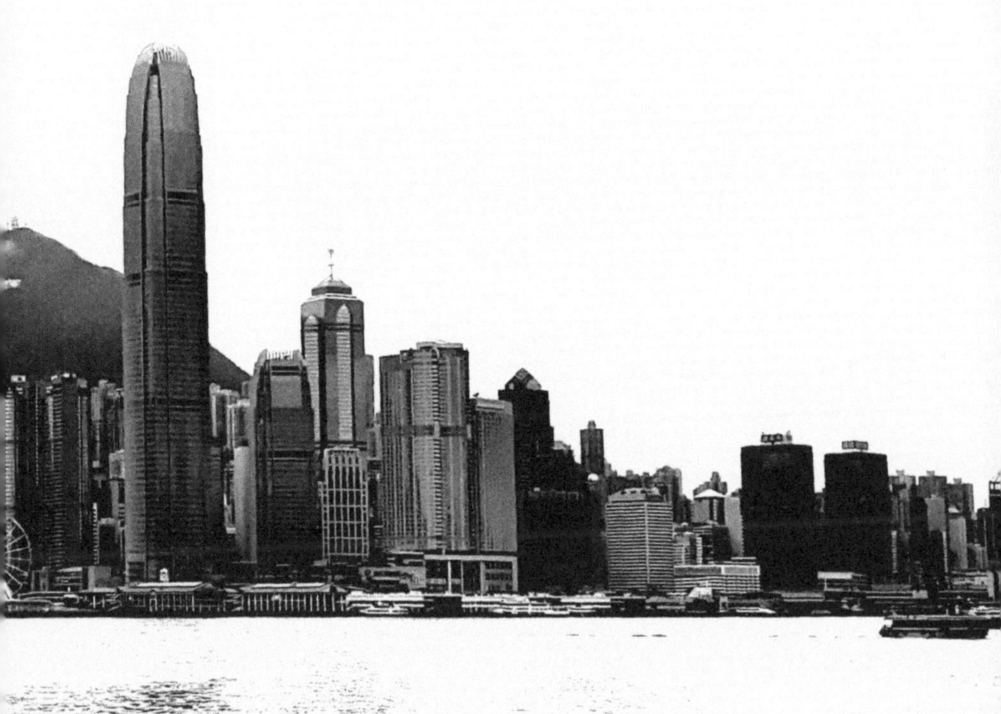

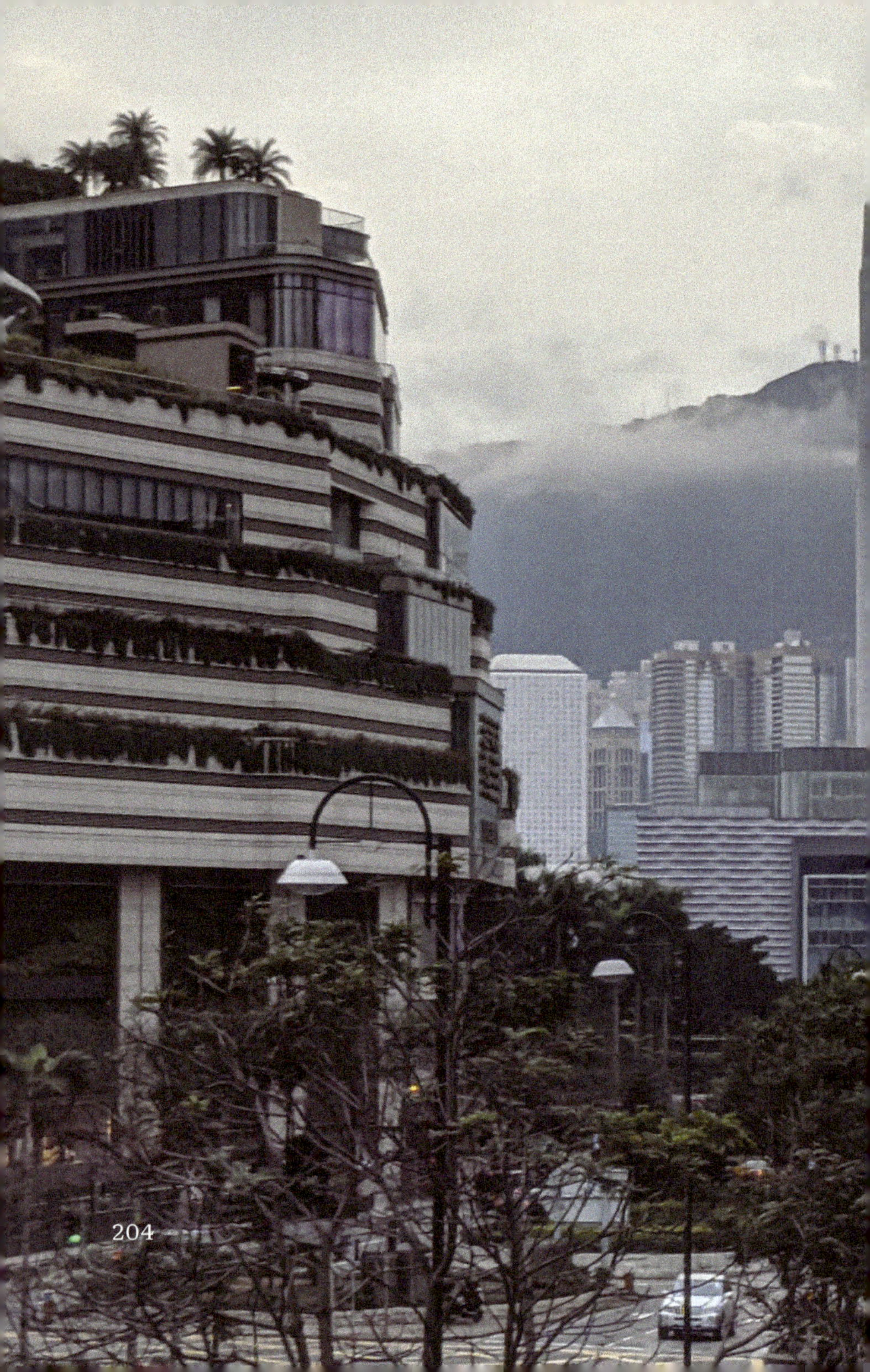

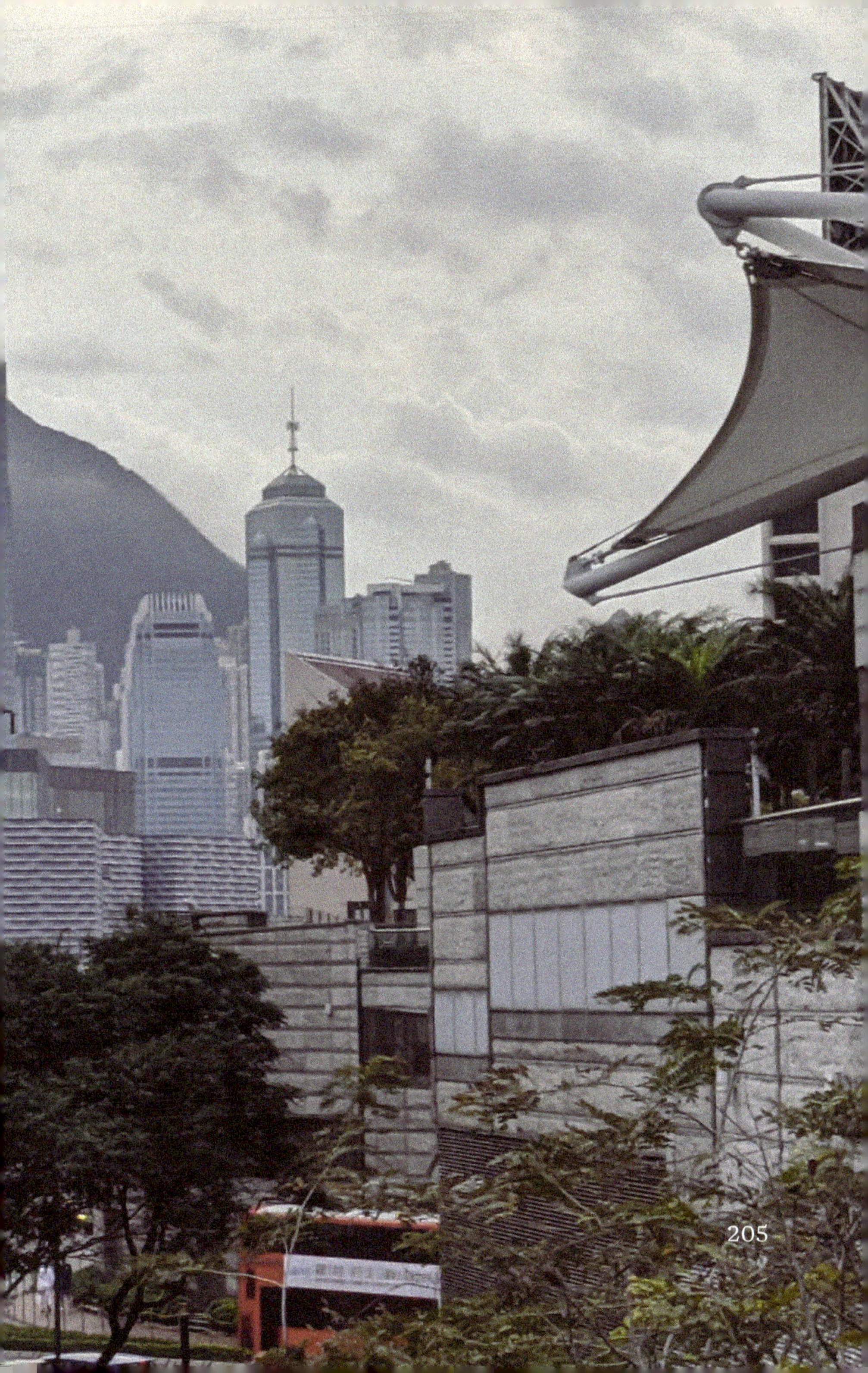

popular legitimacy; incapable of persuasion, it has only violence at its disposal. Yet, at least for the time being, the opposition has little coordination and no obvious answer to the disorganisation that the repression is causing. However, two activists I speak to believe that, contrary to appearances, the movement is not retreating. Each says that it has downed tools, so to speak, to rest, regroup and wait for the virus threat to pass. They have no doubt that another political offensive is coming. Time will tell. There are still protests almost every day about the government's response to the coronavirus, or its attempts to open quarantine stations in or near public housing estates. While they are generally small, they have occurred in far-flung areas of the territory previously untouched by mobilisations.

The level of anti-government anger continues to rise, however—something you would have thought impossible last November, when resentment was ubiquitous and seemingly peaking. Seventy-five percent of respondents to a January Hong Kong Public Opinion Research Institute survey were dissatisfied with the government's response to the outbreak. Chief Executive Carrie Lam's support has sunk to twenty-one percent, the lowest on record for any leader. '[The movement has] not given up in any way. It is just a combination of the virus, and frankly everyone is fucking exhausted,' the Hermit says. 'Every time there has been a chance for people to show where they stand, they have consistently shown they stand with the frontliners … The larger protests will resume in the warmer weather, once the virus emergency passes. Just small wildcat events until then, to keep them aware that this isn't over.'

While there are different takes on how precisely to characterise the current period, and how much action we can expect in the coming months, one thing everyone seems to agree on is that, all things being equal, the annual 1 July demonstration (marking the anniversary of Hong Kong's handover from Britain to China) this year will be a huge display of democratic opposition to the government and to Beijing.

'I'm not yet thirty years old, and I have a second chance—who gets that?' Leo can't quite believe that 2019 came so soon after 2014. That year's Umbrella Movement was the first radicalisation of a generation whose political existence has been framed by the reversion of Hong Kong to Chinese rule. For eleven weeks, thousands of students occupied different sections of Hong Kong Island and Mong Kok demanding universal suffrage. But it ended badly: repression, imprisonment or exile for almost all the key movement leaders. Many

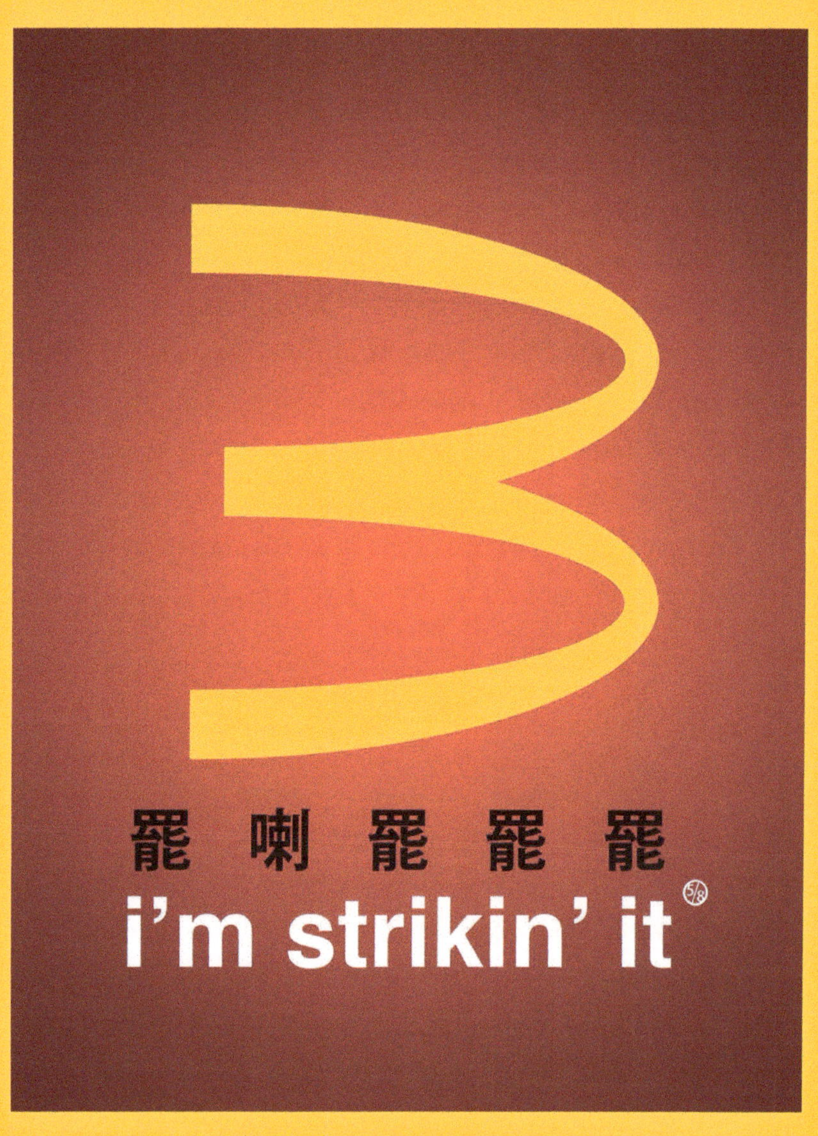
罷 喇 罷 罷 罷
i'm strikin' it

participants gave up hope. But now there's a second coming. And as a labour organiser, researcher and trainer with the Hong Kong Confederation of Trade Unions, Leo notices the terrain shifting.

Of interest is the spike in union registrations. According to the Labour Department, seventeen new unions were formed from October until the end of last year. Leo says the real number is about fifty, but most haven't finished the paperwork to be formally registered. There are about thirty thousand new members, two-thirds of whom have joined the Hospital Authority Employees Alliance, which was registered in December and has already had a week-long strike involving up to nine thousand new members. It now covers almost one-quarter of the Hospital Authority's eighty thousand employees. It's hardly a labour insurgency—you need only seven people to form a union here, a legacy of British colonialism's 'kill them with kindness' attitude to the union movement, which has resulted in craft-style fracturing and weakness, with eleven federations and almost nine hundred individual unions in a city of seven and a half million people. But given the Hong Kong labour movement's unenviable record of civility (save a few notable exceptions), this uptick has people talking.

The general strike has become part of young Hong Kongers' political imagination, Leo says. Last June, the government sent to the Legislative Council a bill that, if passed, would have allowed residents to be extradited and tried on the mainland. This was the spark lighting the fire of mobilisations throughout the rest of the year. From the beginning, the online forum LIHKG was ablaze with calls for a general strike. But they weren't coming from the unions—it was the university students and high-schoolers. And while the 'general strike' that they mustered in November was an heroic, citywide student and youth rebellion without a working-class mobilisation behind it, in the background, seeds were being planted.

Sometime in July, people started industry-based chat groups on Telegram, a popular encrypted messaging app used by most participants in the movement. 'They started calling it the TG Union—the Telegram Union. We couldn't tell how many groups or how many people were involved. This form of organising is very loose. But at least it was a start,' Leo says. 'They started thinking about themselves as workers. This was new in the Hong Kong political movement.' On 2 August, the civil servants' TG group organised a forty-thousand-strong demonstration against police violence. The same day, the health workers' TG group organised a rally of ten thousand. Both groups now are registered unions.

'Those two assemblies inspired people to think, we should do something like this in my industry,' Leo says. 'On 5 August there was an actual strike. It was very important. A total of

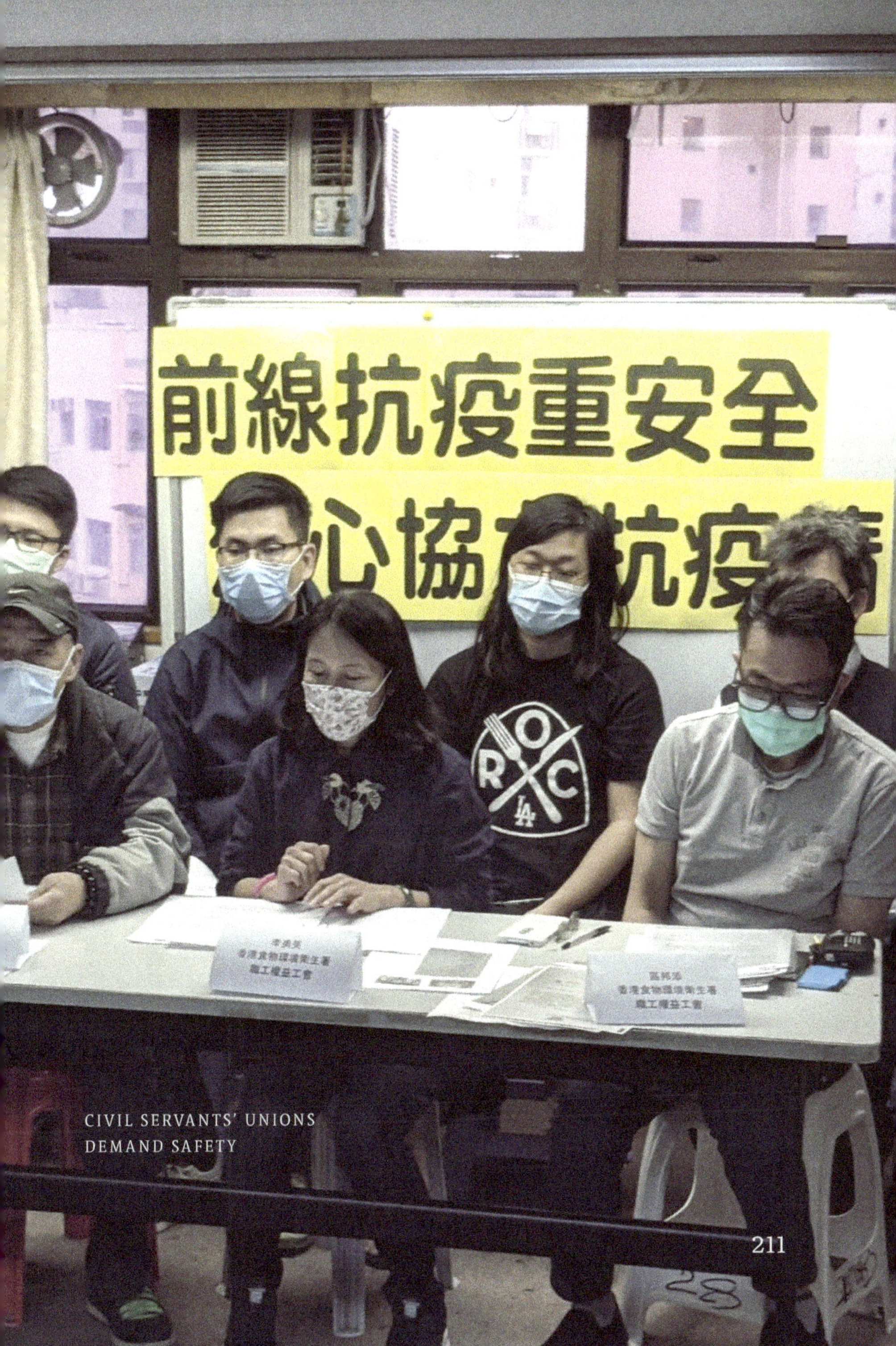

CIVIL SERVANTS' UNIONS
DEMAND SAFETY

maybe three hundred and fifty thousand people didn't go to work; big assemblies [protests] were held in seven locations. But because of the lack of core organisation, you couldn't tell how many people were protesting from each industry, how many were actually on strike, rather than just taking a sick day and things like this. The assemblies were not organised by the unions, but by the young people and TG groups. People could see that the strike was powerful, but not enough—not big enough, not long enough.'

There was a lot of online discussion about why the strike didn't win any concessions. The students felt that they still needed a proper general strike. So those most determined to have a citywide shutdown were the least able to carry it out—by definition, a general strike involves workers refusing to work, using their economic power to paralyse a city, or a country, and provoke a political crisis. The students tried to substitute in November by throwing themselves all over town, shutting down key arterial roads, blocking train lines, setting up barricades and fighting police. Who could blame them? If they were to wait for the older generation to rise up, they would have been waiting a long time. In fact, their militancy was an inspiration across Hong Kong. Many non-students felt ashamed that they had let the young people down.

It was precisely at this time that the wave of new unions began registering. The Telegram channel had grown to more

多一個您罷工，
少一個他被消失。

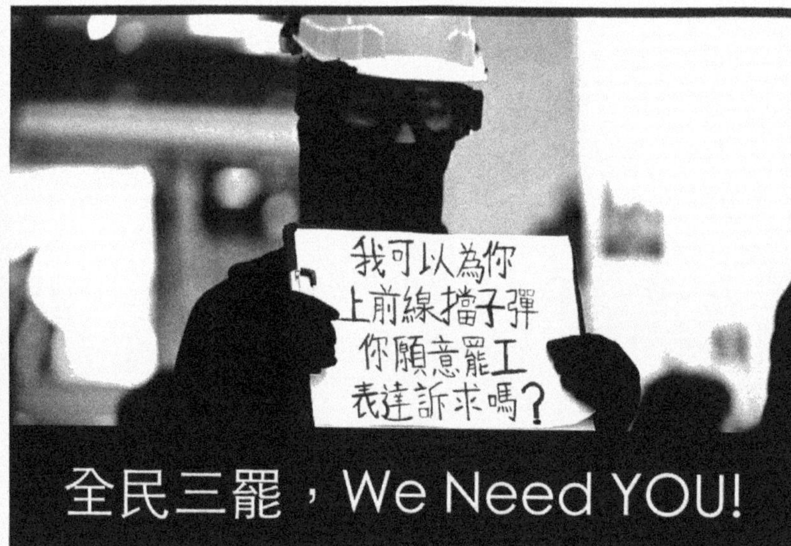

2019年6月至今，五個月了，
大家一直好好好好好嬲。
大家話，愈嬲愈要行出來
但愈行出來，就愈多人被濫捕。
最後，政權、黑警、黑社會有無驚過？
無，仲更無法無天。

香港人，真係無嘢可以做？
與其被政權瘋狂濫捕，
不如抓住政權嘅春袋 - 經濟

二百萬三罷
聯合陣線頻道
Telegram群組

香港人
罷工！

than seventy thousand subscribers with a permanent group of people giving advice on how to join and how to form a union. 'People are starting to see that getting organised is a way to put pressure on the government. Not many are joining because they are thinking first about staff rights and conditions. It's political. This is different from before,' Tam Leung Ying, an organiser with two small civil servants' unions, says. Leo agrees: 'People are joining to fight for democracy. This is totally new. We usually start with economic questions and then later move to politicising people through education.'

The new union leaders are young, generally aged under thirty-five, very few being over forty. 'I would think that most were on the street in 2014,' Leo says. '2009 to 2014 was the peak of social movements. We [students] experienced many different activities—a labour strike, land use disputes, high speed rail protests, high school struggles, then, of course, 2014. It was a time of a lot of social movement training if you were young or a student back then. 2019 was our second chance.'

Ask anyone who has made the transition from student campaigner to union militant, and they will explain that most activist skills are transferable, but the challenges are significantly different. If it goes well, perhaps we may look back on this period as the birth of a new union militancy in Hong Kong. If so, that will throw up a range of new challenges, not least of which will relate to the unity of the self-determination movement. Because if workers start to move, the national question may soon become a class question. There are always 'ifs', of course. Time will tell how this aspect of the movement progresses.

CRACKDOWN

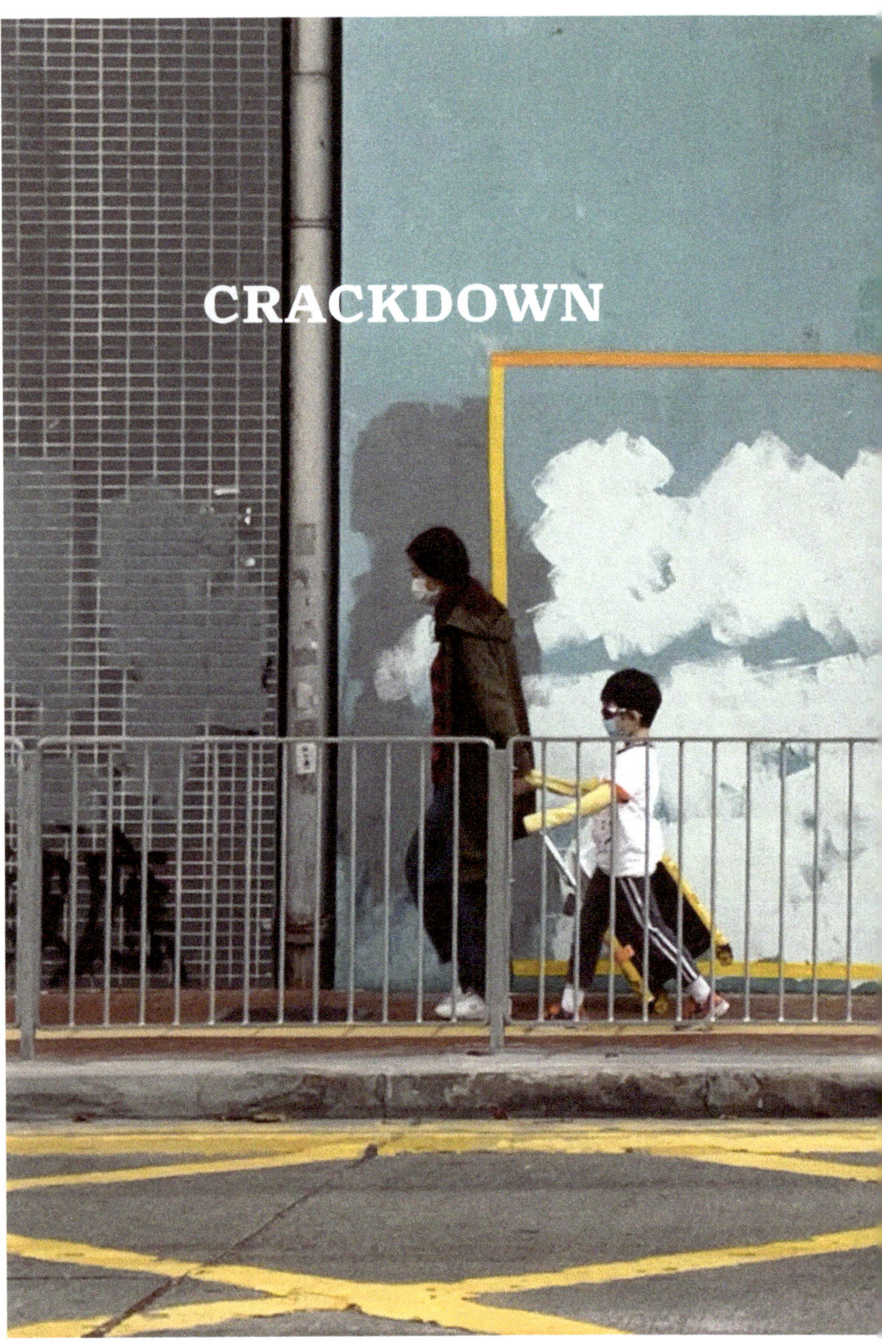

 GIRAFFE LEUNG (2020) 'PAPER OVER THE CRACKS #5'

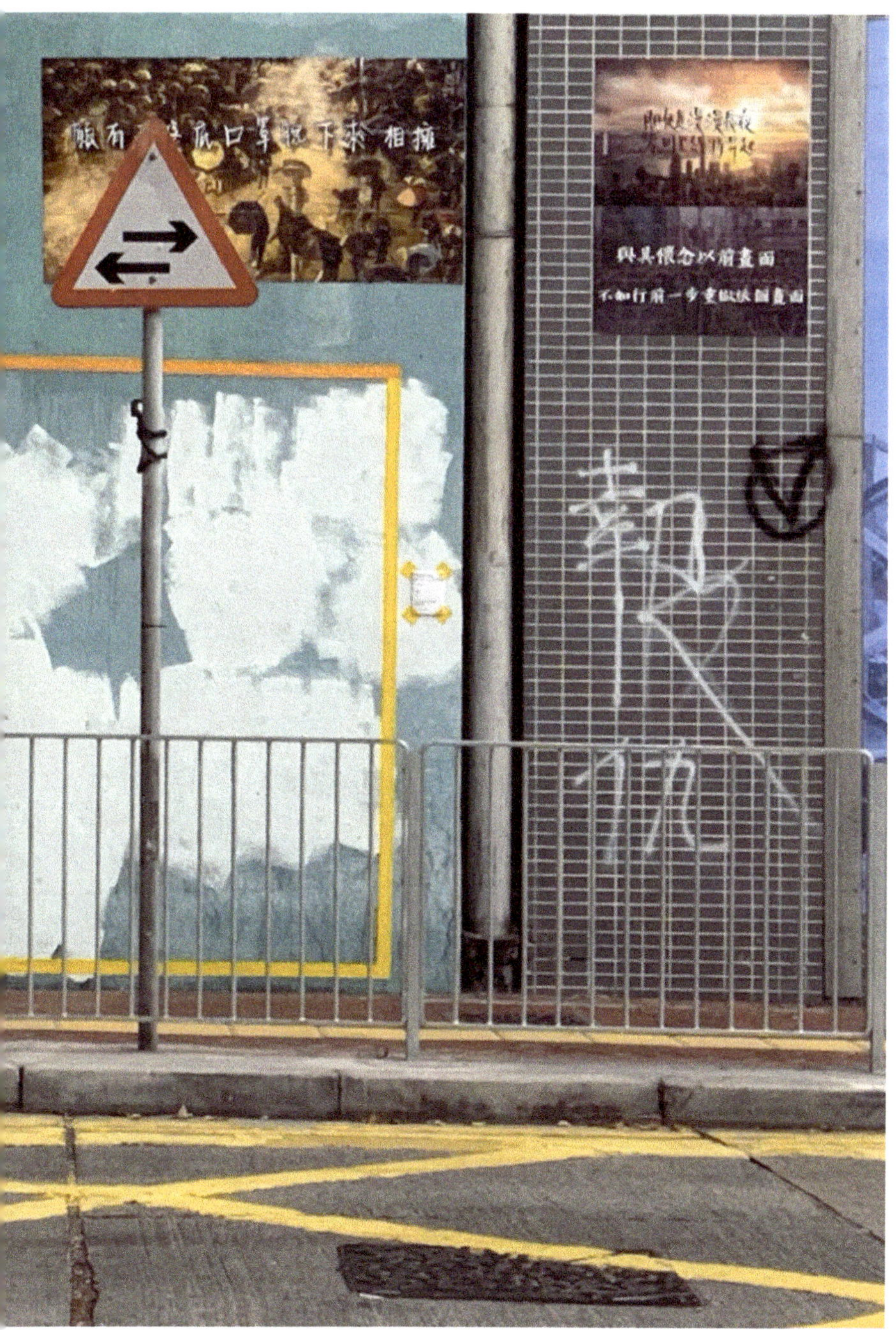
與其懷念以前畫面

CRACKDOWN

The 1 July imposition of a national security law on Hong Kong by the Standing Committee of the National People's Congress, China's legislature, was a hammer blow to the city's pro-democracy movement, which all but disintegrated in the first half of 2020 after months of escalating police violence and government crackdowns under the cover of the coronavirus pandemic. The Chinese Communist Party, impatient with the local government's inability to pass its own laws in the face of mass opposition, bypassed Hong Kong's lawmakers and kept even the loyalist chief executive in the dark about the details. Beijing again used the bogey of a 'political scheme of external forces ... interfering in Hong Kong affairs' as its justification. 'Extremist organisations advocating the so-called "Hong Kong independence" and radical separatist forces have

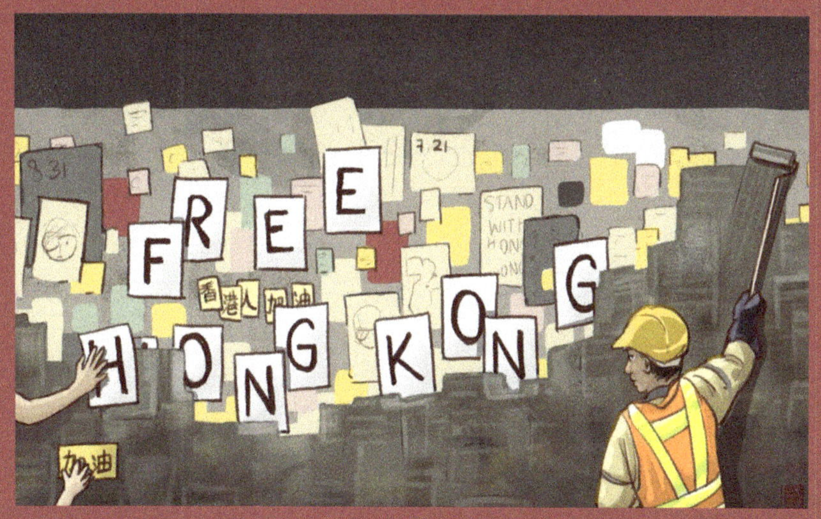

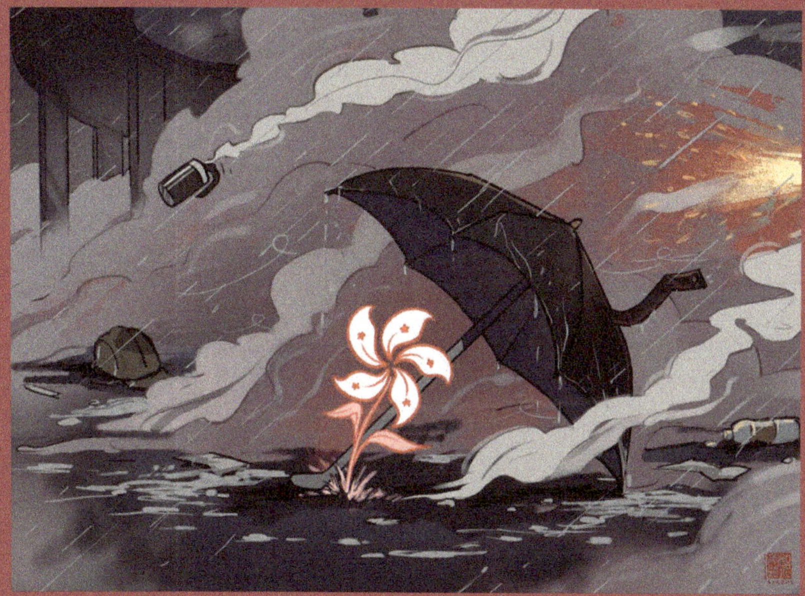

MEI-LI NIEUWLAND
@LIEAPLZ

'HK GOV: REMEMBER, WE'RE GOING FOR "CLEAR AND CLEAN".
HK PPL: BE FAST ENOUGH AND THE WET PAINT CAN BE USED AS GLUE :)'

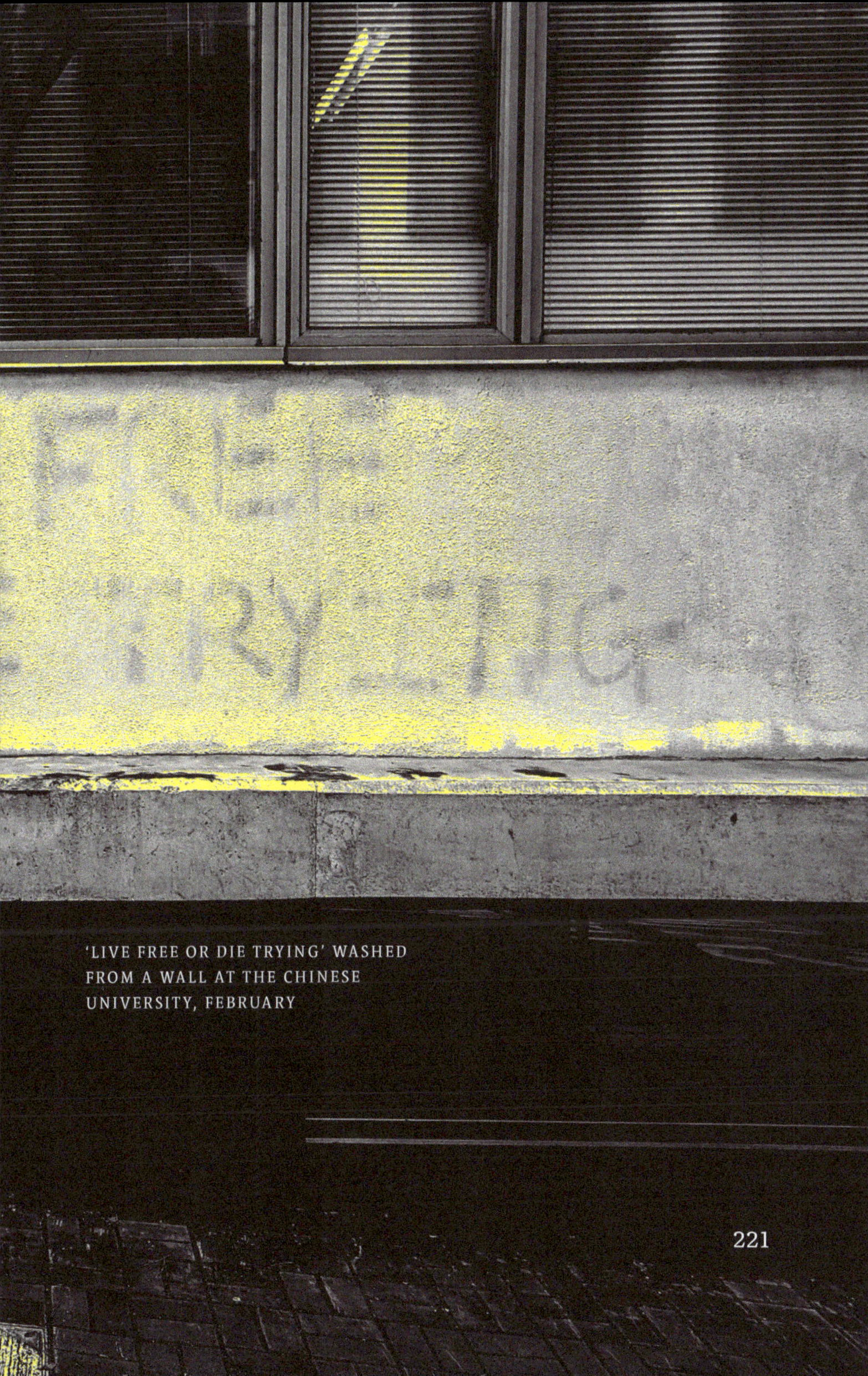

'LIVE FREE OR DIE TRYING' WASHED FROM A WALL AT THE CHINESE UNIVERSITY, FEBRUARY

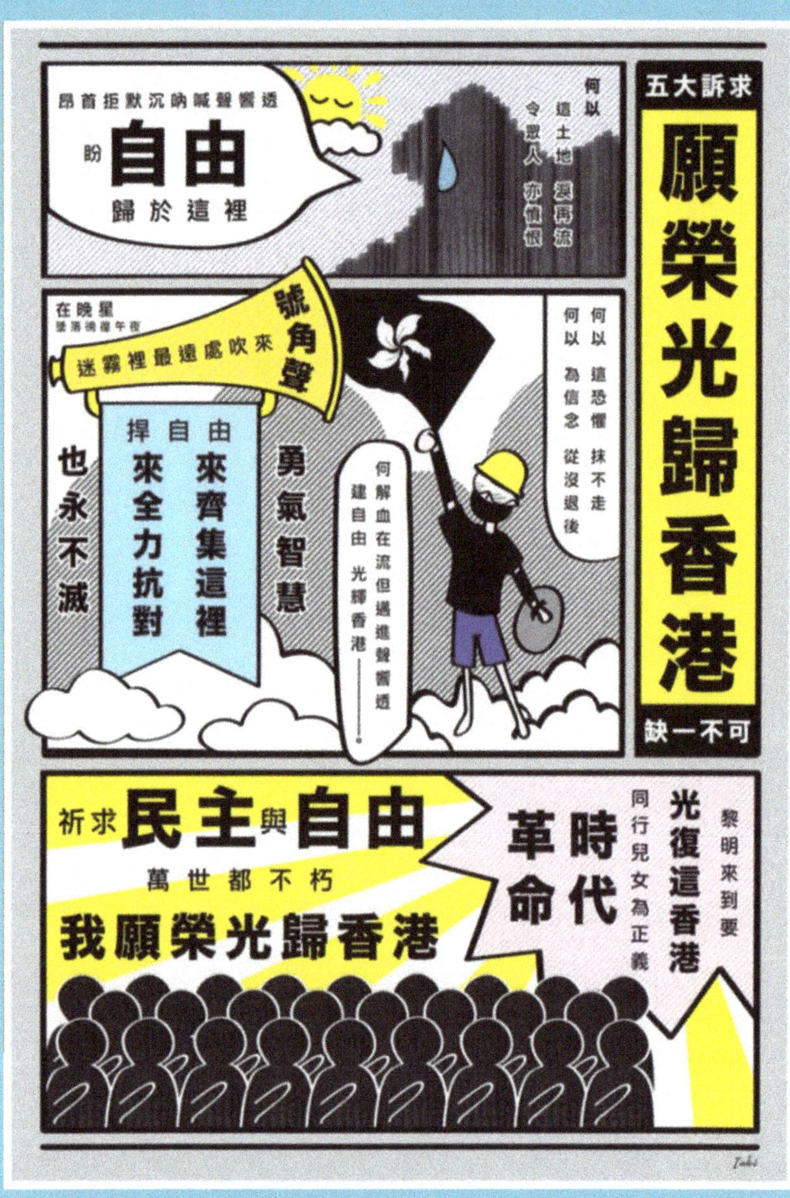

A POSTER WITH LYRICS OF 'GLORY TO HONG KONG': A PROTEST ANTHEM SUNG AT DEMONSTRATIONS AND BANNED AT SCHOOLS committed shocking violent crimes that are in the nature of terrorism,' the state-run Xinhua news agency reported in June after the Congress resolved to assert itself.

The Safeguarding National Security law outlines criminal acts of secession, subversion, terrorism and collusion in sweeping terms that give authorities a broad remit to arrest and potentially prosecute democratic activists on the flimsiest of pretexts. Unlawful attempts to organise, plan or participate in the disruption of the functioning of government or 'damaging the premises and facilities used by' government are among the offences listed as subversion. The crime of collusion includes unlawfully 'provoking hatred' toward the central government in Beijing. Sabotaging transport or control systems—such as 2019's attacks on traffic lights and on the MTR after it became a means of transporting police to protest sites—is now terrorism. Activities prohibited in the name of national security would have been carried out by perhaps tens of thousands of supporters of the pro-democracy movement. In some instances, defendants can be extradited for trial in mainland courts.

'Hong Kong inherited a lot of draconian, British colonial-era laws that enabled the government to crack down on organisations, protests and gatherings,' noted Ho-fung Hung, a sociology professor at Johns Hopkins University, in a July interview in the university magazine. 'But it didn't have the tools to prosecute people based on their speech, their opinion and their associations with other people. The Chinese came in—in 1997—and wanted to change that. The Chinese government wanted to impose some kind of national security law that outlaws certain kinds of opinion and speech and associations with other people deemed subversive to the Chinese state ... The Hong Kong government has always been able to arrest people for so-called illegally assembling ... but they cannot arrest people for the articles they write, for the speeches they make and for merely knowing and having connections with people that are deemed subversive to the government.'

People assisting or inciting those facing primary charges also face potential jail time, putting in Beijing's crosshairs any solidarity movement that again emerges. On the first day of the law's operation, local police charged at least ten people, including a fifteen-year-old carrying a flag advocating Hong Kong independence. Presumably, the police reasoned that the schoolgirl was 'organising, planning, committing or participating in' the separation of Hong Kong from China. For a 'principal offender', such a crime is punishable with life imprisonment under the articles on secession. Further, Beijing established a mainland security intelligence division in Causeway Bay, the Office for Safeguarding National Security, whose spooks are immune from local oversight when carrying out their duties. And if the national security law anywhere contradicts local laws, the former prevails. The legal firewall between Hong Kong and the mainland has been irrevocably breached.

'This next period will be dark. It will be the most difficult period,' Winnie Yu, president of the Hospital Authority Employees Alliance, says over the phone from Hong Kong prior to the full details of the new law being made public. 'Some colleagues are talking about emigrating. But for others this is not an option, they can't afford it. Many of us will stay and fight. I'm not very optimistic, because our enemy is the Chinese Communist Party. It is so powerful. But we have to stay united and stay strong.' Winnie is part of the new generation attempting to build a democratic opposition within the labour movement. The hospital employees, registered in December, grew rapidly to cover around one-quarter of the sector and led a strike against the government in February. But the broader movement's attempts to turn deep-seated anger into large-scale action have had diminishing returns. A citywide survey of union members to gauge the mood for strike action against the security law failed to draw a significant response, with fewer than nine thousand members voting. Of those, most were for holding a general strike, but in a city of seven and a half million, it was nowhere near enough. 'Most union members are strongly against the security law, but there are hesitations about going on strike or taking other industrial

組織工會
集結力量
Power in A Union

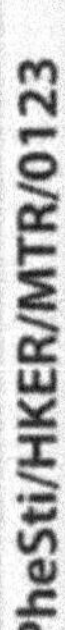

PheSti/HKER/MTR/0123

actions,' Winnie says, citing fear and demoralisation.

Mobilisations did occur in response to the law's enactment. Despite a huge police presence, thousands protested on Hong Kong Island, filling side streets as the authorities blocked main streets. Three hundred and seventy reportedly were arrested. 'There is an anger here. Desperation, demoralisation—but also anger and hatred. The good news is that there is still a will to fight and resist. At least ten thousand took to the streets, which was more than I had expected,' Au Loong Yu says over the phone a day later. But his expectations had been incredibly low. It was a bad sign that so few turned out against the biggest attack on democratic rights since the reversion of the territory to Chinese sovereignty.

'The weaknesses in the movement were there from the beginning. But after a year, it is just as atomised as before,' Au says. 'Civil society here is very weak. No layers of activists to give cohesion to the movement in a downswing. In a police state, things are even worse in the absence of this. The frontal attack from Beijing—no one was prepared for this, not politically prepared, and we are organisationally weak. Among the pan-democratic parties, it was quite alarming that very few [of their leaders] took the initiative to march on the streets. Just three or four of them—a real failure here. And there are no new organisations [emerging] from the young people to take the lead.'

Authorities were so confident that they had weathered the year-long storm that, scarcely a week later, police commanders slashed riot squad numbers by two-thirds.

While the movement may not have been prepared, the signs had been apparent. April, the thirtieth anniversary of the promulgation of the Basic Law, ushered in a new wave of attacks against those defending the limited freedoms, both outlined and promised, enshrined in the document. Police arrested more than a dozen veterans of the democracy movement for their roles in last year's protests. And China's Liaison Office declared that it was not bound by a clause prohibiting the Chinese government from interfering in local affairs. The office was established in 2000, replacing the New China News Agency, and has long been known to coordinate Communist Party cells and mobilise electoral support for pro-Beijing candidates in the city. But this was an unprecedented public announcement.

In May, nearly four hundred protesters were arrested as authorities continued to crack down on civil disobedience. And twenty-one-year-old lifeguard Sin Ka-ho, the first protester to plead guilty to rioting outside the Legislative Council

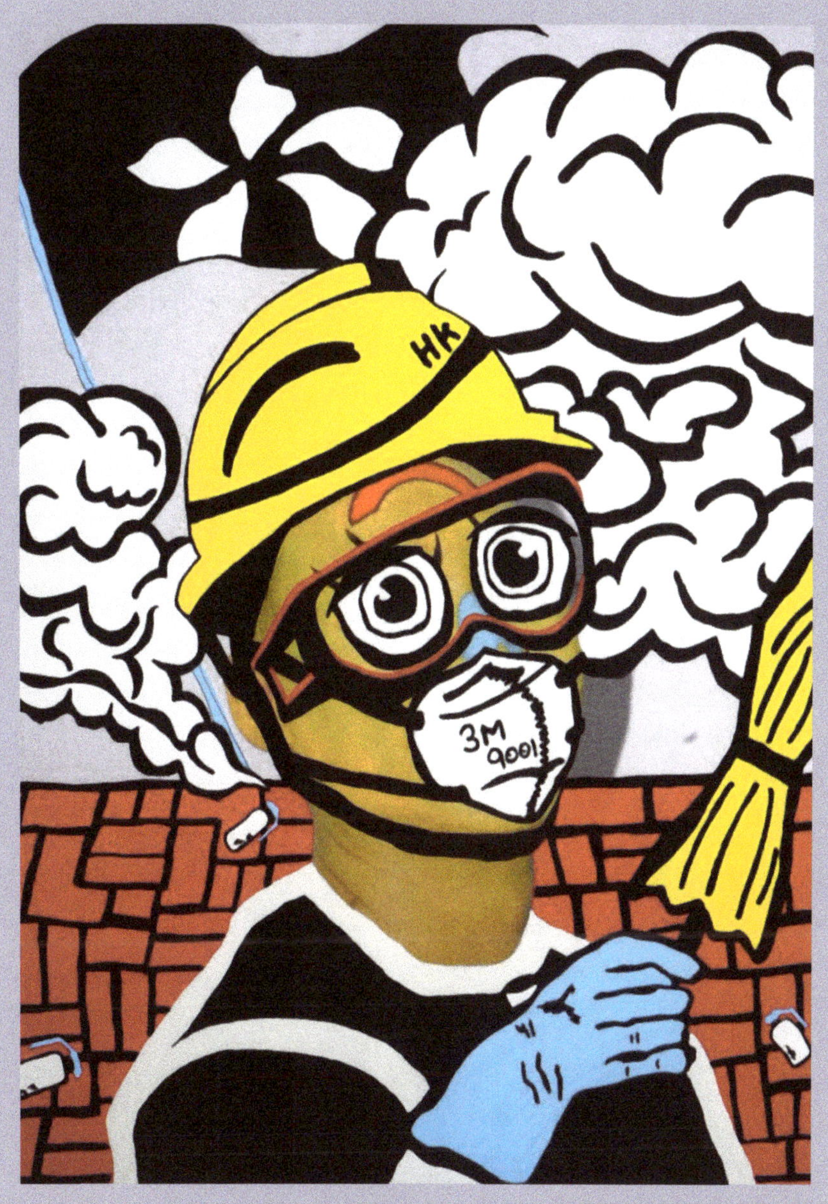

'PROTESTERS'
JAN PAN CHAN (2019)

on 12 June 2019, was sentenced to four years' jail—ominous signals to demonstrators that the state was far from compromising. The city budget passed, providing a twenty-five percent boost to police funding, and the Independent Police Complaints Council released a one-thousand-page report on police conduct during last year's protest movement. Despite receiving nearly two thousand complaints, the council found that law enforcement acted according to guidelines. Later in the month, the government passed a law outlawing the mocking of the Chinese national anthem. 'Anyone who publicly and wilfully alters the lyrics or the score of "March of the volunteers", performs or sings the anthem in a derogatory manner, or insults the song, [faces] a penalty of up to HK$50,000 and three years in jail,' warned a *Hong Kong Free Press* explainer.

With the imposition of the national security law, the character of the resistance in Hong Kong perhaps is irrevocably changed. The Communist Party talks about a 'second return' of the territory. Part one was the 1997 handover, which Beijing now considers a failure. Part two is the city's incorporation into the so-called Greater Bay Area—a megalopolis comprising Guangzhou, Shenzhen, Zhuhai, Foshan, Dongguan, Zhongshan, Jiangmen, Huizhou, Zhaoqing and Macau. In an era of perpetual encroachment, the pro-democracy camp's protests now will be direct challenges to the central government, not simply to local authorities. The pan-democrats

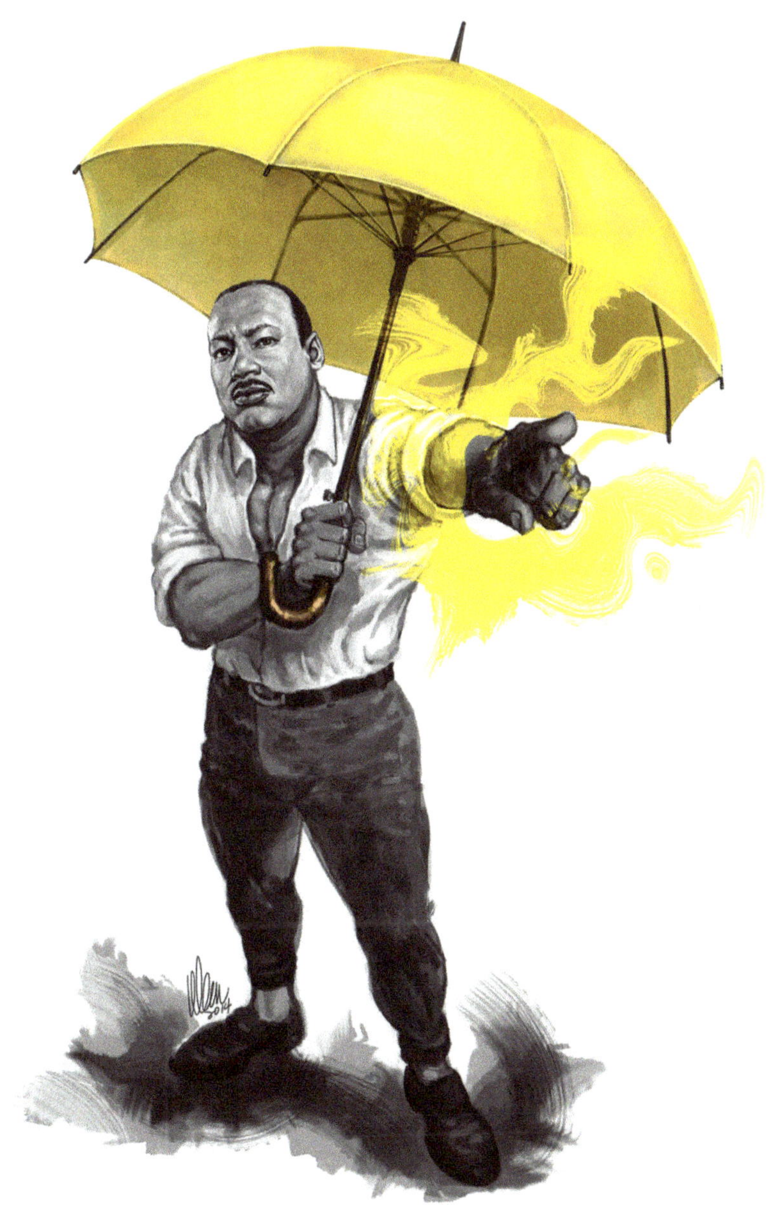

TMAN

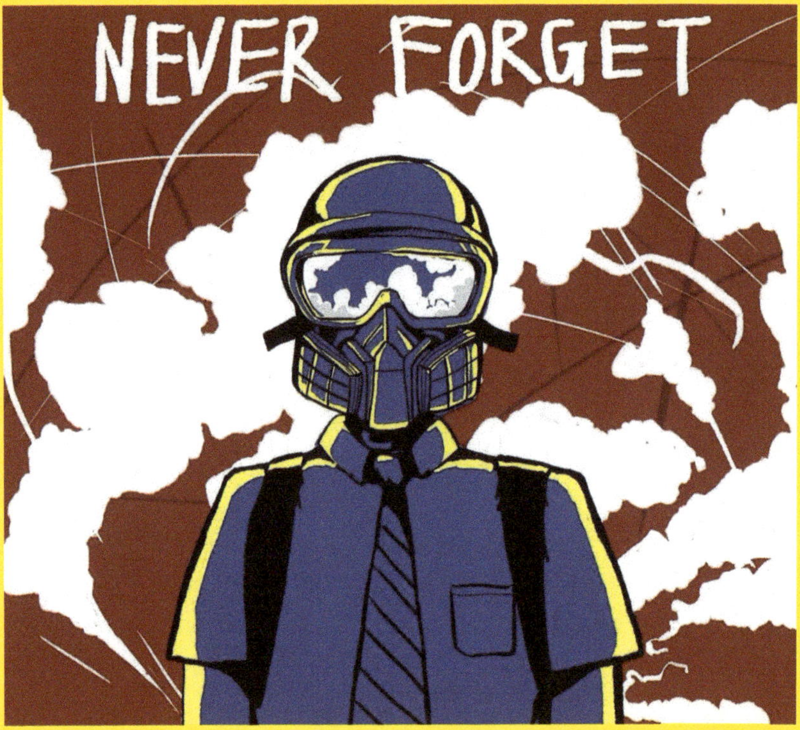

NEVER FORGET

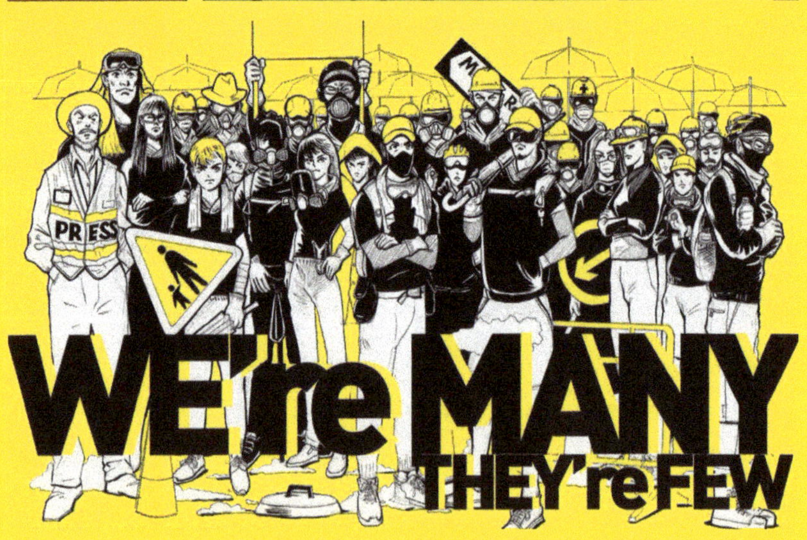

invested a lot of hopes in Legislative Council elections. But the structure of the legislature and the rules for taking office are stacked against the democratic forces—a dozen candidates were disqualified by returning officers at the end of July before the government, again using the pandemic as a pretext, postponed the poll for an entire year.

Are there realistic paths to victory for those wanting to preserve the city's freedoms and obtain a greater say in their own government? 'It's hard to feel any optimism about the Hong Kong struggle's future right now,' Jeff Wasserstrom, author of *Vigil: Hong Kong on the brink*, wrote in June, 'but it's worth noting how hard it would have been to feel optimistic about Solidarity's chances as its leaders were arrested and Poland fell under martial law at the end of 1981'. Solidarity (Solidarność in Polish), which emerged in 1980, was a mass movement against bureaucratic rule, whose leaders suffered persecution before triumphing in 1989, winning the country's first free elections in four decades and releasing the country from Stalinist authoritarianism.

There are many reasons not to draw an analogy between Hong Kong and Poland. Solidarność was an independent trade union with a membership of ten million, and as such was an expression not only of democratic sentiment, but of the power of Poland's organised working class. While the independent trade union movement in Hong Kong has made strides, thus far it has been peripheral to the democratic movement—hence the central feature of the resistance has been street protests, rather than strikes or the formation of industry-based democratic structures to bypass the anti-majoritarian system of government in the city. Further, Solidarność evolved during a period of economic crisis in Poland and of existential crisis in the Soviet Union, the weaknesses of which were exposed by the failing occupation of Afghanistan and an economy stuttering under the weight of a renewed Cold War with the United States. The economic situation is deteriorating in Hong Kong and China, primarily because of the pandemic. But, relative to its global competitors, China appears stronger than ever and the Communist Party supremely confident—a rising power unlike the failing Eastern Bloc.

Yet the comparison seems apt in other respects. The movements in both places were against a purported communism, and were lauded by conservatives and maligned by some socialists in the West who, ignoring the democratic content of the outpourings, focused primarily on Central Intelligence Agency conspiracies and the 'counter-revolutionary' implications of the victory of anti-communism. (The United States did aid Solidarność, but this should have been as relevant to the question of Western socialist support for the democratic movement as Irish Republican Army collaboration with German military intelligence was to the question of Irish national liberation.)

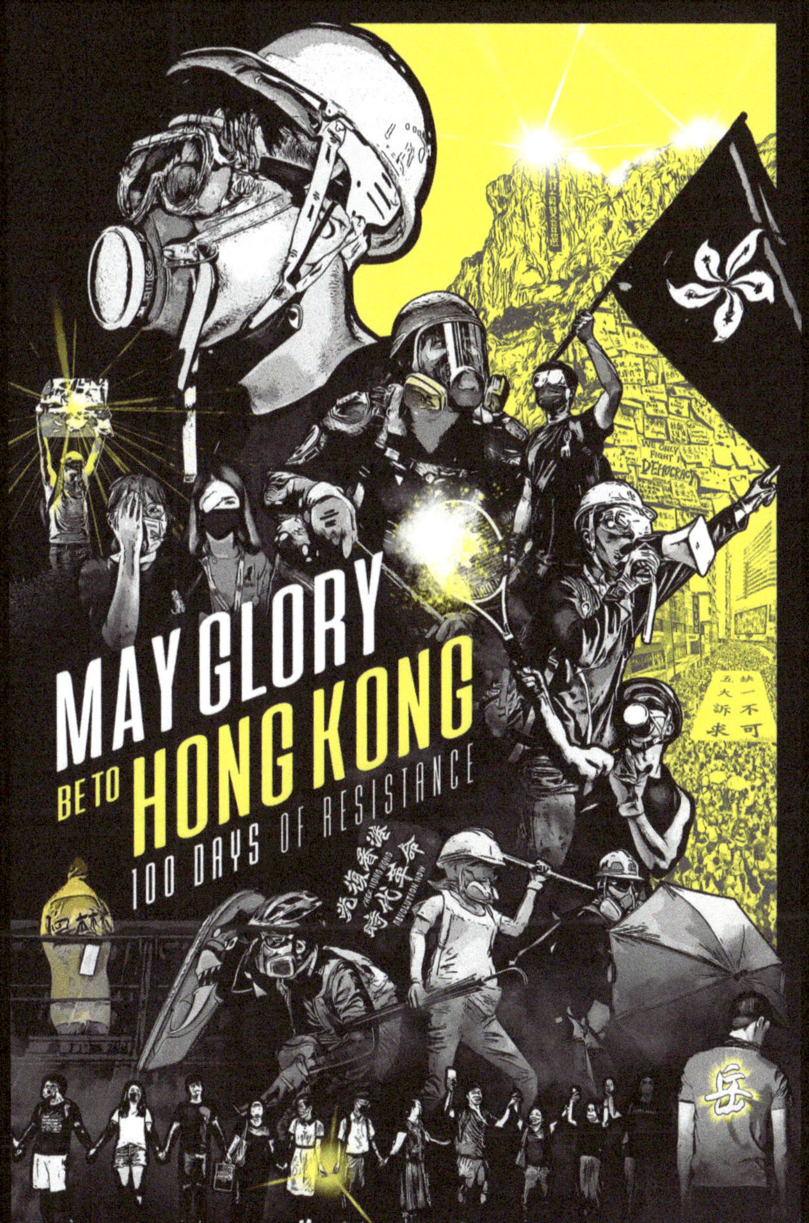
MAY GLORY
BE TO
HONG KONG
100 DAYS OF RESISTANCE
光復香港
時代革命
五大訴求
缺一不可

More important is that Hong Kong's democratic fate, like that of Poland, ultimately may rest on the crippling of its overseer. Polish workers gained their limited freedoms not only through their own struggle, but through the collapse of the entire Eastern Bloc of Stalinist rule with the spread of revolutionary movements in 1989 to Hungary, East Germany, Bulgaria, Czechoslovakia and Romania. The Chinese Communist Party may seem more secure in its position than its Russian counterpart. But it is as vulnerable to rebellion as any totalitarian regime built on exploitation. At some point, the cohesion of Chinese society will be tested, and with it the rule of the mandarins in Beijing. When that happens, the young Hong Kongers who have fought so valiantly may find their greatest and perhaps most unexpected ally in the Chinese working class. The fear of Hong Kong becoming 'no different from Shenzhen', expressed by Joshua Wong at the start of this book, may be transformed into a desire among radicals to emulate that city if the Pearl River Delta one day rises in its own rebellion against one-party state capitalism.

This is a point that the small and marginalised socialist left in Hong Kong has argued, and organised around, for decades. With the lines of demarcation between Hong Kong and China being erased, it is a point more salient than ever. 'The game has changed and so must the Hong Kong movement,' Vincent Wong and JS wrote at *Lausan*, a left-wing website, when the far-reaching nature of the Communist Party's moves against Hong Kong's democratic opposition became evident in May. 'With the fate of Hong Kongers now more intimately tied with those who are marginalized and oppressed in the mainland, Hong Kongers must realign their struggles with Chinese mainlanders who are similarly oppressed by the Chinese state. Now is not the time to look to the West. Now is the time for solidarity with Chinese workers, Chinese activists, and all who are oppressed in China.'

FURTHER READING

Antony Dapiran, *City on fire: the fight for Hong Kong*

Au Loong Yu, *Hong Kong in revolt: the protest movement and the future of China*

Au Loong Yu interviewed in *Spectre* journal, 'The death of Hong Kong's autonomy: beyond the crackdown'

Ching Kwan Lee and Ming Sing (eds), *Take back our future: an eventful sociology of the Hong Kong Umbrella Movement*

Jason Y. Ng, *Umbrellas in bloom: Hong Kong's Occupy Movement uncovered*

Jeff Wasserstrom, *Vigil: Hong Kong on the brink*

Promise Li in *Spectre* journal, 'A left case for Hong Kong self-determination'

Kong Tsung-gan, *As long as there is resistance, there is hope: essays on the Hong Kong freedom struggle in the post-Umbrella Movement era, 2014-2018*

Kong Tsung-gan, *Liberate Hong Kong: stories from the freedom struggle*

Zuraidah Ibrahim and Jeffie Lam (eds), *Rebel city: Hong Kong's year of water and fire*

WEBSITES

Borderless movement: borderless-hk.com

Lausan: lausan.hk

www.ingramcontent.com/pod-product-compliance
Ingram Content Group UK Ltd.
Pitfield, Milton Keynes, MK11 3LW, UK
UKHW062307290726
14090UKWH00018B/926